The experience of free banking

For many years central banking reigned supreme and was virtually unquestioned. However the instability of central banking has led to a resurgence of interest in free (or *laissez faire*) banking. Far from being an untried ideal, free banking systems have existed in many countries in the past and these experiences give us a valuable opportunity to see how free banking works in practice.

This book contains the widest summary to date of the experience of free banking in Australia, Canada, China, Colombia, France, Scotland, Switzerland and the USA, as well as a world overview. Competition in banking was suppressed because it would lead to rapid inflation, because it would de-stabilize the banking industry, or, more generally, because banking was a natural monopoly anyway. These case studies provide an historical laboratory in which these assumptions about free banking can be tested, and explode for good the myth that central banks are really necessary.

Kevin Dowd is a lecturer in Economics at the University of Nottingham. He is also a Fellow of the Durell Foundation and an adjunct scholar at the Cato Institute. He is the author of *Private money* (IEA, 1988) and *The State and the Monetary System* (Phillip Alan, 1989).

The experience of free banking

Edited by
Kevin Dowd

1992

London and New York

First published 1992
by Routledge
11 New Fetter Lane, London EC4P 4EE

Simultaneously published in the USA and Canada
by Routledge
a division of Routledge, Chapman and Hall, Inc.
29 West 35th Street, New York, NY 10001

Typeset in Times by Selectmove Ltd, London
Printed and bound in Great Britain by
Biddles Ltd, Guildford and King's Lynn

British Library Cataloguing in Publication Data
Dowd, Kevin, *1958–*
    The experience of free banking.
    I. Title
    332.1
    ISBN 0–415–04808–7

Library of Congress Cataloging in Publication Data
    The experience of free banking / edited by Kevin Dowd.
    p. cm.
    Includes bibliographical references and index.
    ISBN 0–415–04808–7
    1. Free banking – Case studies. I. Dowd, Kevin.
HG1588.E96 1992
332. 1–dc20   91–18087
                                                        CIP

Contents

List of figures and tables

FIGURES

TABLES

Foreword

The idea for this book was initially suggested by Chris Tame of the Libertarian Alliance. Historical free banking came to prominence in the early 1980s with Lawrence H. White's work on Scottish free banking, but it quickly became apparent that the Scottish experience was only one of a number of historical free banking episodes that had long been neglected by economists and monetary historians, and researchers were soon discovering more (and still are). He suggested it would be a good idea to bring some of these experiences together to see what could be learned from them, and this book is the result. I should therefore like to thank Chris for the initial idea, and Alan Jarvis of Routledge for his support and patience in seeing the project through to completion. Thanks are also due to Kurt Schuler for his helpful advice, and last, but certainly not least, to each of the authors who were kind enough to contribute to it. I hope these essays will persuade others of the importance of free banking and encourage them to explore it further.

Notes on contributors

Howard Bodenhorn is an assistant professor of economics at St. Lawrence University and the author of various articles in professional journals.

Kevin Dowd is a lecturer in economics at the University of Nottingham, an adjunct scholar at the Cato Institute and a Fellow of the Durell Foundation. He is the author of *Private Money: The Path to Monetary Stability* (London: Institute of Economic Affairs 1988), *The State and the Monetary System* (Hemel Hampstead: Philip Allan 1989).

Adolfo Meisel is an economist at the Banco de la República in Bogotá, and has a Ph.D. from the University of Illinois. He has published articles on banking and is a contributor to *El Banco de la República: Antecendentes, Evolución y Estructura*, (Bogotá: Banco de la República 1990).

Philippe Nataf is an associate professor of economics at the University of Paris IX (Dauphine). He also teaches at the University of Paris. He is the author of *An Inquiry into the Free Banking Movement in Nineteenth Century France, with Particular Emphasis on Charles Coquelin's Writings* (San Diego: William Lyons University 1987) and has published articles through the History of Economics Society and elsewhere.

Kurt Schuler is a graduate student in economics at George Mason University, Fairfax, Virginia.

George A. Selgin is an assistant professor of economics at the University of Georgia, an adjunct scholar at the Cato Institute and a fellow of the Durell Foundation. He is the author of *The Theory of Free Banking: Money Supply Under Competitive Note Issue* (Totowa, NJ: Rowman & Littlefield 1988) and of numerous articles in professional journals.

Ernst Juerg Weber is a lecturer in economics and research associate at the University of Western Australia. He is the author of various papers in academic journals.

Lawrence H. White is an associate professor of economics at the University of Georgia, an adjunct scholar at the Cato Institute and a Fellow of the Durell Foundation. He is the author of *Free Banking in Britain: Theory, Experience, and Debate 1800–1845* (New York: Cambridge University Press 1984). *Competition and Currency: Essays on Free Banking and Money* (New York: New York University Press 1989), and of numerous articles in journals.

1 Introduction

The experience of free banking

Kevin Dowd

Since 1975 we have witnessed a remarkable resurgence of interest in free (or *laissez-faire*) banking. For many years the philosophy of central banking had reigned supreme and virtually unquestioned, and even economists sympathetic to *laissez-faire* – for example, Mints (1950), Hayek (1960) and Friedman (1960) – readily accepted that 'money' and banking should not be left to the unfettered competitive process. A conventional wisdom ruled which held that competition in banking should be suppressed because it would lead to rapid inflation, or because it would destabilize the banking industry, or (somehow) because banking was a natural monopoly anyway. There was controversy over how much power the central bank should have and what it should try to do, but no respectable economist suggested that central banking itself was unnecessary or harmful until Hayek finally despaired of it in 1976 and began to argue that the only way to achieve monetary stability was to denationalize money (Hayek 1976). Hayek's suggestion attracted considerable interest, and free banking became the focal point of a major research effort. Although the idea seemed novel and even bizarre, it soon became apparent that free banking systems had actually existed in the past and that free banking had a long and respectable history. Lawrence H. White's *Free Banking in Britain* (1984b) showed that Scotland had experienced something like free banking until 1845, and this experience of free banking appeared to be very successful. Some US states had also experienced 'free banking' in the years before the Civil War, and Rockoff (1974), Rolnick and Weber (1983, 1984, 1986) and others re-examined these episodes and found that they were considerably more successful than traditional accounts had indicated. Free banking experiences were later uncovered in Canada (Schuler 1985), China (Selgin 1987a), Spain (Garcia 1989) and Sweden (Jonung 1985), and it soon became obvious that there were many others which later economists had also forgotten.

This book is the first attempt to pull at least some of these episodes together and provide accounts of the experience of free banking in a variety of different countries.[1] It begins with an overview by Kurt Schuler of the world experience of free banking which looks at no fewer than sixty different historical episodes. These experiences lasted from a number of years in some cases to the best part of a century or more in others, but they all had in common at least a certain amount of bank freedom, multiple note issuers, and the absence of any government-sponsored 'lender of last resort'. Most existed in the nineteenth century, and, as far as we can tell, most if not all can be considered as reasonably successful, sometimes quite remarkably so. Free banking ended because it was suppressed for essentially political reasons, more often than not because it was a barrier to the government's desire to extract seigniorage revenues, and not because it 'failed' economically. The overview is followed by nine further chapters on the specific free banking experiences of Australia (Dowd), Canada (Schuler), Colombia (Meisel), Foochow city in China (Selgin), Revolutionary France (Nataf), Ireland (Bodenhorn), Scotland (White), Switzerland (Weber), and the United States (Dowd). These episodes give a reasonable cross-section of free banking experience. They include some of the longest-lasting experiences (Australia, Canada, China and Scotland) as well as several of the shortest (Colombia and France). They include episodes where free banks operated under a very stable political framework (e.g. Australia) as well as others where political conditions were quite unstable or even revolutionary (China and Colombia, and France, respectively). They include cases where banks enjoyed a considerable though never unlimited degree of freedom from government interference (e.g. Australia before the early 1890s, and Scotland), and at least one (the USA) where banks sometimes operated under quite restrictive legal conditions. They also include the most obviously successful cases of free banking (Canada and Scotland) as well as two episodes (Australia and the USA) which experienced bank failures that helped give free banking an undeserved bad name later on.

While much of this research is still in a relatively early stage, by now we do know enough to draw certain conclusions with a reasonable degree of confidence. One can think of these experiences as a series of experiments, and certain broad outlines are clearly visible even though none of the experiments was conducted under perfect (i.e. pure *laissez-faire*) conditions. Perhaps the clearest results relate to the older conventional view about free banking, and this view is decisively rejected on all three counts.

First, historical experiences of free banking were *not* prone to inflation. In apparently every case, free banks issued convertible currency whose value was tied to the value of some real commodity, usually gold. The price level was therefore tied to the relative price of the 'anchor' commodity, and if the banks had any ability to influence prices at all, it was distinctly limited. Inflations and deflations did occur, but they occurred in response to changes in market conditions for the anchor commodity (e.g. when there were gold discoveries) and these changes had similar effects on all economies on the same monetary standard regardless of whether they had free banking or not. Price-level changes depended primarily on the monetary standard, in other words, rather than on the regulatory regime under which the banking system operated,[2] and there is little or no indication that competition between unregulated banks was itself an inflationary force. If anything, free banks continued to issue convertible and therefore relatively sound currencies precisely because they were free, and a bank that made its issues inconvertible would have presumably lost its market share to a competitor whose currency continued to be convertible. It is worth noting that no free banking system ever abandoned convertibility, and wherever convertibility was abandoned it always took explicit government intervention to do it. One might note too that the government-induced abandonment of convertibility was always followed by later monetary expansion and inflation. The claim that competition among unregulated banks would lead to an explosive money supply and rapid inflation thus has no support in the historical record, and indeed, inverts the truth that rapid inflations have always been associated with government interventions to suppress competition.

Second, the historical record gives little support to the claim that free competition tends to destabilize the banking system. Overissues were usually disciplined by the banks' clearing systems which provided a rapid and effective reflux mechanism to return excess notes and deposits to their users; there is also some evidence that interest rates were more stable under free banking regimes than elsewhere (Pope 1989: 24); and in the absence of either government-sponsored liability insurance or a lender of last resort, banks needed to be careful in their lending policies since they could not expect others to shoulder their losses and bail them out. Banks did sometimes fail under *laissez-faire* conditions, but these failures were almost always limited and do not appear to have been contagious. Free banking systems were rarely subject to major banking crises, and there is evidence that the crises that did occur were usually caused by major external factors such as a crisis in a regulated banking system nearby or by government intervention of some sort. (Recall that free banking was never entirely free.) The Scottish and Canadian free banking systems were highly stable, for instance, and it appears that such instability as they experienced was usually caused by crises in nearby London or New York where banking was considerably more regulated. *Ante bellum* 'free banking' in the USA was also quite free, at least in some states, and most 'free bank' failures can be traced to the combination of a requirement that 'free banks' hold state debt and the fact that holders of this debt sometimes suffered heavy losses because certain states repudiated it. The one case where a free banking system clearly did experience a major crisis was in Australia in 1893, but even that crisis was heavily influenced by government interventions and the idea that the crisis was due to *laissez-faire* is based on a partial and questionable reading of the historical record. In short, there is little evidence to support the idea that free banking is destabilizing, and the impressive records of the Canadian, Scottish and other experiences, appear to refute this idea more or less decisively.

Third, the historical experience of free banking flatly contradicts the idea that the issue of currency is in any sense a natural monopoly. Historical free banking systems seem always to have shown some tendency towards economies of scale – branch-banking would displace unit-banking, for instance – and there would be a tendency for a small number of 'big' nation-wide banks to emerge that would engage in all the major banking activities, including the issue of notes. But economies of scale were never sufficiently pronounced that a single bank would emerge dominant in any one of these activities. More banks would issue deposits of one sort or another than issue notes, but any of the handful of big banks would also issue notes, and none of them ever seriously threatened the others' market shares.[3]

In addition to dispelling earlier misconceptions about free banking, the historical experience also indicates that free banking systems were efficient and highly advanced for their time. Competition was fierce, and the fight for market share developed bankers' entrepreneurial skills and promoted a willingness to innovate. Competition among the Scottish banks led them to introduce the cash credit account, an early form of overdraft, for example, as well as the payment of interest on deposits. Competition also gave an impetus to the development of branch-banking which enabled banks to exploit economies of scale as well as making them safer by facilitating the spreading of risks. There is little evidence that rivalry was ruinous, and the early note duels – attempts to put each other out of business by collecting a large number of notes and unexpectedly demanding redemption – soon gave way to clearing arrangements and other forms of mutually beneficial co-operation (e.g. facilities to lend to one another). Spreads between borrowing and lending rates were generally small which suggests that the banks had low operating costs and had expanded to their economic limits. And banks only earned normal profits, so it appears the economic surplus created by banking was completed away from their customers.

The sophistication and efficiency of the banking system in turn provided a stimulus to economic development. Free banking systems intermediated between savers and borrowers at relatively low cost, and thus helped to promote both saving and investment. Competition among banks ensured that interest rates on loans were low and that no significant class of borrowers of acceptable risk was denied credit. Commerce and industry consequently had access to credit that was both inexpensive and relatively easy to obtain. Banks provided the public with loans as well and promoted habits of thrift by offering them higher returns on their savings than they could obtain elsewhere. Banks also issued media of exchange that were more convenient and easier to keep than specie, so 'barren' holdings of monetary specie could be converted into goods that could be consumed or invested instead, and the cheaper payments system provided by the banks facilitated exchange and gave a further boost to industry and commerce. The effects of free banking on economic development are illustated by Scottish experience.[4] In 1745, per capita income in Scotland was about half what it was in England at the time. However, a century later – a century that corresponds to the heyday of Scottish free banking – Scottish per capita income had risen to almost English levels despite England's own rapid growth. Scotland suffered from a number of obvious disadvantages relative to England: – greater distance to markets, an inferior infrastructure, and fewer raw materials. It had the edge over England only in its banking and educational systems, and contemporary writers – including Adam Smith in *The Wealth of Nations* – believed that the Scottish banking system had contributed in a major way to the country's economic development. The impact of banking freedom on development is also confirmed indirectly by the work of Sylla (1972), which presents evidence that banking restrictions retarded the development of parts of the south and west of the USA in the period after the Civil War. Free banking was thus a major contributor to economic growth.

NOTES

1. Cameron (1972) and Cameron *et al.* (1967) presents two volumes of case studies of historical banking systems and several of these were also free banking systems (e.g. Scotland). The majority were not, however, and the focus of his volumes is banking and development rather than the effects of the regulations under which the banking system operated.
2. It is conceivable, none the less, that the evolution of free banking might have been inflationary if it had led to a falling monetary demand for gold which led in turn to a reduction in its relative value and, hence, a rise in the price level (i.e. free banking might have affected prices through its effect on the market for the standard commodity). There appears, however, to be little or no evidence to support this conjecture.
3. The argument that the currency supply is a natural monopoly is usually used to provide some sort of justification for legal restrictions to establish a currency monopoly, but it actually provides nothing of the sort. Even if it were correct, it would indicate that legal restrictions are unnecessary and, if they are unnecessary, they are presumably also unjustified. In any case, the existence of a natural monopoly does not imply that 'natural' market barriers to entry need to be supplemented with additional legal restrictions.
4. This argument is a modified version of that made in Cameron (1972) pp. 94–5.

2 The world history of free banking
An overview

Kurt Schuler

CENTRAL BANKING AND FREE BANKING

The inability of central banks to prevent inflation in recent years has led a growing number of economists to rethink government's role in issuing money. Milton Friedman and Anna Schwartz, in their article 'Has government any role in money?' (1986), answered that it has very little role, while Friedrich A. Hayek has called for the outright abolition of central banking (1978: 106–7). They and others who question the desirability of central banking argue that money is best supplied competitively for the same reasons that competition is best for supplying other goods. Several writers have developed new models of competitive money supply ('free banking') and compared them with models of money supply under central banking (Vaubel 1984a; White 1984b: 1–22; Selgin 1988; Christ 1989; Dowd 1989: chs 1–4). The new models cast doubt on standard justifications for central banking, among them the claims that the production of reserves is or evolves into a natural monopoly, that competitive supply of money creates harmful 'external effects' that are absent under central banking, that a lender of last resort is necessary to keep a panic-prone banking system from collapsing, and that central bank policies stabilize output.

Other writers have taken a different tack, and have searched for historical cases of banking systems where money was supplied competitively, without a central bank, under conditions that to varying degrees approximate the *laissez-faire* ideal of the models. There have been many such systems. At present, the best-known and best-investigated cases are a handful that occurred in Europe and North America.[1] However, many others existed. During the nineteenth and early twentieth centuries, many countries had free banking for some time at least, and these experiences can shed light on some of the issues raised in the modern free banking controversy.

This chapter sketches the origins, performance and decline of free banking around the world, and offers some broad conclusions about free banking's record. There is not enough space to prove all my conclusions exhaustively, but, the examples I give, the table of cases of free banking (see p. 40–5), the works listed in the bibliography, and the other chapters in this book will enable sceptics to consider all the evidence and to judge for themselves the claims I make.

Free banking's historical record is more than a matter of mere antiquarian interest. It has radical implications for present-day monetary policy. The nature of banking is essentially the same today as it was when free banking was widespread. The techniques are more varied and sophisticated, but a bank's job is still to intermediate loanable funds between lenders and borrowers. If free banking worked well in the past, it should also work well today, and the fact that our current central banking is an old and familiar system does not necessarily make it the best system.

In the present context, I take 'free banking' to mean a banking system with competitive note issue, low legal barriers to entry, and no central control of reserves. Those are the minimum requirements that theoretical writings on free banking usually mention. It is sometimes hard to say at what point increasing restrictions on those and related liberties make a banking system no longer free. Consequently, some writers use the term 'free banking' to refer only to a theoretical ideal that has never existed and perhaps never could, or they use it to refer only to some of the historical cases mentioned in this chapter. However, a more liberal use of the term seems appropriate here, because all the banking systems that I call 'free' are certainly much closer to the theoretical ideal of free banking than they are to central banking, or to intermediate systems such as monopoly note issue without a central bank.

THE ORIGINS OF FREE BANKING

A recent article by George Selgin and Lawrence H. White (1992) builds on Carl Menger's (1871) theory of the origin of money to describe how invisible-hand processes can result in a sophisticated banking system as the product of a step-by-step evolution whose origins stretch all the way back to barter. Media of exchange, money, coinage, rudimentary banking with transferable liabilities, and advanced banking with features such as regular note exchange and clearing-houses can result from the narrow pursuit of profit by individuals, with no thought of the wider implications of their actions. Their accounts imply that free banking is a spontaneous economic development, and that we should observe free banking systems springing up frequently where legal restrictions do not prevent it.

Selgin and White's theoretical picture fits the historical facts well. Private competitive bank-note issue originated in China soon after the year 1000. (The first attempt by government to take advantage of the trail blazed by private note issue by monopolizing the note issue for its own benefit occurred shortly thereafter, in 1023 (Yang 1952: 51–3).) Bills of exchange circulated like bank notes in Japan by the late 1600s (Shinjo 1962: 11), and, independently, the private institution that later became Sweden's central bank opened in 1656 as Europe's first large note-issuing institution. Merchants' scrip issues sprang up time and time again in many countries as an improvised response to the demand for a circulating medium other than coin (see, for instance, McIvor (1958: 14–15); Timberlake (1987); Hargreaves (1972: 46–52)). However, scrip issuers typically did not carry on other banking functions, such as making large-scale loans or accepting demand deposits.

WHERE AND WHEN FREE BANKING EXISTED

As Table 2.1 at the end of the chapter shows, there have been about sixty historical cases of free banking. They lasted from a few years to over a century. Free banking systems varied widely in the degree of government regulation they had. The table lists certain common forms of regulation. It is suggestive rather than exhaustive. For instance, it omits prohibitions of non-banking business or limits on mortgage lending, which were generally unimportant compared to the listed regulations in their effect on the performance of free banks in the nineteenth century. Small-note prohibitions were common, but only in a few cases did they seem to have hampered free banks greatly. Regulations limiting banks' note issues to some multiple of their capital or reserves were also common, but these imposed ceilings were frequently too high to be economically binding.

Ranging free banking systems along a spectrum, from least-regulated to most-regulated, a number of them, including those of Belgium, Revolutionary France, Bolivia and Rhodesia (Zimbabwe), apparently had none of the forms of regulation that the table lists. The Scottish system, the most thoroughly investigated case of free banking and the one that both advocates and critics often point to as closest to the theoretical ideal, had certain minor regulations, which Lawrence H. White discusses in his chapter in this book. The free banking systems of the British colonies were only slightly more regulated than the Scottish system. Many Latin American countries also had little formal regulation limiting the kind of business banks could do, but they frequently suffered government-imposed currency debasements. Among the most regulated free banking systems were the English system and the bond-collateral systems of the United States and some other countries. The bond-collateral systems required banks to hold specified bonds as a precondition for issuing notes.

Free banking was common in the British Empire, the Orient, and the Americas. Conversely, it was rare in northern and eastern Europe, Africa, the Middle East, and colonies of countries other than Britain. The reasons merit explanation.

The banking system of the United Kingdom, with its patchwork of freedom and regulation, was the outcome of piecemeal legal accretions. In return for loans to the government, the Bank of England, founded in 1694, quickly accumulated unique legal privileges. It had sole custody of the government's bank account. It was, until 1858, the only note-issuing English bank whose stockholders had limited personal liability for its debts should it fail; until 1826, the only note-issuing bank allowed to have more than six stockholders and, after 1826, the only note-issuing bank with more than six stockholders allowed to issue notes in the London region. Hundreds of note-issuing banks with six or fewer stockholders were founded outside of the London region; they tended to be very small because the restriction on the number of stockholders severely limited their ability to raise capital. London had no note-issuing bank besides the Bank of England, though it did have a number of large merchant banks. However, the unique privileges that enabled the Bank of England to combine note issue with a large stockholders' capital meant that for decades it was larger and more important than any of its potential rivals (Clapham 1945). It became a quasi-central bank in the 1700s, and a fully fledged central bank in the 1800s, because of its privileges over and above other English banks. It grew into its current role as a non-profit, government-owned regulatory agency and lender of last resort by expanding its privileges and shedding the commercial banking functions that it originally had in common with other banks.

The Bank of Scotland, founded in 1695, and the Bank of Ireland, founded in 1783, at first held sway in their regions as local semi-monopolies, modelled on the Bank of England. The Bank of Ireland got its privileges in return for a loan to the Irish government (Hall

1949: 34–5). The Bank of Scotland, oddly, was prohibited from lending to the Scottish government. It lost its legal monopoly of Scottish note issue when its charter came up for renewal in 1716, because Parliament suspected that its directors supported the Jacobite claimant to the British throne, and it tried in vain to prevent the rival Royal Bank of Scotland from receiving a charter in 1727 (Checkland 1975: 58–9). A third bank, the British Linen Company, received a charter in 1746. The chartered banks tried to persuade Parliament to outlaw the unchartered, unlimited-liability note-issuing banks that began to spring up from around 1750. Their plea fell on deaf ears, however, and the principle of unrestricted entry became established by 1765 (Checkland 1975: 119–20). Unlike England and Ireland, there was no limitation in Scotland on the number of partners that an unchartered bank could have, and some unchartered banks eventually became larger and had more stockholders than the chartered banks.

The banking systems of the British colonies resembled the unfettered Scottish system rather than the heavily regulated English system. Entry into the banking business on equal terms with existing firms was even easier in many colonies than it was in Scotland, though other regulations were typically more severe. Whereas in Britain bank charters (which granted limited liability to stockholders) were a rare legal privilege, they were more common in the colonies. The most developed colonial systems – Canada, Australia, New Zealand and South Africa – granted charters to almost anyone of good character who could meet the minimum capital requirements. The first colonial banking system, that of India, began in 1683, though it did not start to become a modern, competitive system until the 1770s (Bagchi 1987: 32, 45). Banking in other British colonies did not begin until the early 1800s. By 1840, all larger British colonies, including such minor outposts as Guyana and Mauritius, had locally chartered banks. No colony consciously imitated the Scottish system; rather, local political pressures led even those that at first granted monopolies to open the field. For instance, Upper Canada (Ontario), New Brunswick and Nova Scotia had monopoly banking for ten to fifteen years, and the chartering of new banks became one of the chief subjects of political debate, in part because the existing banks were instruments of the parties in power. Reform leaders trained their rhetoric on the monopoly banks and eventually got bank charters for their own parties. Once the precedent was established, keeping out subsequent competitors became increasingly difficult. Competitors effectively mobilized borrowers disgruntled with existing banks, or people seeking the pride of having a locally owned bank in their own areas, to apply pressure on local legislatures to grant charters (see chapter 4).

Since competing locally chartered banks already existed in the colonies, the British government was often willing to grant royal charters to British bank promoters who wanted to establish banks in the colonies and who agreed not to compete in Britain with the Bank of England or other banks.[2] The dual system of charters lowered still further the barriers to entry into colonial banking. The first British colonial bank was the Mauritius Bank, chartered in 1831 (Baster 1929: 268).

By 1845, when Sir Robert Peel's Bank Charter Acts established central banking throughout the United Kingdom, free banking was firmly entrenched in the colonies. British attempts to quash competitive note issue were unsuccessful in those colonies that had a measure of home rule. The legislature of the Province of Canada (Ontario and Quebec) in 1841 defeated the plan of a British governor who adhered to Currency School doctrines for a monopoly bank of issue (Breckenridge 1894: 85–7). The British governor of New Zealand imposed a monopoly bank of issue in 1850, despite strong local opposition, but when New Zealand achieved home rule in 1856 the legislature abolished the bank, and banks that had formerly done only deposit business immediately began to issue notes as well (Hargreaves 1972: 54–61). Only in colonies lacking home rule was Britain gradually able to impose monopoly note issue, beginning with Mauritius in 1849 and not ending until 1951 with the British Caribbean colonies.

In the 1830s, Scottish banking methods began to influence colonial banking practices. 'Cash credit' lending (a form of overdraft borrowing), payment of interest on deposits, and more accurate forms of accounting spread to the colonies as British overseas banks and emigrating British bankers brought their experience to new lands (Checkland 1975: 393, 492, 511–12; Shortt 1986: 311–12, 327; Bagchi 1987: 494).

Free banking in China and Japan developed independently of free banking in Europe. The first Chinese banks were founded shortly after the year 1000. Chinese banking had management procedures and lending customs that were quite different from those of European banks. However, after western banks came to China beginning in the 1840s, Chinese bankers opened some 'modern-style' banks that imitated European practices, among them dispersed stock ownership. Modern-style, old-style and western banks issued notes side by side. By treaty, western banks were exempt from most Chinese laws, and hence operated virtually unregulated. Native banks faced little formal regulation until 1907, but were subject to occasional pressure to make loans to the government at below-market rates (Yang 1952: 81–91).

Japanese note-issuing banking began in the 1600s, and, like Chinese banking, became influenced by western practices in the 1800s. In 1872, Japan adopted a bond-collateral banking system for native banks patterned on that of the United States. The reform was mandatory, and unlike the voluntary changes in the Chinese system, it did not leave room for old-style banking (Soyeda 1896: 424–5). Some foreign banks also issued notes in Japan (Cribb 1987).

Elsewhere in Asia, free banking did not exist until western banks opened branches. The Banco Español Filipino had a monopoly of note issue in the Philippines during Spanish rule. After the Spanish–American War passed control of the Philippines to the United States, the bank lost its privileges, and the competing Philippine National Bank was founded in 1916 (Conant 1927: 589–90). The Thai government allowed one French and two British banks to issue notes for several years before claiming note issue for itself (King 1988: 129–32, 236).

In Britain and its colonies, and in Asia, private, competitive note issue generally preceded any government note issue. In the Americas, on the other hand, government note issue often preceded private note issue, but unhappy experience frequently made government note issue politically unpopular, causing governments to leave note issue to competitive banks. Countries in the Americas that suffered currency debasement under government note issue in the eighteenth and early nineteenth centuries included Canada (French playing-card money and later British Army Bills), the United States (Revolutionary War 'Continental Currency'), Costa Rica, Guatemala and Colombia. In Mexico, Argentina and Brazil, government-owned banks of issue that were little more than engines of inflationary finance took the place of direct government issue in depreciating the currency. When governments abandoned note issue, private, competitive banks filled the void with notes convertible into gold or silver, at least while governments avoided further involvement with the monetary system. Of countries in the Americas that were independent by 1900, only Haiti, Nicaragua and Santo Domingo (the Dominican Republic) never experienced free banking.

British-chartered banks played an important role in the free banking system of the Americas except in the United States. They preceded local free banks in Newfoundland, Mexico and Colombia, and were also extremely prominent in Argentina, Peru and Uruguay. Local banks with significant British ownership existed in Costa Rica and El Salvador. The Colonial Bank, one of the corporate ancestors of Barclays Bank, served British colonies around the Caribbean in competition with local banks and two Canadian banks (Barclays Bank (1938: ch. 2) Joslin (1963). Restrictions on the activities of foreign banks were typically lower in the 1800s than they are today, and British banks in Latin America usually enjoyed the same rights as local banks, including the right of note issue.

Europe, which had many overseas banks with extensive branch networks, hindered banks at home with branching restrictions. Excluding the tiny countries, only Scotland, Sweden and Belgium permitted unfettered nation-wide branching of free banks from the start of their free banking periods. England and Ireland in the 1820s abolished their rules limiting note issue to banks with six or fewer stockholders, thereby permitting banks to raise the capital necessary for nation-wide branching, but banks that wanted to establish London or Dublin branches had to renounce the right of note issue. (No cross-border branching was allowed among England, Scotland and Ireland.) Spain, Italy, Greece, Portugal and France during its second free banking period (1815 to 1848) all had local note-issue monopolies. Note-issuing banks were forbidden to establish branches outside their monopoly region, though deposit-only banks were sometimes exempt from the restriction. Germany's note-issue system was particularly complicated, because its states had no uniform banking law or monetary standard before they were unified in 1871. Some states had monopoly banking, while others had competitive issue. Competition in Germany was more intense than it appeared on the surface. The main purpose of several of the banks in small states was not to do business in their home territory, but to circulate their notes in Prussia or other large states nearby. To facilitate 'foreign' circulation, some banks printed denominations in terms of coinage standard both of their home state and of the state where they hoped the notes would circulate (Cameron 1967: 158). In Switzerland, cantonal laws prevented nation-wide branching for many years, though some cantons had multiple issuers. In countries with branching restrictions, competition among note brands lacked the vigour that it had in Scotland or Sweden, but could still be powerful because some of the regions with monopoly issuers were small enough to ensure that the cost of using and redeeming notes issued in nearby regions was low.

Free banking never reached some areas of the world. Parts

of Africa and the Middle East were so economically backward that they had no note-issuing banks at all during free banking's heyday in the nineteenth century. Instead, moneylenders and traders performed prototypical banking functions, including issuing scrip. Russia, Austria-Hungary, the Ottoman Empire, Persia, Egypt, the Netherlands and Denmark granted note-issue monopolies as a way of helping state finances. Norway, which belonged to Denmark until 1914, and Iceland, which remained a dependency until 1944, set up monopoly note-issuing banks in imitation of Denmark. Finland did likewise when it became independent of Russia in 1917. The Balkan nations that broke away from Ottoman rule in the late nineteenth century also set up monopoly note-issuing banks.[3] Most countries that had monopoly note-issuing banks allowed competition in bank deposits, but fixed-rate convertibility between notes and deposits and the demands for notes made by deposit customers, made the monopoly notes into a kind of reserve (high-powered money) for the deposit banks. The note-issuing banks thus became rudimentary central banks, though not until later did they develop other characteristics that are now typical of central banks.

The prevalence of monopoly note issue in colonies of European powers other than Britain was related to that other vestige of mercantilism, the colonial trading company. Just as they organized privately owned colonial trading monopolies, France, the Netherlands, Portugal and Germany organized private colonial monopoly note-issuing banks, which generally had a monopoly of deposits too. Whereas Britain by the end of the nineteenth century had monopoly issue at home and free banking abroad, the other countries, practising a more uniform policy, had monopoly issue everywhere. The sole exception was the Portuguese colony of Macau, where local Chinese traders issued notes long before Portugal's monopoly colonial bank established a branch, and continued to issue notes until definitively outlawed in 1944 (Ma 1987).

COMPETITION AND CO-OPERATION UNDER FREE BANKING

Free banking systems displayed several interesting common characteristics. One is that they showed no tendencies towards concentration of note issue in a single bank. *All* free banking systems had more than one note-issuing bank, even in such tiny places as Malta, Mauritius, and Fiji. Single issue never lasted after legal barriers to entry fell. Even where people had been long accustomed to using the notes of a single bank, competing issues soon found ready acceptance. Government-issued notes never drove free banks' notes out of circulation, except when punitive taxes or outright prohibition hindered competition. The most striking example of unrestricted banking's inherent tendency toward competitive issue was Brazil, which thrice abandoned monopoly note issue and each time saw competitive issue spring up immediately from banks that had formerly done deposit business only. In Scotland, eleven years elapsed between the expiration of the Bank of Scotland's monopoly and the founding of the first competitor, the Royal Bank of Scotland, in 1727. However, that was the longest lag of any free banking system, and the sequel is worth remarking: Scotland became the most hotly competitive banking market of its time. (Perhaps the lag was so long because Scotland was too economically backward to support more than one bank in the early 1700s.)

The mature free banking systems of countries that permitted nation-wide branch banking generally had two to twenty large, strong banks. Competition compelled most small banks to merge so that they could take advantage of the economies of scale that their larger rivals enjoyed. In Scotland, for instance, there were 29 issuing banks in 1826, and 19 at the end of the free banking era in 1845 (White 1984b: 35, 37). In Canada, the peak was 51, in 1875; by 1932, there were only 10 banks (Neufeld 1972: 78–9). Other countries that allowed nation-wide branch banking exhibited similar patterns of consolidation. The hundreds of small, poorly capitalized banks that existed in England and the United States, and the dozens in Switzerland and Germany, were the feeble offspring of legal restrictions. China, Japan and some very small places (such as the English Channel island of Guernsey) where 'everyone knew everyone else' were the only countries that allowed nation-wide branching yet had predominantly unit banking systems for decades. Chinese and Japanese customers strongly valued family and geographical ties to particular banks, so branch banks did not have the marked advantages over unit banks that they enjoyed elsewhere. Despite the small number of banks in most mature free banking systems, consolidation never reached such a point that only one bank was left to issue notes. Note issue showed no more sign of being a natural monopoly than deposit taking was then or is now.

Competition was a surprise to many early bankers, who often mistakenly believed that trade could not support a rival in their neighbourhood. For example, the Bank of Scotland and the Swedish Risksbank were piqued that other firms set up right under their noses and took business away from them (Checkland 1975: 58–62; Jonung

1989: 12, 27). In Canada the Quebec Bank regarded its home city as a private preserve, and tried to persuade the legislature to close the Bank of Montreal's branch there (Denison 1966: vol. 1, 150).

The first banks frequently nurtured jealousies that did not disappear until they realized that the competition was there to stay. Some initially refused rivals' notes, but they soon came to understand that it exposed them to an asymmetrical reserve drain. Rivals who accepted their notes had a claim against their reserves, which the rivals would periodically present for redemption, but if they refused to accept rivals' notes, they had no offsetting claim against the rivals with which to replenish their reserves. Some banks then changed tactics, and practised 'note duelling' – collecting large quantities of rivals' notes and presenting them suddenly, at irregular intervals, for immediate redemption (usually in gold or silver). The Scottish banks had the longest note duelling period, nearly half a century (Checkland 1975: 118). Note duelling was rarely successful in forcing other banks to suspend convertibility. Typically, note duelling vanished and regular note exchange developed much more quickly than it did in Scotland, as banks came to realize that regular note and cheque exchange was mutually beneficial because it reduced the need for reserves all around. Mentions of note duelling are rare for banking systems that began in the mid-nineteenth century or later, so evidently its drawbacks were common knowledge among bankers by then.

All free banking systems developed regular clearing arrangements, though few had formal clearing-houses. Informal, bilateral clearing was cheaper than multilateral clearing until the number of banks or the volume of liabilities to be cleared became great. Free banking systems without branching restrictions often had just a handful of banks, so multilateral clearing had little advantage over bilateral clearing. The author of a handbook for Canadian bankers stated near the turn of the century that there was little gain to be had from establishing clearing-houses in cities with fewer than seven banks (Knight 1908: 137). The internal workings of individual banks' branch networks achieved economies of scale that, up to a point, were comparable to those of a clearing-house in processing notes and cheques for redemption. Branch banking combined with regular bilateral exchange was often a satisfactory alternative to a clearing-house.

In Europe, credit clearing arrangements preceded note-issue banking. The trade fairs of Champagne became the centre of clearing for bills of exchange by the 1300s (Roover 1974 [1954]: 203). Japanese banks had clearing arrangements by the 1600s and Chinese banks by the 1700s (Yang 1952: 86; Crawcour 1961: 357). The Scottish banks began nation-wide multilateral clearing, centred in Edinburgh, in 1771 (Munn 1981b: 25). (Bilateral exchanges in each case began long before.) The impetus for the Scottish clearing-house was an upstart bank's desire to distinguish itself from the stodgy practices of the older Edinburgh banks, which refused to accept the notes of many rural issuers. Most of Scotland's thirty-one banks joined the clearing arrangement, directly or through correspondents, not long after it opened. Other early multilateral clearing arrangements sprang up where there were similarly large numbers of banks. Systems that had branching restrictions, such as those of the United States, England and Switzerland, were especially likely to have multilateral clearing, since they tended to have many more banks and thus higher average transportation costs for bilateral note redemption.

Clearing-houses often developed beyond their initial role as note exchanges and became vehicles for co-operative action. They established consensus among members on certain matters for which a uniform policy was desirable, such as procedures for handling out-of-town cheques or efforts to detect fraud. In a few instances, they became the chief organizations through which banks marshalled reserves to face local panics. The New York City clearing-house played a particularly important role in mitigating panics from 1857 to 1907 (Timberlake 1984). A large group of Mexican free banks in 1899 founded the Banco Central Mexicano to act as a clearing-house and a lender to banks facing local panics (Conant 1969: 485–6). Despite its name, the Banco Central was not a central bank in the present-day sense: it had no monopoly of note issue (in fact, it did not issue notes), and in no sense controlled the money supply of its members.

Though clearing-houses were vehicles for co-operation among free banks, attempts to use them to form cartels were largely unsuccessful. In Scotland, Canada, Australia, Switzerland and Singapore, the uniform interest rates that clearing-houses or bankers' associations set for their members gave way to rate wars as soon as any bank (usually a smaller one seeking to compensate for the more limited range of services that it offered customers) spotted a competitive opportunity, and action to punish renegades was futile (Johnson 1910: 134–5; Landmann 1910: 41–5; Conant 1969: 305–6; Nelson 1984: 112–13; Pope 1989: 79).

Checkland (1975: 452), voicing a claim that could easily be made about many other free banking systems, states that the Scottish system during the free banking era was to some extent a cartel.

As evidence, he adduces the generally uniform interest rates that the banks set. However, uniformity may equally well indicate that vigorous competition enforced the 'law of one price'. Clear-cut evidence of cartelization would be persistently higher loan interest rates, lower deposit rates, or higher profit margins than the more fragmented English banking system had. None of these characterized Scottish banking. Interest-rate-setting agreements never lasted long, as Checkland himself admits (1975: 391). (After Scotland's free banking era, when no new note-issuing banks were allowed, matters may have been different.) Even though there were few banks in Scotland and in many other banking systems when the systems reached maturity, the number was large enough to ensure effective competition. As long as legal barriers to entry are low, few competitors need not imply lack of competition. In industries such as banking where there are economies of scale, one should not expect to see the thousands of firms that inhabit unrealistic textbook expositions of 'perfect' competition.

The notes that free banks issued generally circulated at par nation-wide, except where the size of the country, poor transportation, or legal restrictions on branch banking made note redemption quite costly. Even Canada, despite its immense size and sparse population, had nation-wide par note acceptance by 1889 (Breckenridge 1894: 245–6), four years after railways finally linked the country from coast to coast. Par note redemption usually came into being quite early in the free banking periods in small countries.

ASPECTS OF FREE BANKING'S PERFORMANCE

In assessing a banking system's performance as part of the wider economy, economists typically look at how well it fosters economic growth, intermediates efficiently between lenders and borrowers, maintains stability of prices or exchange rates, avoids problems of fraud and counterfeiting, prevents overissues of credit and discourages bank runs and panics.[4] The least regulated free banking system did well by those standards. The more regulated ones sometimes did not, and in many cases regulations seem to have caused their poor performance.

Economic growth

The sole study that examines the relation between banking systems and growth rates is favourable to free banking. In a comparative survey of seven banking systems, Rondo Cameron *et al.* (1972: 97, 290, 304, 307–8; 1982) gave the Scottish system, which was the most free of all, the highest marks for promoting growth. Cameron contended that the assimilation of the Scottish system to English practices that occurred after Peel's Bank Act of 1845 contributed to Scotland's relative industrial decline in the late nineteenth and the twentieth centuries.

Efficiency at intermediation

There is little systematic work on how efficient various types of banking systems were at intermediating between lenders and borrowers. However, bank profits and spreads between deposit and loan interest rates under free banking generally do not seem to have been higher than they were in nearby central banking systems, suggesting that free banking was at least as efficient as central banking at intermediation.

Exchange-rate and price stability

Free banking systems maintained exchange-rate stability by giving people the right to convert bank notes and deposits into gold or silver at a fixed rate. Free banks issued notes denominated in the main currency of the region where they hoped the notes would circulate. There was not a proliferation of different monetary units; in fact, during free banking's heyday in the 1800s and early 1900s there were fewer major monetary units than there are today. Dozens of countries had local monetary units equivalent to either the silver dollar, the gold dollar, or the gold pound sterling. By making the units official, governments in most cases merely recognized conventions that markets had already established.

The commercial customs and the legal framework of the nineteenth century made free banking inherently a regime of convertibility. Free banks had strong competitive incentives to maintain convertibility as a way of attracting customers (Dowd 1989: 7–8). Except when governments allowed banks to renege on their previous contractual obligations to convertibility, there seem to have been no cases of free banking systems issuing fiat-money liabilities carrying no promise of fixed-rate convertibility. Temporarily inconvertible bank currencies sometimes circulated alongside convertible bank currencies of rival banks at a discount, as during the panic of 1857 in the United States (Hammond 1957: 466), but the tendency was for all free bank currency to be convertible. Fiat money nowhere permanently supplanted convertible currency as the voluntarily preferred medium of exchange, and sometimes, as in the case of the California 'gold banks' of the 1860s and 1870s, people successfully defied government attempts to impose fiat money on them (Greenfield and Rockoff 1990). Notes of banks that had failed or suspended payments kept value only to the extent that people expected eventual payment in gold- or silver-denominated assets. Whatever economists today may say about the theoretical advantages of floating exchange rates, the voluntary practice of the nineteenth century strongly favoured the stability that fixed-rate convertibility afforded.

Free banking's success at maintaining peacetime convertibility (at least, in countries where governments enforced the redemption rights of noteholders and depositors) suggests that free banking was what enabled the gold standard to persist before the First World War. George Selgin (1988: 40, 96) has argued that where commercial bank liabilities are convertible into a 'base money' (such as gold) whose supply is limited, free banks must quickly respond to changes in their reserves. Central banks, as the holders of base money for the whole banking system, do not lose reserves as quickly when they overissue, and so have more leeway in responding when losses come. The discipline that regular clearing imposed, enforcement of the laws of contract between banks and their noteholders and depositors, and free banks' lack of power to make their notes legal tender (hence, the absence of a 'time consistency' problem), explain why free banking systems rarely abandoned specie convertibility during peacetime. Free banks at times attempted to manipulate exchange markets, but without the limited success that central banks on a gold standard sometimes had with reserve sterlization policies. For instance, Scotland's Ayr Bank failed in 1772 partly because it could not prop up exchange rates between Scotland and London (Checkland 1975: 128). It may be that because much of the world had free banking during the time of the classical gold standard, the gold standard was indeed automatic then, contrary to the belief of many writers who have examined its workings (for a listing, see Bordo 1984). During and after the First World War, many countries switched to central banking or introduced measures to control the supply of commercial bank reserves, and the gold standard may have lost its automatic character as a result. (It may also have been important that, before the First World War, central banks acted more like the privately owned entities most of them were, rather than, the government appendages they all later became.)

Because free banking was inherently a regime of convertibility into gold or silver (or copper, in China), long-run price stability was greater than it has been under central banking, which has often begun as a regime of convertibility but has always become one of fiat money. Even a casual look at historical trends in price indexes (for instance, the tables in McCallum 1989: 247) confirms that long-run price stability was greater under free banking.

Counterfeiting and fraud

Counterfeiting and fraudulent note issue were not serious problems under free banking. Even where there were many contemporary complaints about counterfeiting or 'wild-cat' banking, subsequent research suggests that the complaints were exaggerated (Rockoff 1975a: 13–33. The complaints arose in systems that had hundreds of note brands because they restricted branch banking (England before 1826, the United States, France during the Revolution[5]) or during periods when a banking system as a whole suspended convertibility with the government's blessing (e.g., Canada in 1837). Accounts of branch banking systems rarely mention instances of counterfeiting and fraudulent note issue during periods of convertibility.

Frauds by bank employees happened, of course. But there is no evidence that fraud was so widespread that it undermined the stability of any free banking system, though it occasionally caused individual banks, usually small ones, to fail. Certainly free banking offers nothing to compare with the massive fraud in the American savings and loan industry over the past few years.

LIQUIDITY AND THE LENDER OF LAST RESORT

The most common argument that economists make for the desirability of a central bank is that commercial banks need a higher authority to prevent them from reckless credit expansion in good times and to serve as their lender of last resort in bad times. The argument originated with Walter Bagehot (1912 [1873 chs 6–7]). In its current form, it claims that depositors and noteholders cannot adequately discipline commercial bank credit expansion by themselves because they lack the necessary information.[6] Therefore, banking systems without a central bank are supposedly prone to occasional sudden demands for redemption, which they cannot meet, when people try to convert notes and deposits into the reserve asset as a way of testing the solvency of banks. A central bank can regulate commercial banks to prevent them from overexpanding credit, or help them surmount crises by lending generously to them (Goodhart 1988: chs 5,7).

I believe that economists have misread the historical evidence that they adduce in favour of central banking. Free banking systems were on the whole more stable than central banking systems during peacetime and no less stable than central banking systems during wartime. As we shall see later, the English and American free banking systems, which economists often cite as examples of free banking's instability, were among were the most regulated of all free banking systems. The far less regulated Scottish and Canadian free banking systems had much better performance under similar economic conditions. Most free banking systems experienced *no* peacetime system-wide panics, and even heavily regulated free banking systems developed arrangements that provided liquidity without a lender of last resort.

Where the law enforced contractual obligations to convertibility, free banking systems did not habitually hold inadequate reserves to meet redemption demands, as Richard Cothren (1987) has suggested they might. No account of any free banking system that I am aware of mentions any attempt by free banks to expand credit in concert with one another; each bank was too much concerned with guarding its own reserve. Individual banks overextended credit and sometimes went broke by being overly bold, but that is a danger under any fractional-reserve banking system.

Free banking systems developed several means of providing themselves with liquidity during crises. One was the local interbank lending market. It was extremely rare for free banks in a system to be so heavily 'loaned up' that none was willing to lend to banks that were illiquid at the moment but had sufficient assets to repay a short-term loan. Other banks were often willing to rescue a troubled bank, either for a high interest rate on a loan or, in severe cases, for control of the bank. Sometimes a single bank assumed all the risk, while at other times they formed syndicates. As I have mentioned, in the United States and in Mexico, clearing-houses mobilized the reserves of their member banks during crises. In the Australian crisis of 1893, the Melbourne clearing-house did likewise (Pope 1989: 22). Unlike current central banking systems, free banking systems did not have a policy that some banks were too big to let fail. Solvent banks sometimes expressed fear about the effect on public confidence of an insolvent rival's failure, but on the other hand, some very large troubled banks were in such straits that nobody would take over their management, so they had to declare bankruptcy.

In certain countries, banks that could not raise sufficient funds in local markets borrowed in a larger market in another region of the country or across the border. Thus Scottish banks and British overseas banks borrowed in London, Swiss banks in Paris, Canadian banks in New York, and so on. Some writers have contended that free banking systems were 'satellites' of the central or semi-monopoly banks in the large money markets (the Bank of England, the Bank of France, the Federal Reserve System and perhaps the US Treasury) (Goodhart 1988: 52). Many claim that the Bank of England was in fact the lender of last resort to the whole world during the classical gold standard's heyday, and that it was what enabled the classical gold standard to persist.

However, the Bank was not even the lender of last resort to Scotland, let alone to the four corners of the earth. Checkland's history of the Scottish banking system (1975: 409–10, 444) mentions only one occasion when the Bank of England acted like a lender of last resort to a Scottish bank. In 1830, when war with France threatened, the Royal Bank of Scotland arranged a long-term credit with the Bank of England. However, during the panic of October 1836, the Bank of England made the Royal Bank repay the loan. Charles Munn (1981a), in his history of the smaller Scottish banks, makes no mention of the Bank of England being a lender of last resort to them. Kevin Dowd (1990a) also disputes the claim that Scotland's banking system was a 'satellite' of the Bank of England.

Scotland, and much of the rest of the world, certainly did business in the London money market. The larger Scottish banks kept deposits with London correspondents, in part because they were forbidden from establishing branches in England. But London would have been the financial centre of the British Isles, and of the world, whether the Bank of England had existed or not.

The United Kingdom was the greatest commercial nation of the nineteenth century, and London was its centre. Other financial centres, among them Montreal,[7] Shanghai, Osaka and Stockholm, had no central bank at the vortex and were none the worse for it. Indeed, that London was the storm centre of so many eighteenth- and nineteenth-century panics suggests that the Bank of England's effect on the world financial system may have been detrimental. All eighteenth- and nineteenth-century panics were apparently worse in England than in Scotland (Cameron 1967: 98), except the Scottish crisis of 1878, well after the free banking era, which occurred when a large Glasgow bank failed.

Another means of providing liquidity, which Scottish banks used especially widely for a time, was an option clause. A standard Scottish option clause permitted a bank to delay gold payment of notes and deposits for up to six months, during which it paid 5 per cent annual interest, a higher than normal rate and the legal maximum.[8] The delay gave the bank time to liquidate assets at good prices rather than at fire-sale losses. The Bank of Scotland originated the option clause in 1730 after the Royal Bank of Scotland's note duelling tactics made it suspend convertibility temporarily (Checkland 1975: 67).[9] The option clause suffered undeserved bad publicity from Adam Smith (1937 [1776]: 309–10), who, though he otherwise approved of free banking, claimed that banks' abuse of the option clause disrupted Scotland's internal exchange rates. The British Parliament outlawed the option clause in 1765, and outlawed notes under £1, as a way of favouring the three chartered banks, who suffered less from the measures than their smaller, unchartered rivals (Checkland 1975: 118–21). Agreement to the option clause was voluntary; people who disliked it could hold the notes and deposits only of banks that did not have it. Advantageous as the option clause could have been though, it was rarely used elsewhere (Hammond 1957: 178 describes one case), though some banks in the United States even today have 'notice of withdrawal' clauses, which allow them to delay redemption but do not impose a penalty rate of interest.

As an unsatisfactory substitute for contractually specified suspension of convertibility, free banking systems sometimes imposed inconvertibility involuntarily on noteholders and depositors, with express or tacit government approval. Most involuntarily imposed suspensions happened during wartime. Governments recognized that compelling banks to maintain convertibility would choke off credit as the public rushed to withdraw gold and silver from bank reserves.

The precarious situation that free banks faced in wartime was not the product of free banking's own instability, but of events that gold- or silver-standard central banking systems could not handle either. If anything, central banking systems historically have been more prone to suspend convertibility than free banking systems. For example, the Bank of England, which has one of the better records among central banks, suspended convertibility from 1696 to 1697, 1797 to 1821, 1914 to 1925, 1931 to 1946, and 1971 to the present – a total of seventy of its 296 years. In 1825, 1839, 1847, 1857 and 1866, it avoided suspension only by borrowing from the Paris money market or breaching the ceiling of uncovered note issue laid down in the Bank Charter Act of 1844. The

Bank of France likewise suspended during the revolution of 1848, the Franco-Prussian War of 1870 and the First World War. During the Great Depression, central banks that had been on the gold standard abandoned it for long as fifteen years. And all of them again abandoned it in 1971 under pressures that they could easily have surmounted, had they had more political willpower; no war or great economic calamity had occurred.

PANICS

Absence of system-wide panics (bank runs) is a good indicator of the stability of banks as a group. In considering whether free banking systems were prone to panics, though, one must carefully distinguish between wartime and peacetime panics. There are few cases of banking systems, whether under free banking, central banking, or other arrangements, that maintained fixed-rate convertibility into gold or silver during wartime. Both the countries that had free banking and those that had central banking suspended convertibility during the First World War, for example. In countries that had convertible government-issued notes circulating alongside bank notes, such as Canada, the free banks and the government alike suffered convertibility runs.

There is a chicken-and-egg problem in trying to assess why wartime convertibility runs happened, either under free banking or under central banking. It could have been because people were fearful that the issuing banks would fail, or because people anticipated that governments would suspend convertibility as a prelude to inflationary war finance. If the option clause had been widespread, it would be easier to tell the difference between the two causes of runs: countries where most banks used the option clause should have had only runs on *individual* banks in wartime. The option clause should have been a sufficient deterrent to *system-wide* wartime bank panics, as it was before it was outlawed in the Scottish free banking system. However, since such test comparisons are lacking, it seems wise to restrict the evidence about systemwide panics under free banking to peacetime cases only.

Systemwide peacetime panics in free banking systems were infrequent. There were occasional runs on individual banks whose solvency the public doubted, but they rarely spread to other banks that had no business connection with the first bank to suffer a run. Even more rarely did they ever turn into general runs for gold or silver from the banking system. Instead, people switched funds from banks that they perceived as risky to those that they perceived as safe, leaving the banking system's total gold and silver reserves unchanged. System-wide peacetime panics under free banking occurred in England in 1825 and 1836–7; in the United States on a half-dozen occasions from 1819 to 1907; in Ireland and Canada in 1836–7; in Belgium in 1848; in Ceylon (Sri Lanka) in 1884; in Argentina, Uruguay and Paraguay in 1890–1; in Australia and New Zealand in 1893; and in Chile in 1898. Let us briefly now briefly examine these cases, except for the English and American panics, which we shall consider later.

Ireland

A credit stringency gripped the British Isles in the autumn of 1836, following a decision by the Bank of England to raise its discount rate from 4.5 per cent to 5 per cent and to stop lending to unlimited-liability 'joint-stock' banks. Irish banks suffered a run in November after one of their number failed – the Bank of England had earlier refused to lend to it – but they did not suspend (Ollerenshaw 1987: 42–3).

Canada

By the spring of 1837, the credit stringency in the British Isles spread to the New World as British demand for New World products dropped. All but a few banks in the United States suspended specie payments in May; banks in Canada, except Upper Canada (Ontario), followed suit. In the Maritime provinces, banks resumed by the end of the summer. In Lower Canada (Quebec), banks resumed soon after their US counterparts in May 1838. The governor of Upper Canada refused to let banks in the province suspend, and as a result, a wave of business failures, far more severe than in the other provinces, swept over the land as banks contracted credit (Shortt 1986: 333–45; Schull and Gibson 1982: 35). (Here is a case where an option clause would have been advantageous, both to banks and to their borrowers, in helping buy time for more orderly liquidation.)

Belgium

The French revolution of February 1848 forced the Bank of France to suspend convertibility. The Belgian public took that as a signal to stage a run on Belgian banks, and an Antwerp bank failed. To prevent a greater crisis, the Belgian government allowed the two biggest banks to suspend convertibility and made their notes legal tender. However, the notes did not depreciate against silver, which was Belgium's monetary standard at the time. The two big banks lent liberally to smaller banks and industry, and by June the storm passed (Cameron 1967: 135). Nevertheless, Belgium established a central bank in the belief that it was the only way to avoid another crisis.

Ceylon (Sri Lanka)

The Oriental Bank Corporation, which had three-quarters of Ceylon's note circulation, failed in 1884. Its demise came at the end of a long slump in the market for Ceylon's principal export, coffee, which brought a decline in the bank's fortunes. To avert panic, the governor guaranteed the bank's notes (Gunasekera 1962: 61–70). The other note-issuing bank in Ceylon could not easily expand its issue to fill the gap in supply that the Oriental Bank failure created because, as was typical of British colonial banks, its charter prohibited its note circulation from exceeding the amount of its capital (Nelson 1984: 186).

Australia

Australian land values began to drop in 1888, as the collapse of a building boom, caused by an influx of foreign investment, threw large new projects onto the market. Near the end of 1889, the first of what was to become a chain of mortgage company failures occurred; the failures continued until 1892. Some small banks also closed their doors, but not until January 1893 did a big bank fail. Runs on other banks followed, and by May, 13 of the 26 banks in the system suspended convertibility into gold. The other banks did not suspend convertibility, though, and all but one of the banks that suspended reopened within two months (Gollan 1968: 28–33; Pope 1989: 18; and Dowd, chapter 3 in this book).

New Zealand

The Australian crisis hurt the Bank of New Zealand, which was weak from a series of losses it had suffered since the late 1880s. The crowning blow was the failure of one of its largest borrowers. The bank asked the government to rescue it, which the government did. The other banks in the system suffered runs because the public suspected them of weakness, but they met all demands to pay out gold (Sayers 1952: 326–7).

Argentina

Argentina's currency during its free banking period consisted of fiat government notes and bank notes nominally backed by gold government bonds, but in reality unbacked. In November 1890, the Bank of England came to the rescue of Baring Brothers, the largest underwriter of Argentine bonds. News of the Barings failure prompted a drain on banks owned by Argentina's national and provincial governments, which failed in April 1891. The British-owned London and River Plate Bank was one of the few to survive a run on private banks in June. Argentina centralized the note issues of the failed banks in a government agency that was supposed to restore gold convertibility, but did not (Joslin 1963: 125–8; Quintero-Ramos 1965: 86).

Uruguay

In Uruguay, the government bank failed in April 1890. The failure of another bank in August 1891 sparked a system-wide run. The London and River Plate Bank, which maintained convertibility while its rivals were suspending, then emerged as the strongest in the country. Uruguayan political opinion was hostile to what it considered foreign domination in banking, and a central bank was founded in 1896 on the wreckage of the old government bank (Joslin 1963: 136–7).

Paraguay

Most of Paraguay's foreign trade passed through Argentina, and Argentina's troubles caused a run on Paraguay's banks, which then suspended convertibility. By 1891, the government bought three banks and took over their inconvertible note issues, and it did not restore convertibility (Rivarola Paoli 1982: 209–17).

Chile

The threat of war with Argentina in 1898 led to rumours that the government would abandon the gold standard, which had been re-established a few years before after a long period of inconvertibility.

A scramble for gold ensued in Santiago. When it started to spread to the rest of the country, the government allowed the banks to suspend convertibility. Once it had done so, the government was tempted to increase its own note issues, which had been responsible for the previous period of inconvertibility, and Chile did not return to the gold standard until 1913 (Subercaseaux 1922: 116–17). Conant (1927 [1896]: 514) blamed the crisis on the exchange-rate system, which, like the Japanese and Argentine systems, attempted to keep government currency convertible by selling gold bonds to banks that wanted to issue notes.

Some recent economic models of bank runs (Diamond and Dybvig 1983; Gorton 1985a) have suggested that runs on individual banks and on the banking system might be common where there is no central bank or government deposit insurance. According to these models, bank runs can arise randomly, and once they do, they become self-fulfilling prophecies: since no fractional-reserve bank ever has enough reserves on hand to meet convertibility demands from all its customers at once, a small number of withdrawals can generate a mad rush by other customers to withdraw before a bank's reserves are depleted. Free banking's history does not support the results of these models. The panics that we have just examined all had readily identifiable causes. In a detailed investigation of runs on individual Canadian banks from 1867 to 1925 (Schuler 1988), I did not find any that seemed random. Runs were caused by bad news about a bank's asset holdings (for instance, failure of a major debtor), or by troubles affecting banks with similar portfolios. Only in about half the cases did banks suspend convertibility or fail. Runs did not spread to banks that were utterly dissimilar from the first bank to experience trouble. Large size was a deterrent to runs: runs sometimes spread from large banks to small banks with similar characteristics, but did not spread from small banks to large banks. The free banking systems of other countries seem to have had similar experiences to Canada.

CAUSES OF FREE BANKING'S DEMISE: SEIGNIORAGE

If free banking worked so well, why did it disappear? Broadly speaking, its demise had three causes. In some countries, governments squeezed out competitive note issue to extract monopoly profits (seigniorage) from their own note issues. In others, theoretical arguments for monopoly note issue carried the day. In still others, a bank failure or a suspension of gold or silver convertibility discredited free banking. Although in a number of cases those causes were mingled, for the sake of simplicity Table 2.1 at the end of the chapter assigns one cause as predominant.

Central banking did not always appear when free banking disappeared. There was often a long interval of monopoly note issue without central banking, as under the 'currency boards' established in many British colonies. Even where a central bank existed, it sometimes took many years to acknowledge its role as regulator of and lender of last resort to commercial banks. Until the Bank of England rescued Baring Brothers in 1890, for instance, some of the Bank's directors continued to resist Walter Bagehot's suggestion that it should not behave as an ordinary commercial bank.

I now want to examine the reasons why free banking ended in some of the leading nations.

China

Several times, from the eleventh to the twentieth centuries, Chinese governments outlawed free bank-note issue to force acceptance of their own note issues. In 1935, China abolished free banking for the last time as part of a policy to confiscate private silver stocks and to impose government fiat money as the monetary standard.

France

The first western country to replace free banking with monopoly issue was France, whose initial free banking era lasted just seven years. The Revolutionary government foreswore note issue after its *assignat* fiat currency collapsed in 1796. Several free banks soon sprang up in Paris. They succeeded in maintaining convertibility where the government had failed. Napoleon held stock in one, the Bank of France, and in 1803, he stripped competing banks of their right to issue notes (see chapter 7).

Sweden and some other cases

Heads of state elsewhere rarely had the personal financial motive for favouring note-issue monopoly that Napoleon did, but they did have motives of political self-preservation. When war or extravagant peacetime expenditures threw a government into debt, concentrating note issue in a favoured bank that would lend to it, or emitting government notes, was often less unpopular than raising taxes.

The use of the printing press as a tool of government finance was commonplace. Nine of the approximately sixty free banking episodes listed in Table 2.1 ended because of overt seigniorage considerations. Sweden, where no note-issuing bank failed during seven decades of free banking, seems to have been one. Legislative hostility towards competitive note issue was not the result of any theory of monetary policy or unfavorable experience with free banking in Sweden (Jonung 1989: 16, 29).

CAUSES OF FREE BANKING'S DEMISE: THEORETICAL RATIONALES

Britain

Britain was the prototypical case of central banking triumphing because its partisans seemed to have the stronger arguments. In an intense debate that lasted for two decades up to 1845, hundreds of economists, bankers and politicians argued for and against free banking (see White 1984b: 51–80). The so-called Currency School believed that the depressions and bank failures England suffered in 1825–6 and 1836–7 showed the instability of competitive note issue. (English banks did not suspend convertibility into gold during either panic.) The Currency School argued that the cause of business cycles is that unregulated note currency behaves differently from purely metallic currency. As a remedy, they advocated centralizing note issue with the Bank of England and subjecting the Bank to an iron-clad rule requiring it to hold 100 per cent marginal gold reserves for all notes issued above a fixed ceiling.

Among the Currency School's opponents, the Free Banking School pointed to the Scottish banking system's performance. They argued that Scotland's comparative immunity from the crises that beset England was evidence that English note issue was too much regulated rather than too little regulated. (A third group, the Banking School, was silent on this aspect of the debate.) In over a century of free banking, Scottish noteholders and depositors lost only £32,000, whereas losses in London (which had fewer inhabitants than Scotland) were twice as much in 1840 alone (Aytoun 1844: 678, cited in White 1984b: 41). The Free Banking School argued that a system of large, competing note-issuing banks would be more stable than the system that existed at the time in England. To that end, they advocated abolishing the law that English note-issuing banks could have no more than six stockholders, which the British Parliament did in 1826. They also advocated, but unsuccessfully, abolishing a provision of the new 1826 law, which forbade banks with more than six stockholders from issuing notes if they established branches in the London region, the Bank of England's seat.

The Currency School's arguments convinced the government of Sir Robert Peel, which in the Bank Charter Acts of 1844 and 1845 forbade new banks in England, Wales and Scotland from issuing notes and froze the circulation of existing note-issuers other than the Bank of England, at a total of £8.5 million, which was approximately their average circulation at the time (Capie and Webber 1985: 211). The 1844 Act fixed a ceiling above which the Bank of England had to hold 100 per cent gold reserves against its note issue at £14 million (the Bank's note circulation was then about £21 million). However, the Act provided that the Bank of England could partly absorb the 'uncovered' note issues of banks that failed or gave up the right of note issue. The Bank of England thus became the central bank of England, Wales and Scotland. A similar law for Ireland in 1845 made the Bank of Ireland in effect the central bank there. (A few Scottish and Northern Irish banks continue to issue notes today, but beyond a combined uncovered issue of less than £5 million, they must have reserves at the Bank of England at least equal to the amount of their note issues, and they are prohibited from issuing notes for more than £5.) The Bank of England eventually absorbed the note issues of all English and Welsh banks. Two Bank of England officials drafted the 1844 Bank Charter Act (Clapham 1945: vol. 2, 178–9).

The Currency School was preoccupied with note issue, and it failed to understand that deposits are just as much as part of the money supply as notes. The English financial crises of 1847, 1857 and 1866 exposed the flaw in Currency School doctrine. The Bank of England averted runs only by temporarily exceeding the legal limit on its note issue. Although free banking would have automatically accommodated changes in the public's demand to hold notes, there was little thought of returning to it, because, as Walter Bagehot (1912 [1873]: 68) remarked, it would have seemed as great a break with tradition as abolishing the monarchy. Through the fixed-rate convertibility of commercial bank deposits into Bank of England notes, the Bank came to exercise control over commercial banks.

British Colonies

After Peel's Bank Charter Acts, all non-self-governing British colonies eventually wrote a form of Currency School doctrine into law. They established colonial currency authorities or currency boards, which in some cases held gold or silver, but more frequently sterling-denominated assets, equal to 100 per cent of their monopoly note issues. In Mauritius, Ceylon and the Bahamas, currency boards were the result of local government distrust of bank-note issue after a local bank failed. Elsewhere, though, the main reason for currency boards was the triumph of Currency School ideas (Hanke and Schuler 1992).

France

In the late nineteenth century, several European countries had contests between partisans of free and central banking that mirrored the British monetary debates. Economists there appropriated whole-sale the ideas of the Currency, Banking and Free Banking schools, and frequently referred to English or Scottish banking experience to illustrate their arguments. In France, vigorous debate occurred when France annexed Savoy in 1860. The Pereire brothers, who directed the huge investment bank, Credit Mobilier, tried to challenge the Bank of France's note monopoly by taking over the note-issuing Bank of Savoy. However, the Bank of Savoy had to give up its note issue, so the effort came to naught.

Germany

In Germany, the Reichsbank was founded in 1875 to standardize the disparate coinage and note systems that had existed in the German states before unification. However, other means could have accomplished the goal just as well. Unrestricted private minting would have led to a uniform coinage, albeit one produced by multiple competing firms, as in the United States before 1864. Similarly, unrestricted branch banking would have led to nation-wide par acceptance of all banks' notes, as it did in Scotland and other systems. German officials mistakenly believed that a central bank was necessary for a discount policy, and proponents of free banking were unable to convince them of the self-correcting nature of the price – specie flow adjustment. The statutes governing the Reichsbank consequently imitated Peel's Bank Charter Acts (Smith 1990 [1936]: 68).

United States

Central banking in the United States, as in England, resulted from dissatisfaction with the existing system's flaws. The American banking system was among the most regulated of all 'free' banking systems. Legal barriers to branch banking prevented the United States from developing the large, stable nation-wide banks that characterized most free banking systems elsewhere. There were marked regional differences in bank stability before the American Civil War, and banking systems generally experienced less trouble in states where regulation was less extensive. The New England states, which had few significant regulations except for prohibitions of branch banking, were known across the country for sound banking, and they weathered the panics of 1819, 1837 and 1857 with little difficulty. They suspended convertibility only in 1837, whereas banks in other regions suspended convertibility on many other occasions before the Civil War. The private Suffolk Bank of Boston developed into a central clearing agent for banks all over New England, and its strict policies kept the note issues of other banks closely in line with the demand to hold notes. In other regions, local authorities often aided local banks in frustrating outsiders' attempts to exercise the legal right to convertibility on demand (Hammond 1957: 178–80, 549–56).

The first nation-wide bank charter laws, passed during the Civil War, prohibited banks that wanted to issue notes from having any branches, and required them to hold government bonds as collateral for their note issues. The bond-deposit requirement severely constrained note supply during seasonal peaks of demand for notes. In 1873, 1893 and 1907, note shortages developed, and notes went to a premium against deposits (for example, a cheque for $100 would only 'buy' $97 of notes). Retail trade would have ground to a halt had not clearing-houses and other issuers created emergency notes, which were illegal but immensely useful (Sprague 1977 [1910] Timberlake 1984).

Canada had an entirely different experience from the United States, just as Scotland had had a different experience from England. Canadian bank-note issues were limited to the amount of the bank's paid-in capital, but for many years the ceiling was too high to have any effect. Canada was little affected by the American panics of 1893 and 1907, and Canadian bank notes circulated widely in the United States during these panics (Denison 1966: vol. 2, 260, 284–5). Many American observers admired the Canadian system's branch networks and its 'asset-based'currency, so called because banks did not have to hold any special collateral against note issues. The

1894 Baltimore convention of the American Bankers' Association proposed remodelling American note issue along Canadian lines, but anti-gold standard agitation and opposition from small banks opposed to competition from branch banks prevented the plan from receiving a hearing (Hepburn 1968 [1903]: 381).

Though Canada suffered no actual note shortage in 1907, Canadian banks were approaching the legal ceiling on their note issues, which raised the spectre of American-style shortages in the future. In 1908, Canada amended its banking law to allow note issue of up to 115 per cent of bank capital during the months of peak demand, and in 1913 loosened note-issue limits still further. The changes proved adequate to prevent troubles. The United States, on the other hand, resolved the problem of inelastic note supply by passing the Federal Reserve Act in 1913. In the American debate over the solution to inelastic note supply, most bankers, economists, and politicians sought intellectual guidance from European central banking systems rather than from Canada's free banking system. As an interim measure to ease note shortages, the 1908 Aldrich–Vreeland Act authorized clearing-houses to issue emergency notes without specific collateral. When the First World War broke out in August 1914, the Federal Reserve had not yet begun operations, and clearing-house currency issues efficiently met the increased demand for notes, with no currency premium. Milton Friedman and Anna J. Schwartz (1963: 172) have commented that Aldrich–Vreeland currency had the elasticity that the Federal Reserve brought, without the Fed's inflationary potential. Abolishing bond-deposit requirements would have made the Federal Reserve's original rationale superfluous.

Other countries

The First World War was a great divide in free banking history. Most nations that had free banking suspended convertibility during the war. Canada, New Zealand, South Africa and other countries took a step towards central banking during the war when they imposed inflationary war finance measures. After the war, the 1920 Brussels and 1922 Genoa monetary conferences of the League of Nations recommended that central banks be established in the new nations created after the war and in older countries. The League's recommendation proved influential. Free banking by then had no significant support among economists. The chief reason appears to have been that economists had little understanding of the difference between free banking and central banking. The controversy over gold versus silver as the monetary standard, and then the debate over quantity theory of money, diverted attention from the earlier Currency School–Banking School– Free Banking School debates, which, as a practical matter, the Currency School seemed to have won.

The Great Depression was the crowning blow to free banking. Even countries that suffered no bank failures, such as Canada and New Zealand, introduced central banking, because prevailing opinion held that it might be able to help end the Depression. Central banking evidently did not end the Depression, but there was no thought of returning to free banking. One by one, governments imposed central banking on the remaining free banking systems. The last place where free banking existed was, apparently, South West Africa (Namibia), where free banking lasted until 1962 (Crossley and Blandford 1975).

CAUSES OF FREE BANKING'S DEMISE: CRISES

Central banking in the countries just discussed originated in government cupidity or in unwillingness to solve contemporary banking troubles by deregulation. However, there were countries where free banking passed from the scene because financial crises created a demand for more bank regulation. A previous section touched on the crises that led to the end of free banking in Argentina, Belgium, Ceylon (now Sri Lanka), Chile and Uruguay. This section examines the remaining cases: Japan, Italy, Mauritius, the Bahamas, Southern Africa and Hong Kong.

Japan

The bond-collateral system that Japan introduced in 1872 was intended to support the country's monetary system. Banks were to buy bonds from the government with gold. The government was then supposed to use the gold to restore convertibility of its inconvertible notes. However, it never realized these intentions, and printed increasing quantities of notes to finance its expenditures. In 1876 government notes traded at a discount to their face value in gold and silver. The expense of supressing the Satsuma rebellion the following year led to further inconvertible issues. Banks were released from buying gold bonds as collateral against bank note issues; instead, the government encouraged banks to prop up the price of inconvertible bonds that it had issued to compensate former feudal lords. The inflation of the late 1870s provoked discussion of how to return to the gold standard, and the government decided to scrap bond-collateral issues and its own inconvertible issues, replacing them with the notes of a central bank, the Bank of Japan, which opened in 1882 (Soyeda 1896: 425–8; Conant 1911: 12).

Italy

The collapse of the Banca Romana in 1893 prompted Italy's government to reappraise its free banking system. The banks of issue in the various states had come into competition with one another as the country achieved unification. The former monopoly issuer in the Papal States, the Banca Romana, was bankrupt, but the national government propped it up for political reasons. That situation continued for over twenty years, until in 1893 the economist Maffeo Pantaleoni made public a secret government audit revealing the true state of the bank's finances. The Banca Romana failed, and two other note-issuing banks hastily merged with the Bank of Italy. Legislation passed in the aftermath of the failure preserved plural note issue, but the Bank of Italy effectively supervised the other two note-issuing banks and the Bank of Italy became the monopoly note issuer in 1926 (Ferraris 1911).

Mauritius

In the British colony of Mauritius, one of the two local banks failed in 1847 (Crick 1965: 302). It is possible that the other bank's charter limited its note issue sufficiently to prevent it from filling the added demand for notes. The government decided, however, that a state monopoly note issue would be safer than private one, though it left deposit banking competitive.

Bahamas

In the Bahamas, the only locally chartered bank failed in December 1916 (a British colonial bank also circulated notes in the Bahamas) and the Bahamas government reacted in the same way as the Mauritius government.

Southern Africa

In South Africa and in Bechuanaland (Botswana), where the only banks were branches of South African banks, there was an inflation during the First World War when the country in effect abandoned the gold standard and made bank notes legal tender. A central bank was proposed as the remedy and it opened in 1920 (Conant 1969 [1896]: 805).

Hong Kong

Hong Kong ended free banking in 1935 in the wake of China's unexpected decision to abandon the silver standard, which disrupted the basis of their trade. The government confiscated the banks' silver, and tied the Hong Kong dollar loosely to the British pound, which itself was no longer convertible into gold at a fixed rate.

CONCLUSIONS

Free banking was far more widespread than economists have hitherto recognized. There were approximately sixty cases of it. The spontaneous evolution of free banking in all countries that had banking but lacked monopoly note issue indicates that free banking was indeed 'the natural system', as Walter Bagehot had earlier argued (1912 [1873]: 67).

On balance, free banking was stable. Only in a handful of episodes did the banking systems as a whole suffer runs or suspend convertibility into gold or silver during peacetime. All of the runs had identifiable causes and none was random. (Present-day central banks do not suffer runs for reserves, but they have cast off the 'nominal anchor' of convertibility that once guaranteed relative stability in the value of central bank liabilities.)

There was no apparent tendency towards monopoly in any free banking system. Many systems saw a similar pattern of a large number of banks entering the field in early years, only to fail or merge with others until few were left. However, the ranks never diminished until just one bank was left; there remained plural note issue. The attempts of free banks to form cartels were always unsuccessful, since cartels were undermined by uncooperative or cheating banks.

Central banking was an imposition, not the outcome of the natural evolution of free banking. Free banking systems showed no apparent tendency to develop a lender of last resort – or to need one. The experience of the little-regulated banking systems of Scotland and Canada indicates that deregulation would have solved the problems that plagued the heavily regulated English and American free banking systems. Curiously, it was regulation that drove Britain, the United States and other countries to adopt central banking. Nor do free banking systems seem to have had significant public-good problems

Table 2.1 Free banking episodes

(1) Country	(2) Free banking era	(3) Restrictions on bank freedom	(4) Reason free banking ended	(5) Central banking began	(6) Main sources
Europe					
Belgium	1835–1851	none	crisis	1851	Chlepner 1943; *banque en Belgique* 1980
France	1796–1803	none	seigniorage	1848	E. White 1990*;
	1815–1848	E, F	seigniorage		Nataf, ch. 7, this vol.*
Germany	1821–1833	E, F	theory	1875	Riesser 1911;
	1836–1875	E, F	theory		Klein 1982
Greece	1839–1920	A, F	theory	1928	Kyrkilitsis 1968; Freris 1986
Italy	1837–1894	A, E, F	seigniorage	1926	Ferraris 1911; Nardi 1953; Fratianni and Spinelli 1984, 1985
Luxembourg	1873–1883	none	theory	1922h	Weiller 1981; Croisé and Link 1988
Malta	1809–1865	unknown	theory	1964	Crick 1965, ch. 13(b)
Portugal	1850–1891	E, F	seigniorage	1891	Essars 1896, part 6
Spain	1844–1874	E, F	seigniorage	1874	Tortella Casares 1977; Garcia Ruiz 1989*
Sweden	1831–1901	C, e, g	seigniorage	1901	Flux 1910; Jonung 1989*
Switzerland	1834–1907	C, e, F	theory	1907	Landmann 1910; Weber, ch. 11, this vol.*
United Kingdom:					
Channel Islands	c.1797–1914	none	theory	1914	McCammon 1984
England, Wales	c.1668–1844	C, E, F	theory	1844	Gilbart 1865; Pressnell 1956
Ireland	c.1693–1845	c, E, F	theory	1943	Bodenhorn, ch. 8, this vol.*
Isle of Man	1802–1961	d	theory	1961	Clay 1869; Quarmby 1971
Scotland	1716–1845	c, g	theory	1845	L. H. White 1984, and ch. 9, this vol.*

Table 2.1 Free banking episodes (continued)

(1) Country	(2) Free banking era	(3) Restrictions on bank freedom	(4) Reason free banking ended	(5) Central banking began	(6) Main sources
North America					
Bahamas (UK)	1888–1916	unknown	crisis	1974	Conant 1927, ch. 18
British Honduras (Belize) (UK)	1904–1937	b	theory	1981	Conant 1927, ch. 18; Wyeth 1979
British West Indies (UK)	1837–1951	none	theory	1964	Barclays Bank 1938, Crossley and Blandford 1975
Canada (UK)	1817–1914	b, d	theory	1934	Schuler, ch. 4. this vol.*
	1914–1933	A, B			
Costa Rica	1863–1884	A, B	seigniorage	1936	Soley Guell 1926; Villalobos Vega 1981
	1902–1921	a, d	seigniorage		
Guatemala	1877–1926	A, B	theory	1926	Prober 1957; Quintana 1971
Honduras	1886–1889	none	theory	1950	Castillo Flores 1974; Cruz Reyes 1981
	1912–1950	b, d			
Jamaica (UK)	1837–1958	b	theory	1961	Barclays Bank 1938; Crossley and Blandford 1975
Mexico	1864–1925	e, f	theory	1925	Conant 1910; Bett 1957
El Salvador	1880–1934	a, D	theory	1934	Canales 1942; Rochac 1984
United States	1782–1863	c, D, E, F	theory	1914	Dowd, ch. 11, this vol.*
	1863–1914	B, C, D, F			

Table 2.1 Free banking episodes (continued)

(1) Country	(2) Free banking era	(3) Restrictions on bank freedom	(4) Reason free banking ended	(5) Central banking began	(6) Main sources
South America					
Argentina	1887–1890	A, B, D	crisis	1935	Williams 1920, chs. 7–8; Quintero-Ramos 1965, chs. 3–4
Bolivia	1887–1914	none	theory	1929	Benavides M. 1972, ch. 12; Cabezas Villa 1941
Brazil	1836–1853	A, B	seigniorage	1920	Calogeras 1910; Franco 1973; Pelaez 1981
	1857–1866	A, B, E	seigniorage		
	1889–1892	A, B, D, F	seigniorage		
British Guiana (Guyana) (UK)	1837–1951	b, d	theory	1966	Conant 1927, ch. 18; Thomas 1965
Chile	1849–1850	none	theory	1925	Ross 1910; Subercaseaux 1922
	1854–1898	A, B, C, D	crisis		
Colombia	1871–1886	A, B	theory	1923	Torres Garcia 1980; Echeverri 1989*; Meisel Roca 1989*
Ecuador	1860–1927	A, B	theory	1928	Carbo 1978; Estrada Ycaza 1976
Paraguay	1889–1907	A, b	theory	1944	Rivarola Paoli 1982; Fernandez 1982–4
Peru	1862–1887	A, B, d	theory	1922	Ferrero 1953; Alcazar 1957
	1914–1922	unknown			
Uruguay	1865–1896	b	crisis	1896	Lezana 1956; Joslin 1963, chs. 3, 7
Venezuela	1882–1940	b	theory	1940	Crazut 1970; Pardo 1973

Table 2.1 Free banking episodes (continued)

(1) Country	(2) Free banking era	(3) Restrictions on bank freedom	(4) Reason free banking ended	(5) Central banking began	(6) Main sources
Africa					
Bechuanaland (Botswana) (UK)	1897–1921	none	crisis	1975	Onoh 1982, chs. 4, 5
Mauritius (UK)	1832–1849	unknown	crisis	1967	Crick 1965, ch. 13(e); Nelson 1984
Rhodesia (Zimbabwe) (UK)	1892–1939	none	theory	1956	Henry and Siepmann 1963, ch. 10; Reserve Bank of Zambia, 1983
South Africa (UK)	1837–1921	d, f	crisis	1921	Arndt 1928; Sayers 1952, chs. 10–11
South West Africa (Namibia) (RSA)	1915–1962	none	theory	1962	Crossley and Blandford 1975
Asia					
Ceylon (Sri Lanka) (UK)	1841–1884	b, C	crisis	1938i/1950	Gunasekera 1962
China	c. 1004–1935	G	seigniorage	1942	Yang 1952, ch. 9; King 1965. ch. 4; Selgin, ch. 7, this vol.*; Shiu 1990*
	1644–1935	G			
Hong Kong (UK)	1845–1935	c	crisis	1988	King 1957, ch. 5; King 1987–8
India (UK)	1806–1861	c, d	theory	1934	Bagchi 1987
Japan	1600s–1882	A, B, D	crisis	1882	Soyeda 1896; Shinjo 1962
Macau (Port.)	1800s–1944	e	theory	1980	Ma 1987
Malaya (Malaysia) (UK)	1850s–1908	b, c	theory	1958	Chiang 1966; Drake 1967

Table 2.1 Free banking episodes (continued)

(1) Country	(2) Free banking era	(3) Restrictions on bank freedom	(4) Reason free banking ended	(5) Central banking began	(6) Main sources
Philippines (US)	1916–1942	A, b, E	theory	1949	Stanley 1974
Singapore (UK)	1846–1908	b, c	theory	1958	Nelson 1984; Lee 1986
Thailand	1888–1902	none	seigniorage	1942	Tavedikoul 1939; King 1988, vol. 2: 129–32, 236
Australia and Oceania					
Australia (UK)	1817–1911	b, e	theory	1911	Butlin 1953, 1986; Pope 1989
Fiji (UK)	1860s–1914	unknown	theory	1975	Crick 1955, ch. 2; Rogers and Cantrell 1989
New Zealand (UK)	1840–1850	c	theory	1934	Sayers 1952, ch. 9; Chappell 1961;
	1856–1914	c, b			Hargreaves 1972
	1914–1933	A, B	theory		

NOTES

Column (1):

Port. – Portuguese colony
UK – British colony for part or all of free banking period
US – territory under American administration during free banking period
RSA – territory under South African administration during free banking period

Column (3):
Capital letters indicate severe restrictions, lower-case letters, mild ones. List is suggestive rather than exhaustive.

a – government-induced suspension of specie payments begun in peacetime, usually caused by government currency debasement
b – government legal-tender note issues alongside free bank note issues
c – note issue restrictions (economically binding issue ceilings, small-denomination restrictions)

Table 2.1 Free banking episodes (continued)

d – economically binding reserve or bond-collateral requirements
e – barriers to entry (chartering restrictions, limits on number of stockholders, minimum capital requirements that significantly limited competition)
f – branching restrictions
g – other (economically binding usury laws, frequent forced loans to government, etc.)

Column (4):
crisis–bank failure or suspension of payments prompting note issue monopolization
seigniorage–the government attempt to raise revenue by monopolizing the currency
theory–laws passed to impose a theoretical ideal (such as British Currency School programme)

Column (5):
Many countries had monopoly note issue but no fully fledged central bank for awhile after abolishing free banking.
h – the Belgian central bank became Luxembourg's central bank
i – the Reserve Bank of India was Ceylon's central bank from 1938 to 1950

Column (6):
* The author discusses the episode as a case of free banking.

Episodes requiring further investigation:
Gibraltar to 1914, Liechtenstein, Morocco 1865–1906

that are often held to make central banking necessary. As Vera Smith wrote in her study of nineteenth-century banking controversies,

> An examination of the eventual decision in favour of a central banking as opposed to a free banking system reveals in most countries a combination of political motives and historical accident which played a much more important part than any well-considered economic principle.
>
> (Smith 1990 [1936]: 4–5)

Of course, free banking was not perfect; in a world populated by imperfect people, no institution can be. Some bank managers made inept decisions; some noteholders and depositors suffered losses. Overall, though, free banking was quite robust, and it proved itself able to thrive in a great variety of economic and cultural conditions.

The often-heard claim, first made by Bagehot (1912 [1873]: 68), that central banking is irreversible, rests more on assertion than on solid theory or careful historical investigation. In the past, free banking has replaced monopoly note issue or monopoly banking in countries as diverse as Scotland, New Zealand, Costa Rica and Brazil. Central banking persists today only because government self-interest and received economic theory have combined to impose it. Not long ago, most economists considered telephone systems to be natural monopolies, and justified state ownership of the telephone system in many countries on the grounds that it was more efficient than private ownership. Today they know better. Perhaps they will change their minds about natural monopoly in banking when they consider the historical record of free banking.

NOTES

The best compilation of free banking episodes is still *A History of Modern Banks of Issue* by Charles Conant, first published in 1896. The sixth edition (1927) was reprinted in 1969. Other world surveys are Sumner, W. G. (ed.) (1896), Huebner (1854), Levy (1911), Dierschke and Mueller (1926) and Willis and Beckhart (1929). More limited surveys are Kindleberger (1984) (Western Europe); Sayers (1952) and Crick (1965) (the British Commonwealth); Cameron (1967 and 1972) (some European countries, Japan, and the United States); Young (1925) (Central America); Onoh (1982) (Africa), and King (1957) (British East Asia). Hahn (1968: 43–4 and 62–81), and Kock (1974) have world lists of central banks. Pick (1986) and other numismatic publications are useful for information on otherwise obscure cases of free banking. The British government's colonial reports often have brief descriptions of colonial banking. Finally, of course, there are primary sources such as bank archives, newspapers and statutes.

1 Earlier surveys of cases of free banking are Cameron (1967 and 1972), Vaubel (1978: 362–401 and 1984a), Selgin (1988: 5–15), and Goodhart (1988).

2. There were exceptions. The Colonial Office rebuffed persistent requests for royal charters to operate in India from the 1830s to 1851 (Baster 1929: 92–109), and in southern Africa from the 1830s to the 1860s (Sayers 1952: 354).

3. For an outline of the free banking and central banking history of many countries, see Conant (1927).

4. One should remember, though, that like any institution that arises from the voluntary co-operation of many people, free banking served a variety of ends. To suggest that any single quality taken in isolation should be the standard for judging free banking systems is to imply that bankers and consumers in the free banking era should have had the same tastes that we do.

5. The French *caisses patriotiques*, which issued small-denomination notes, faced no explicit branching restrictions, but the national government's hostility towards them made expansion risky. The government outlawed them in 1792, less than two years after they came into being (White 1990: 271).

6. Roland Vaubel (1984b) rebuts the related argument that money itself has characteristics that justify supressing competition between issuers of money to solve 'public goods' problems (made for example, by Brunner and Meltzer 1971: 802).

7. Official monthly statistics show that from 1871 (when reporting began) to 1927, the Canadian banking system as a whole was *never* a net debtor to 'banks and banking correspondents, elsewhere than in Canada and the United Kingdom' (Curtis 1931: vol. 1, 31, 45), a category that included Canadian banks' New York activities. During the American panic of 1907, Canadian banks actually increased their New York loans (Rich 1988: 122).

8. After adopting the option clause, the Bank of Scotland used it only once, in 1745, when Bonnie Prince Charlie's rebellion provoked a general suspension of convertibility (Checkland 1975: 73). Apparently, the existence of the option clause was by itself enough to deter bank runs. An option clause would have benefited Scottish noteholders during the Restriction period of 1797 to 1821, when all British banks suspended convertibility. Instead, noteholders received no interest. Banks had less incentive to resume payments, because suspension imposed no additional costs.

9. For an exposition of the rationale of the option clause see Dowd (1988).

3 Free banking in Australia

Kevin Dowd

Australia experienced one of the most interesting historical experiences of free banking. Australian banking was relatively free for almost a century, from the establishment of the first banks in the second and third decades of the last century until well into the twentieth, and fully fledged central banking only arrived with the establishment of the Reserve Bank of Australia at the comparatively late date of 1959. The Australian experience of free banking is of particular interest to students of banking history because the legal framework within which banks operated was perhaps the least restrictive of any on record, and the banking system was largely free of significant government intervention until the 1890s. Australia never had 'pure' *laissez-faire* in banking, but Australian banks operated under relatively innocuous legal restrictions compared to many 'free banks' elsewhere, and the legal restrictions that did exist were frequently disregarded anyway. The comparative purity of the Australian case ought therefore to give us a reasonably fair indication of how well the theory of free banking has worked in practice.

Australian free banking is also of interest for another reason. In the early 1890s Australia experienced a banking crisis of a severity never witnessed in Australia before or since, a crisis whose severity superficially compares to that of the English crisis of 1825–6 or the banking collapses of the US during the early 1930s. But unlike these other crises, the Australian one occurred while banking was still in some ways quite free, and many writers have argued that the freedom of Australian banking contributed in a major way to its severity. Unrestricted competition led banks to over-extend themselves, so the argument goes, and the collapse of the land boom in the late 1880s left them exposed to a crisis that most of them lacked the resources to ride out. Had there been a monetary authority to limit competition and ensure that prudential standards were maintained, on the other hand, then the banking system would not have over-reached itself to the extent that it did, and the ensuing collapse ought to have been avoided. Generations of Australian economists have consequently believed that the crisis of the 1890s demonstrates that unregulated banking is inherently unstable, and have concluded that some form of government control is needed to keep this instability in check.

The Australian experience is unique in that it is the *only* recorded case where free banking has been associated with a major banking collapse. Free banking systems elsewhere witnessed occasional bank failures, but none ever experienced a crisis comparable to the Australian one, and the supporters of free banking need to reconcile their theory that banking *laissez-faire* is stable with the claim that the Australian banking crash indicates that it is not. Contrary to received opinion, however, the Australian experience is in fact quite consistent with the predictions of free banking theory. The depression of the 1890s was fundamentally a 'real' phenomenon driven by forces outside the bankers' control, and these forces overwhelmed the banks as well as the 'real' economy. The bank failures were also heavily influenced by government intervention, especially in Victoria, and these interventions destabilized the banking system and encouraged banks to suspend to take advantage of new laws which allowed them to reconstruct on advantageous terms. The evidence on reserve ratios and capital adequacy also provides little support for the hypothesis that the bank failures were caused by the banks' previous over-expansion. It is in any case somewhat misleading to talk of bank 'failures' in an unqualified way when virtually all of these banks were subsequently able to re-open successfully. The timing of events lends also further support to the view that the primary direction of causation was from the real economy to the banking system, and the timing of the downturn is quite inconsistent with any claim that a banking 'collapse' pushed the economy into a steep depression. The crisis of 1893 was not what it might appear to be.

THE EARLY HISTORY OF MONEY AND BANKING IN AUSTRALIA

The blueprint for the first Australian colony in New South Wales in 1788 made no allowance for the provision of money or banking. Its monetary arrangements were consequently almost all *ad hoc* temporary makeshifts. Foreign coins, arriving haphazardly in trade or in officers' purses and convicts' pockets, acquired local acceptability and brief legal recognition. But they did not suffice, and from the simple expedient of settling debts with promissory notes grew, in the first decade of the nineteenth century, the practice of regular issue by all and sundry of small-notes. . . .

Makeshifts and *ad hoc* expedients to provide for payments between government and individuals and amongst individuals thus merged into a pattern. . . . The core of the monetary system was the Commissariat store with its Treasury bills for public and external payments, its Store receipt, its loans in kind; outside its range private local transactions were fulfilled by supplanting its Store receipts with barter and a variety of private note issues.

(Butlin 1953: 4–5)

Once it had established itself the new colony began to prosper. The settlers took to farming and whaling, and by the second decade of the nineteenth century they were already exporting wool to England. The private note issues continued to prosper, and repeated attempts by Governors King, Bligh and MacQuarie to suppress them came to nothing. The first bank – the Bank of New South Wales – was set up under MacQuarie's patronage in 1817, but its note issues were small and had relatively little impact on the non-bank issuers. A number of new banks was set up in the 1820s, however – the Waterloo Company (1822), the Bank of Van Diemen's Land (1823), the Bank of Australia (1826), among others – and

with them died at last, in the metropolitan centres but not in the country, miscellaneous issues by individuals and stores. In the country such issues were progressively pushed further and further outback as banks advanced, to be (virtually) eliminated only after a full century. What the Bank of New South Wales had heralded they made commonplace, 'the ordinary banking business of deposit, discount and exchange'.

(Butlin 1953: 9)

These banks were all unit (i.e. one-branch) banks that operated under the English law that restricted all banks except the Bank of England to be partnerships with no more than six partners, and all partners bore an unlimited liability for the debts of the bank. These banks were initially allowed to issue notes for any amount, but a domestic British ban on notes under £1 was extended to Australia in 1826.

It took some time to resolve the issue of the monetary standard. Foreign denominations circulated side by side with sterling for a number of years. One Governor (MacQuarie) introduced his own dollars – 'holey' dollars, imported dollars with a hole stamped in them – which were over-valued locally and hence circulated by virtue of Gresham's Law, while another, Governor Brisbane, tried in 1822 to have the Spanish dollar made the legal unit of account and the basis of the circulating medium. This attempt was apparently well on the way to success when the UK government intervened and imposed the gold-based pound sterling as the official currency and ordered the colony to use British coins. This was the origin of the Australian pound (Butlin 1953: 8; 1961: 10). Dollars then disappeared relatively quickly in New South Wales, but survived for some time in Tasmania. The value of the Australian pound was now linked to gold, but it could fluctuate by a margin that reflected the costs of shipping gold to or from England to exploit any discrepancy between its par and market values. Arbitrage therefore kept the value of the Australian pound reasonably close to par. The links between the Australian pound and gold were tightened further by the establishment of a branch of the Royal Mint at Sydney in 1855, and later on by the opening of other branches in Melbourne and Perth. The Australian Mints reduced the costs of arbitrage – one could now carry out arbitrage operations without having to ship gold to or from England – and thus narrowed the range within which the value of the Australian pound could fluctuate. The result was that in the sixty years following the establishment of the Mint in Sydney, the value of the Australian pound was almost always within 2 per cent of sterling, and usually much closer.

THE DEVELOPMENT OF AUSTRALIAN BANKING

The transformation of the banking system

The 1830s saw a large pastoral boom – half a continent was occupied in ten years – and the inflow of large amounts of British capital into Australia. The first chartered bank – the Bank of Australasia – obtained its charter in 1835 and a 'flurry of colonial bank formations' followed in the late 1830s (Butlin 1953: 9, 10). The banking system was then rapidly transformed into one that was, 'for its time, mature and sophisticated':

> In place of a few localized unit banks relying on capital for loanable funds, content with a restricted business and averse to

serious competition, there were a number of large banks – all the important colonial banks had greatly expanded – engaged in aggressive competition. A scramble for deposits which had pushed up deposit rates to high levels had established deposit banking as the standard practice. Competition for business as settlement spread had caused abandonment of unit for branch banking. . . . One aspect [of this transformation] was the rapid growth of a systematic foreign exchange market, primarily constituted by the English banks, outside and independent of the Commissariat.

(Butlin 1953: 11)

Branching enabled banks to economize on operating costs (e.g., by holding fewer reserves per branch, and operating an inter-branch reserve market) and enabled them to provide specialist services (such as the provision of foreign exchange) at lower cost. Branch banks were also likely to have a more stable capital value because branching enabled them to protect themselves against adverse conditions in one locality or region by diversifying their risks.

The legal framework

The chartering of the Australasia in 1835 prompted the United Kingdom Treasury to clarify its ideas on colonial banking, and these ideas were set out subsequently in the Colonial Bank Regulations of 1840. These Regulations were meant to provide broad guidelines for colonial governors who were faced with petitions and bills to grant charters. Although they were sometimes modified in practice, the main principles were that bank notes should be payable on demand; the personal liability of shareholders should be limited to twice the value of subscribed capital; following a 'real-bills' view of the business of banking, banks were not allowed to lend on land, or to deal in real estate or merchandise, except to settle debts; there should be no notes under £1; banks should provide regular statistics to the relevant authorities; and there were certain restrictions on total indebtedness. The revised Regulations of 1846 also stipulated that the note issue should be limited to the amount of paid-in capital (Butlin 1986: 89–90)

These conditions were not as restrictive as they might appear. The note and indebtedness restrictions were seldom if ever binding (e.g. Butlin 1986: 93). The ban on lending against land threatened to be more restrictive, but the regulation was always accompanied by the qualification that a bank could subsequently acquire property in settlement of a debt, and it was not too difficult to devise ways to keep transactions strictly within the letter of the law while violating its intent (Butlin 1986: 94). In any case, as Pope noted,

> Formal codes were not, however, taken very seriously. In the vernacular of the times, bankers drove a coach and horses through the hampering limitations of the legislation. The National Bank, almost from its inception [in 1859] lent on land. . . . What the National was doing so too were the others, land based advances possibly accounting for as much as two-thirds of the banks' total advances business by the 1880s. According to Turner '. . . the limitations [of the acts and charters] are practically ignored, in some cases by a special adaptation of the form of the entry, but frequently by an entire disregard of them'.
>
> (Pope 1987: 21)

The legal framework under which banks operated changed further in the third quarter of the century. The colonies became masters of their own banking laws as they became self-governing from 1856. (Western Australia became self-governing in 1890.) Banks with earlier charters were still nominally subject to the previous system of regulation, but

> none of these [regulations] was, in practice, a serious limitation on a bank's freedom and the colonies soon began to diverge from the canon basis provided by the Regulations. In the event, the only requirement that survived in more or less uniform terms was the requirement to make statistical returns.
>
> (Butlin 1986: 92)

One change, from 1863 onwards, was the gradual amendment of colonial banking laws to make shareholders' liability for the note issue unlimited (Butlin 1986: 92–3). Tasmania also started to tax the note issue in 1863 and the other colonies followed suit:

> The only purpose behind these levies was the raising of money. . . . The usual rate, two per cent, was about a half, or a little less, of what was generally accepted as the net profit on issue accruing to the banks. In time this was to make the banks dubious of the advantage of continuing note issue and readier to contemplate acceptance of government monopoly of issue.
>
> (Butlin 1986: 94)

This period also saw the Treasury move towards eliminating the chartered banking system and the Treasury supervision that went with it (Butlin 1986: 89). Charters had been sought earlier because they were the only way to obtain the valuable privilege of limited liability, but a British Act of 1862 had allowed banks access to limited liability without the need for a special charter. (The limited liability was qualified, however, in that it did not apply to the note issue.) The Treasury then took the view that this Act provided all that was necessary, and that a special charter implied Treasury supervision and might be seen to imply some degree of government responsibility for a bank that had a charter. The Treasury therefore tended to refuse new charters and resist the renewals of existing ones.

AUSTRALIAN BANKING FROM THE 1850S TO THE 1880s

The prosperity of the golden decade of the 1850s saw a massive expansion of Australian banking:

> The eight trading banks operating in Australia when gold was discovered, had grown to fifteen by the end of the fifties. At the end of 1850 there was a total of twenty-four branches (including head offices); at the end of 1860 there were 197.
>
> (Butlin 1986: 8)

Some indication of this expansion can also be gleaned from the figures on notes, deposits and bank advances. Note issues grew from £447,000 in the first quarter of 1851 to £3,192,000 a decade later. Deposits grew from £2,932,000 to £14,583,000 over the same period, and advances grew by a comparable amount.

The next decade saw further growth in the banking system, though at a slower rate, as well as

> a flowering of fringe institutions. Most obvious were the building societies, multiplication of which was in response to the housing demand of the new population. . . . Building societies had first appeared in New South Wales in the forties, and in greater numbers in the fifties. But whereas by 1860 in Victoria the total number of mostly short-lived terminating societies had been less than twenty, in the next ten years nearly fifty were established, and the permanent type of society was more usual. Other colonies had a similar story to tell.
>
> (Butlin 1986: 67)

This period also witnessed the rapid growth of savings banks. These were started to encourage thrift, and to counter the excessive drinking and gambling which threatened to leave convict emancipists, in the famous phrase, 'poor, vicious, unmarried'. At mid-century there had been six small savings banks whose main investment was mortgages, but twenty years later their assets had grown nearly ten-fold (Butlin 1986: 69). Savings banks were also encouraged by colonial governments which saw them as a means of securing cheap loans. The British model of using post offices as savings banks

> appeared to offer colonial governments . . . [which suffered] recurrent financial crises, the prospect of a steady flow of funds at moderate rates of interest, not as subject to parliamentary supervision as conventional public borrowing. This was crudely obvious in New South Wales, and not well concealed in Victoria and Queensland.
>
> (Butlin 1986: 69)

The financial system – the 'regular' (i.e. trading) banks, as well as the building societies, the savings and land banks, and other 'fringe' institutions – continued to grow until the early 1890s. All these institutions took in deposits and made advances of one sort or another, and competition for market share was fierce. The 1870s and 1880s witnessed a rapid expansion of branch banking, and institutions looked more and more to Britain to increase their deposits. Interest rates were lower in Britain than in Australia, so deposits in Australian banks were attractive to British investors and a comparatively cheap source of funds for the banks. The ratio of British to domestic deposits in Australia consequently rose from perhaps 10 per cent in the mid-1870s to 40 per cent by the eve of the Depression (Pope 1989: 15–16). The relative market shares of the different types of financial institution also changed substantially over this period, with the trading banks losing ground to the fringe institutions. The trading banks' loss of market share was particularly large in the 1880s, and figures provided by Merrett (1989: 65) indicate that the trading banks' share of financial assets fell from around 90 per cent in 1883 to barely 65 per cent only a decade later. A major reason for their loss of market share was the trading banks' reluctance to participate in the land boom of the 1880s with the same enthusiasm as some of the 'fungoid' banks that mushroomed during that period on the strength of it. This conservatism was to stand them in good stead later when the boom ended and the economy went into depression.

The Australian banking system exhibited a number of distinctive features during this period:

1 The banks formed a hierarchy. By 1892 there were 7 large banks with 100 branches or more spread across at least 2 colonies, there were 5 intermediate banks which tended to be concentrated in a single colony, and which had 50–99 branches each, and there were 11 small banks which tended to be concentrated in a single region, and to have less than 50 branches each (Schedvin 1989: 3; Merrett 1989: 73).

2 Concentration rates were very high – four banks issued about half the deposits throughout this period (Pope 1989: 29) – but no one of these banks ever looked as though it would win the others' market shares. There was therefore no tendency towards natural monopoly. The experience of Australian free banking thus matches free banking experiences elsewhere (e.g. in Scotland, Canada or Switzerland, as the chapters by White, Schuler and Weber make clear) that banking exhibited economies of scale, but never showed any sign of natural monopoly.

3 The note-issuing banks accepted each others' notes from a relatively early stage, and mutual acceptance seems to have facilitated the reflux mechanism whereby notes were returned to issuers, but clearing was often carried out on a bilateral basis. A (multilateral) clearing-house was established in Melbourne in 1867, but Sydney only followed suit at the comparatively late date of 1895. The explanation appears to be that the small number of banks involved implied that the gain from moving from bilateral to multilateral clearing was relatively unimportant.

4 Profit rates appear to have fallen over this period, presumably because of increased competition (Pope 1987: 7–8). Pope also notes elsewhere that bank profits do not appear to be excessive on an opportunity cost basis, and that 'the banks' profit rate lay in the middle of the league of corporate profit earners' (1989: 10).

5 The interest rate margins – the spread between the banks' overdraft rates and their 12-month deposit rates – fell to a margin of around 4 per cent in the early 1870s and then stayed around that level (Pope 1989: 11). Boehm (1971: 211) notes that fixed deposit rates were very similar between the banks over the later part of this period (1884–94), and this evidence appears to suggest that the banks had effectively unified the Australian financial market. Note too that Australian interest rates were only about half as volatile as interest rates in the UK or the USA (Pope 1989: 24–5), and the most obvious cause of this greater interest stability would seem to be the comparative freedom of the Australian banks from disruptive

government or central bank interference.

An interesting feature of the Australian free banking system is that the note issue was never particularly important for Australian banks except in their very early years. The bank note/deposit ratio was 26.1 per cent in 1851, and fell subsequently to 7.4 per cent in 1881, 4.5 per cent in 1891, and 3.9 per cent in 1901 (Pender *et al.*, 1989: 8). These figures are well below contemporary note/deposit ratios for the UK or the USA, and seem to indicate a more mature banking system in which greater use was made of cheques and deposits. It also appeared to be generally accepted that the rapid reflux mechanism provided by the banks' clearing system made note over-issue more or less impossible, and this point was so widely accepted that it was never even controversial in Australia. The Australian attitude to competitive note issue stands in marked contrast to attitudes in countries such as the UK or the USA in the nineteenth century where the argument that competitive banks would not overissue notes was normally a minority view, and, indeed, a view that was considered almost completely discredited by the later part of the century.

Another remarkable feature of Australian free banking was the large number of branches that banks maintained. Branching was a significant form of non-price competition, and banks used branches to gain an edge over their competitors by distinguishing their product by means of its location (Pope 1988). The extent of Australian branching can be gauged from an article in the *Australasian Insurance and Banking Record* (*AIBR*) of 1880 which stated:

> There is . . . in England and Wales a banking office for every 12,000 persons; in Scotland, one for every 4,000; and in Ireland, one for every 11,000 of the inhabitants. Now in Victoria . . . we have a branch of a bank for every 2,760 colonists.
>
> (Quoted in Pope 1988: 2)

The corresponding figure in the US was one for every 9,200. It has long been argued that branches were a major drain on profits. An *AIBR* article of 1877 had earlier stated that

> in a township where there is barely enough profitable business for one branch bank or banking agency, there are often two or three, each with its building and its staff of officers to maintain. . . . But when two branch managers become rival candidates for the patronage of three or four petty traders, we cannot help considering that branch business is overdone.
>
> (Quoted in Pope 1988: 3)

These claims were echoed by the chief executive of the Australasia who at the end of the 1880s could list forty-two branches that earned less than the 5 per cent the bank was paying on its deposits (Pope 1987: 5). Such claims have also been supported by other writers such as Blainey (1958).

These claims should none the less be viewed with some suspicion. The problem is that it is not in a bank's own interest to expand its branch network to the point where it erodes its own long-run profitability, and it is no defence to say that a bank will do it if it thinks its rivals will as well. It is not rational for a firm to choose to incur losses, and this holds true regardless of whether it expects its rivals to inflict losses on themselves or not. The 'evidence' for over-branching also needs to be treated cautiously. The fact that Australia had more branches per capita than other countries might simply reflect their under-branching, or, perhaps, the fact that Australia had a higher per capita real income and consequently a greater demand for financial services. The Australasia's forty-two loss-making branches might also reflect the state of bank profitability at the time or the state of the economy, as well as the bank's own policy. Branches typically made a loss to start with, but were expected to make up for this loss later on. A bank with a lot of relatively new branches might therefore expect a significant number of them to make temporary losses, but those losses did not necessarily mean that the branches lacked viability in the longer term. Note, lastly, that the remaining 'evidence' in favour of over-branching is merely anecdotal, and a recent empirical study by David Pope was unable to find any significant evidence to support it (1988).

A final noteworthy feature of Australian banking during this period is that the banks never managed to establish a viable cartel. They repeatedly tried, but their attempts were always undermined by competitive pressures:

> The banks formed associations and collusive agreements to fix 'terms of business', more explicitly the rates to be charged on deposits, advances, bill discounts and foreign exchange. However, as the manager of the Union Bank (now ANZ) reflected, 'I do not think it has ever been believed that a strict adherence to the spirit and conditions of the [price] agreements has at any time prevailed and there is no Bank that hasn't . . . at some time or another trangressed the strict letter of it' . . . Banks cheated, agreements were ruptured and at times one of the biggest banks, the Bank of NSW (now Westpac), remained outside the agreements.
>
> (Pope 1988: 1, n. 1)

THE DEPRESSION OF THE 1890S AND THE BANK CRASH

The 1880s saw a major land boom, especially in Melbourne, and many financial institutions lent extensively against land-based assets. The boom continued into the late 1880s and the more experienced bankers began to perceive danger and advise caution. A contemporary observer, Nathaniel Cork, later said in a lecture to the (British) Institute of Bankers,

> Many in this audience can testify that the most experienced Australian bankers . . . emphatically discouraged this movement [i.e., jumping on the bandwagon]. They saw the danger to the depositors, the mischief to the colonies, and the fearful risk to the bank's [*sic*] concerned.

(Cork 1894: 181)

An example was the London executive secretary of the Bank of Australasia, Prideaux Selby, who warned the Bank's chief Australian executive in February 1888 that 'you Melbourne people are riding for a bad fall' (quoted in Pope 1989: 16). He had earlier warned against speculative lending on real estate, and had cautioned the Australian managers 'to be in no hurry to let out your spare funds – keep strong – profits must be sacrificed in the interests of safety' (quoted in Pope 1989: 18, n. 21).[1] These warnings were reflected in more cautious policies by a number of banks, including the big ones – the Australasia, the Union, and the Bank of New South Wales – which tried to reduce their exposure to losses in the event that the property market turned down.

Concerted action then followed in October 1888 when the Associated Banks of Victoria[2] raised the 12-month deposit rate from 4 to 5 per cent and announced that advances on speculative real estate were at an end. The interest rise 'abruptly halted the reckless spirit of land speculation' (Boehm 1971: 254), and the chairman of the Associated Banks was able to report by the end of the year 'that the times were acute, that the land-banks were short of funds, that the Associated Banks were slowly gaining more funds but conserving them, and that speculators were short of money' (quoted in Blainey 1958: 137). House prices started to falter, and the property companies the following year were unable to recover their deposit market share from the 'sounder' institutions despite being willing to pay 1–2 per cent more on their deposits (Boehm 1971: 256). Falling land prices then led to the collapse of a number of these institutions in 1889–90. Around the same time, the earlier inflows of British capital started to decline, and Australian terms of trade were already very adverse and becoming more so. The economy's momentum led real output to peak in 1891, but output declined very sharply thereafter. Blainey reports that

> Melbourne felt the scarcity of British money early in 1891. The price of property slumped, smiting the weaker building societies and land-banks. The building industry crumpled, unemployment increased and trade became dull. The cheques passing through the Melbourne clearing-house fell from £150,600,000 in the last half of 1890 to £114,300,000 in the second half of 1891.
>
> (Blainey 1958: 141)

The year 1891 saw the first bank failures and the widespread collapse of the fringe institutions that had gambled their futures on a continuing land boom. The first outright bank failure – the failure of the Bank of Van Diemen's Land – occured in August, and the situation on the mainland rapidly deteriorated:

> Late in July the Imperial Banking Company, a Melbourne mortgage bank, collapsed, to be followed in August by two similar and related institutions. In September there was a burst of failures in Sydney of land banks and building societies. In December the centre of disaster was again Melbourne, with building societies and mortgage banks collapsing in quick succession, including the Metropolitan and Standard Banks.[3]
>
> (Butlin 1961: 285)

Many of the building societies tried to meet the demands for withdrawals by relying on overdraft facilities with the Commercial Bank. The Commercial managed to keep them afloat for a while, but it eventually decided that it could no longer withstand the strain on its own position. It therefore called in its overdrafts in late 1891 and many societies were soon forced to close (Blainey 1958: 143).

The runs prompted – indeed, panicked – the New South Wales and Victorian governments to rush through emergency legislation at the end of 1891 to give beleagured institutions a chance to defer redemptions by removing the right of a single creditor to enforce liquidation. The result in New South Wales was the Joint Stock Companies Arrangement Act (1891) which stipulated that claims could be deferred if creditors holding three-quarters of the company's liabilities agreed to it. The reconstruction scheme would then become binding on all creditors, which meant that no single creditor would (normally) have a veto over it. The Victorian legislature, by contrast, passed the Voluntary Liquidation Act (1891) which stipulated that a company in voluntary liquidation could only be wound up if one- third of creditors demanded it, and these creditors had to have at least a third of the value of the company's liabilities. This Act was widely condemned as making it almost impossible to have a company wound up, and consequently left creditors more or less at the mercy of the directors.[4] (Butlin 1961: 286; Boehm 1971: 266, 301). The main effects of the Act were to damage credit in Victoria and hinder the restructuring of the financial system, and it was subsequently amended at the end of 1892 to bring it into line with the New South Wales Act.

The bank failures continued in early 1892 when the building society connections of the Federal and Commercial Banks gave rise to considerable public concern, and the Associated Banks were pressured to come up with joint action to reassure the public. (Much of this pressure came from the Federal and Commercial Banks themselves, which were members.) The result was a public statement in March in which the Associated Banks announced that they had agreed on conditions on which they would help members. (They did not announce, however, that those conditions required borrowers to provide adequate security, and this requirement effectively nullified the support they were offering.) The announcement managed to allay public fears, none the less, and the Associated Banks remained 'unscathed for the remainder of the year, while many of their former competitors – the mushroom land-banks – were wiped away'. As Blainey continued,

> In Melbourne and Sydney forty-one land and building institutions failed in the space of thirteen months, locking up £18,000,000 of deposits. In new suburbs whole streets of houses were vacant, scores of shops were shut; and in the city entire floors of new skyscrapers were tenantless.
>
> (Blainey 1958: 147)

The crisis then flared up again when the Federal Bank failed in January 1893. The Federal was the smallest and weakest of the Associated Banks, and, indeed, had only been (reluctantly) admitted as an Associated Bank four months earlier. The Federal had unfortunate associations with recent building society and land company failures, and these problems were reflected in a very sharp fall in its share price and a steady and substantial loss of deposits in the second half of 1892. The bank's position was hopeless,[5] and the

Associated Banks' refusal to help it after a thorough investigation of its finances gave it no option but to close. The public seemed to take the news calmly at first,

> but depositors drew some obvious morals. Here was the first of the Associated Banks to fail, and apparently no serious attempt had been made to save it; the misunderstood assurance of mutual aid of March 1892 clearly was no protection. From this time onward the withdrawal of deposits from banks believed to be weak rose to almost panic levels.
>
> (Butlin 1961: 296)

The Commercial Bank was extremely hard hit by this loss of confidence. As noted already, the Commercial had already tried to cut its losses by curtailing credit to building societies at the end of 1891, but its association with institutions that had gambled heavily on land continued to haunt it and encourage a flow of withdrawals that turned into a flood once the Federal failed. Its share price had also fallen sharply since the end of 1891. The Commercial's position became so precarious that the Victorian Treasurer pressured the Associated Banks to bail it out. The Associated Banks themselves disagreed about what should be done. The stronger banks such as the Union and the Australasia had no incentive to support the weaker ones since their own reserve position was strong and they continued to enjoy public confidence. The Australasia, the Union and the Bank of New South Wales had all received substantial deposit inflows since late 1892 – so many deposits flowed in, in fact, that the two Melbourne banks were embarrassed by this 'sign of public confidence' (Butlin 1961: 305) – and this 'flight to quality' was to continue until the final bank failures later in May (Blainey 1958: 145, n. 1). For the weaker banks, however, an agreement was tantamount to the provision of a credit facility at interest rates generally below what they would have had to pay on the market. An agreement was thus equivalent to a transfer from the stronger banks to the weaker ones, and the stronger banks were naturally reluctant to consent to it. An initial statement was put out that the Associated Banks would support each other, but considerable political pressure had been applied and the chief executive of the Australasia had refused to go along with it, and this statement was followed soon after by a 'clarification' on 13 March that so qualified it as to render it virtually meaningless. As Butlin put it,

The fat was really in the fire. Such an assurance . . . [meant]
that the banks were not in fact prepared to give each other any
guarantees at all . . . the sequence [of events] could not have been
better planned to touch off panic. . . . The run on deposits now
became a panic, so far as banks believed to be tottering were
concerned. . . .

(Butlin 1961: 297)

The Commercial was then faced with a run it could not meet. It
applied for assistance from the Associated Banks, but was unable,
or perhaps unwilling, to satisfy the conditions required for a loan,
and it duly suspended on the weekend of 4–5 April.

When it suspended, the Commercial simultaneously announced
plans for its capital reconstruction under the terms of the recent
Victorian legislation. (There was some suspicion, indeed, that its
application for assistance had simply been a feint to provide a
justification for suspending in order to implement a reconstruction
plan that had already been decided upon.) Reconstruction involved
setting up a new bank with the same name as the old; there
were extensive calls on shareholders for more capital; and deposit
repayments were generally deferred, with existing deposit claims
being tranformed into a combination of preference shares and
deposits of varying (and often long) maturities. The 'essence of
the scheme was that the bank asked for time to pay those creditors
who demanded immediate repayment, but it promised to pay them
in full, in interest and principal' (Blainey 1958: 165), and the fact
that depositors raised relatively few objections suggests that they
preferred it to any viable alternative.[6] Small depositors with £100
on current account

were given three £10 preference shares and a fixed-deposit receipt
for £70 when the bank re-opened. If they were short of ready
money they could borrow from the bank on the security of their
fixed-deposit receipt, and within three years they were able to sell
their preference shares at a profit and within seven years they
received full payment for their deposit receipt. For eight weeks,
while the bank was shut, they were seriously inconvenienced, but
thereafter they did not suffer. . . . Reconstruction caused [the
majority of wealthier depositors] worry but neither monetary
loss or inconvenience. They had originally deposited their money
for the long term in order to get a good return and a secure
investment, and they continued to derive these advantages from

their preference shares and fixed-deposit receipts. The rate of interest was higher than they had received before the bank crash and for some years it would be 50% higher than the rate offering for a new deposit in any Victorian bank. They only suffered inconvenience if by chance they had to suddenly marshal their resources in order to meet debts or business losses. Being men of property, however, they could usually raise the money on mortgage.

(Blainey 1958: 165–6)

A curious feature of the reconstruction, and one that was later copied by other suspended banks, was the opening up by the Commercial, four days after it suspended, of trust accounts which enabled deposits and withdrawals to be made without involving any of the funds in the bank's 'old' business. These accounts then undermined the banks that remained open, and there 'ensued the spectacle of depositors in banks still open, hastily withdrawing their funds to escape the threat of reconstruction and promptly depositing in a trust account in the Commercial' (Butlin 1961: 300).

The suspension of the Commercial encouraged others to follow suit. As Butlin observed:

Every surviving bank had thrust before it the great advantages of 'reconstruction': permanent accession of capital; immediate elimination of the mounting tide of deposit withdrawals; and miraculous restoration of confidence. Harrassed and worried bankers . . . followed the lead of the Commercial.

(Butlin 1961: 300)

Twelve other banks suspended over April and May to gain time to reconstruct. The banks that suspended accounted for 56.2 per cent of all deposits held in March, and 61.3 per cent of all notes issued in April and May, and while they would have accounted for smaller percentages over the next two months, these figures none the less give an idea of the order of magnitude of the suspensions (Butlin 1961: 302).

The suspensions were also prompted by government intervention. In Victoria the government imposed a five-day banking holiday from 1 May. The heads of the Union and Australasia Banks strongly opposed the holiday and ordered their banks to remain open to do whatever legal business they could. The *AIBR* reported that the bank holiday proclamation was issued 'in the hope that the public mind might calm down, the principle being unconsciously adopted that in order to put out a fire the right thing is to shower petroleum on it'. It failed to have the desired effect. The *AIBR* continued:

> When Monday morning came, Melbourne was in a state of indescribable confusion and semi-panic and Collins-street presented scenes never before witnessed in the history of the colony. But when it was discovered that the Bank of Australasia and the Union Bank of Australia, ignoring the proclamation, had thrown their doors wide open . . . the excitement gradually abated.
>
> (quoted in Boehm 1971: 307–8)

The two banks' willingness to remain open shored up public confidence in them, and the withdrawals they faced soon abated. The Bank of New South Wales re-opened the next day, and also stood the storm, but the remaining banks that had closed had effectively lost public confidence and were consequently unable to reopen (Butlin 1961: 303–4). The government of New South Wales considered a similar step, but rejected it and decided instead to make bank notes temporary legal tender. The banks in New South Wales were consequently allowed to apply to have their notes made legal tender, but the major banks had no desire to apply – presumably because they felt it would signal to the market that they needed the 'support' of legal tender – and the government ended up making their issues legal tender regardless. The governments of New South Wales and Queensland also made provision for a government note issue to enable the weaker banks to meet demands for redemption.

Whatever effect these measures had, the crisis calmed down by the end of May, and the remaining suspended banks reopened again over the next three months. (The Commercial had already reopened on 6 May.) The bank suspensions hindered trade (e.g. by disrupting the circulation of cheques), and households and businesses experienced difficulties obtaining credit, but the figures for bank advances show no steep decline over this period (Boehm 1971: 214). The real economy reached its nadir in the second quarter of 1893 (Boehm 1971: 26) – annual figures indicate that real GDP in 1893 was 17 per cent lower than it had been in 1891, and the difference between the quarterly peak in 1891 and the trough in 1893 would have been even larger. Prices as measured by the GDP deflator fell by 22 per cent from 1890 to 1894 and thus implied a very sharp increase in *ex post* real interest rates. The economy started to recover in the third quarter of 1893, but recovery was faltering and uneven, and it took nine years for real GDP to surpass its 1891 peak (Butlin 1962: table 13).

Interpreting the bank collapses

A conventional view soon grew up around the bank 'failures' of the 1890s. This interpretation of events was first put forward by Cork (1894) and Coghlan (1918), but later writers 'have fleshed out the details without altering the substance of the story' (Merrett 1989: 62). As summarized by Merrett:

> Speculation fed by the inflow of British capital in the 1880s sowed the seeds of subsequent collapse. Bankers . . . endangered the solvency of their organizations by lending against overvalued real property and shares. The inevitable end of the land boom left the banks exposed. . . . The large-scale failures among the many financial institutions more intimately connected with the property boom and the discovery of fraud by executives and directors cast a pall of suspicion over the safety of the trading banks. Pressure intensified with the closure of both the Mercantile Bank of Australia and the Federal Bank. . . . The unwillingness or inability of the Associated Banks of Victoria to mount a successful rescue operation to save members in distress further lowered public confidence. Panic sprang from the failure of the Commercial Bank. . . . Frightened depositors attacked banks willy-nilly until the crisis had run its course.
>
> (Merrett 1989: 61–2)

Merrett himself seems to opt for a similar story:

> The rapid growth of the banks' balance sheets and the spread of their branches outran the ability of some to devise adequate reporting and control mechanisms. The maturity mismatch between assets and liabilities worsened, asset quality deteriorated, and risks became increasingly concentrated. This increase in average risk in the system was not offset by any strengthening of liquidity standards or capital adequacy. Rather, the reverse occurred. Liquidity ratios declined, as did capital ratios. . . . The growing loss of confidence in particular banks was crystallized by a combination of factors into a general panic in early 1893.
>
> (Merrett 1989: 63)

One of the key issues here is the banks' liquidity and Merrett goes on to argue that the 'inescapable conclusion is that the long decline in liquidity standards seriously undermined the banks' ability to cope with the growing problem of higher risks' (1989: 77). However, as George Selgin points out

> the facts tell a different story. Merrett (1989, p. 75) reports that the aggregate reserve ratio . . . fell from .3217 in 1872 to .2188 in 1877; but his figures for later five-year intervals show no further downward trend. . . . Even the lowest figure compares favorably to those from other banking systems, both regulated and free. It is much higher than Scottish bank reserve ratios for the mid-nineteenth century . . . and about the same as ratios for free Canadian banks in the late nineteenth century and for heavily regulated US banks today.
>
> (Selgin 1990a: 26–7)

He also notes that

> Pope's annual data, presented graphically . . . are more plainly inconsistent with [the falling reserve] hypothesis . . . in the seven years preceding the crisis . . . the average ratio of the thirteen suspended banks rose steadily from about .15 to .16. . . . Pope's reserve figures also show a minor difference only – perhaps two percentage points – between the reserve holdings of failed Australian banks and those that weathered the crisis. This also suggests that 'overexpansion' was not the root cause of the banking collapse.
>
> (Selgin 1990a: 27)

The other key issue is capital adequacy. The figures given in Butlin, Hall and White (1971: table 2) show a fall in the capital ratio from about 20 per cent in 1880 to 12.5 per cent in 1892, but these figures ignore the uncalled liability attached to bank shares, and a number of banks also had a contingent reserve liability which took effect if the bank went into liquidation (Merrett 1989: 82). Merrett himself estimates that this extra capital resource amounted to 'nearly 45 per cent of the conventional measure of shareholders' funds' (p. 81) which suggests that these capital ratios give a considerably understated impression of the 'true' capital adequacy of the banks. It is far from clear, however, that these capital ratios are low enough to say that the banks had grossly over-reached themselves in the way the conventional view maintains. The banks did run into problems later, of course, but those problems do not themselves prove that the banks' capital policies had been reckless. The banks' capital ratio recovered after the crisis, but its subsequent rise was relatively small – it reached a maximum of around 17 per cent in 1897 – and fell again subsequently to pass through its earlier low point in 1903. (And it is interesting to note that there was apparently no concern then with the banks' capital adequacy.) One might reply that the capital ratio ought to be interpreted in conjunction with other factors (e.g. liquidity, or some index of the quality of banks' assets), but that argument only concedes the points that the capital ratio should not be read on its own, and hence, that further evidence is needed to be able to say convincingly that 12.5 per cent was an irresponsible capital ratio in 1892 but not in 1903.[7] The claim that the banks had allowed their capital ratios to fall to reckless levels is also difficult to defend in the light of Pope's chart (1989: figure 8) on core capital adequacy. If this hypothesis were correct, we would expect the capital ratios of failed banks to show a distinct downward trend in the period before they failed, we would expect a model of bank failures to show that the capital ratio had a negative and statistically significant coefficient, and we would also expect there to be a major (and growing) difference between the capital ratios of failed and non-failed banks. In fact, the capital ratio of failed banks appears to *rise* in the two years prior to failure, and their capital ratio reaches a low point *five* years before failure and then recovers. Pope's logit model of the probability of failure also shows that capital adequacy has a 'correctly' signed coefficient in only one out of four cases, and even that is only significant at the 10 per cent level (1989: table 1), so there is little evidence that capital adequacy 'matters' in the way that this hypothesis predicts it should. And note, finally, that the difference between the capital ratios of banks that were to fail and banks that were not is relatively small – under 3 percentage points, and usually considerably less – and shows no tendency to grow as the dates of the failures approach (1989: figure 8).[8]

There is no denying that some bankers made serious mistakes in the run-up to the 'crash' of 1893, but the evidence just reviewed does not prove the claim that these mistakes were the major factor behind the severity of the 'crash'. Nor does the evidence support the claim that the bank 'crash' contributed in a major way to the severity of the depression. If this claim were valid, it would be possible to isolate the channel or channels through which the crash was able to push the real economy down. Several possible channels suggest themselves, but none shows any evidence of having transmitted a major shock from the banks to the rest of the economy:

1 There may have been a major disruption to the provision of credit by the banking system along the lines suggested, for example, by Bernanke (1983). The evidence indicates, however, that while bank advances declined from 1891 onwards, there was no detectable drop in advances that can be associated with the bank failures *per se* (Boehm 1971: 214). This first channel can therefore be ruled out.
2 There may have been a sharp monetary shock. As discussed already, there was a major restructuring of bank liabilities during suspension, and this transformation implied a large fall in liquid deposits – M3 deposits minus deposits converted by reconstruction, or 'Merrett money' – fell by a massive 46 per cent from December 1892 to June 1894 (Schedvin 1989: 5). Schedvin describes this fall as 'exceeding the United States experience of the early 1930s and far greater than any other Australian deflationary shock' (p. 5). Yet there was no major fall in aggregate monetary liabilities at the time of the crash (see Schedvin 1989: figure 1) and depositors who had their claims transformed suffered inconveniences but no major monetary losses (though see also note 6). (In the US in the early 1930s, by contrast, depositors *did* suffer major losses and there was a large fall in the broader monetary aggregates.) If the fall in Merrett money was a major deflationary shock, we would also have expected the shock to be followed by a downturn in the economy. Yet the economy was already recovering in the third quarter of 1893, just after the major drop in Merrett money, and the recovery continued into 1894 – a pattern of output behaviour that would appear to be quite inconsistent with any major deflationary shock in 1893.

What, then, are we to make of the events of the 1890s? The evidence seems to support the following interpretation. The depression itself was fundamentally a 'real' phenomenon. Australian terms of trade had been falling for a long time, but the effects of these terms-of-trade changes were masked until around 1890 by large inflows of British capital (see, for example, Boehm 1971: 271). These inflows dried up in the early 1890s. Investment fell, especially in the building industry (Boehm 1971: 271, 279), and falling investment itself pushed the economy down as well as forcing it to make its long-overdue response to the earlier terms-of-trade changes, and the combined effect was a very sharp downturn. A number of institutions had lent heavily and, in retrospect unwisely, against land, but other institutions, the larger banks especially, saw the danger coming and pulled in their horns. The downturn was so severe, however, that financial institutions were bound to be seriously affected, even those that had consciously restricted their lending against land-based assets. The land banks and building societies were naturally affected most, but the banks as a whole survived quite well until 1892. One might note too that there was no indiscriminate running of financial institutions; there was instead a 'flight to quality' in which depositors withdrew funds from institutions perceived as weak to re-deposit them in stronger institutions such as the big banks, and it is significant that at no time were the big three banks – the Australasia, the New South Wales and the Union – ever in serious danger. The weaker banks started to fail in early 1892, and a full-scale banking crisis blew up in early 1893, but these 'failures' owed much to government intervention. The Victorian and New South Wales governments first intervened to make it more difficult for creditors to liquidate institutions, and this rewriting of the rules encouraged banks to run for the cover of a legal suspension which would allow them time to reconstruct on relatively favourable terms. As Pope noted, 'One interpretation of the "crash" of April – May 1893 is of a rush by banks to seize the vantage ground offered by reconstruction' (1987: 29). The implication is that the failures were a product of the legal framework rather than a symptom of genuine insolvency, and it is surely significant that all – with one arguable exception – were able to re-open successfully afterwards. Nor can there be much doubt that other interventions intended to allay the crisis actually had the opposite effect. The bungling attempts of the Victorian Treasurer to pressurize the Associated Banks in to bailing out the weaker banks backfired at a critical point and needlessly undermined public confidence. The Victorian banking holiday had a similar impact. It amounted to the government bullying the banks to close, and those that obeyed found it very difficult to re-open. The threat of a banking holiday in New South Wales would also have encouraged withdrawals there, and it is questionable that the legal tender measures or government note issues there or in Queensland did much to allay the panic. The bottom line, then, is that the bank 'failures' were caused primarily by a combination of 'real' factors and misguided government intervention, and the 'failures' were not what they might appear to be anyway. It is ironic that a crisis in which inept government intervention played such a major part should have become so widely regarded as a failure of 'free banking'.

This 'new view' of the bank crash avoids a number of drawbacks with the traditional interpretation. First, the conventional view emphasizes banks' reckless lending as a major contributory factor to the crash, but the evidence presented to support this view is weak. The fact that reckless lending took place does not establish that it was an important force behind the crash, and the banks' liquidity and capital ratios provide relatively little evidence that it was. Second, the conventional view fails to give sufficient emphasis to the true nature of the bank 'failures', and, more importantly, it underrates the extent to which those failures were a product of the legal system under which the banks operated. A bank 'failure' was usually no more than a device to reconstruct before opening again, and it seldom if ever meant that an insolvent bank was going permanently out of business. Third, the bank runs were not an indiscriminate attack on the banking system as a whole, and it is misleading to think of there being a 'systemic' crisis. Instead there was a noticeable flight to quality as deposits were transferred from the weaker banks to the stronger ones, so much so, in fact, that the stronger banks sometimes did not know what to do with the deposits they were receiving. Fourth, the standard view misses the significance of the various government interventions discussed in the previous paragraph which unwittingly aggravated the crisis. Last, and of critical importance, if the conventional view were correct, we would expect the banks' over-expansion to be reflected in the behaviour of real economic activity. The bank expansion would promote real economic activity, and we would expect the real economy to fall once the banks' expansion had ended, or soon after. But instead of falling, real output started to rise shortly after the bank 'crash', and there appears to be relatively little correlation between bank lending and real activity. The conventional view predicts that the gun should be smoking, as it were, and yet we can find no evidence that it has even been fired.

EPILOGUE: THE DEVELOPMENT OF CENTRAL BANKING IN AUSTRALIA

The events of the 1890s dealt a very heavy blow to the reputation of the banking profession. 'The crash, and subsequent revelations of fraud and chicanery' by some bankers 'tarnished the image of bankers as responsible guardians of the society's savings' (Merrett 1989: 61). After the suspended banks re-opened,

> it could appear to those who had suffered acutely that, by financial legerdemain, the banks had saved themselves . . . at the expense of thousands of individuals. Suspicion of financial institutions had long been endemic in Australian thinking . . . [and it appeared obvious that] in the 'nineties the banks' escape by reconstruction

72 The experience of free banking

was made at the expense of their customers.

This view combined with an increasingly interventionist ideological climate to have a profound effect on twentieth-century politics.[9] Political parties identified the banks as a major source of economic instability and social injustice, and this view helped to undermine resistance over succeeding decades to the notion that the state should take control over the banking industry (see, for example, Schedvin 1989: 5–6). The drive to establish state control was especially strong on the political left, and state control of the financial system – and, later on, outright nationalization – became a key part of the Australian Labour Party's political platform. The poor public standing of the banks also undermined their bargaining position relative to the political authorities. The politicians could make demands on the banks in the knowledge that they could easily whip up anti-bank feeling and impose more unpleasant measures on them if they resisted. The banks were consequently cowed into submission, and the new Commonwealth government established in 1901 frequently had its way with them without having to resort to the formality of legislation.

The banking system consolidated itself considerably after the crash was over. The number of branches fell from 1,553 in 1892 to a low of 1,223 in 1896 (Butlin 1986: table 38) and a wave of mergers started in the 1890s which was to reduce the number of banks by half in the first two decades of the twentieth century (Schedvin 1989: 6). Bankers became much more conservative. Their first priority was to rebuild their strength to reassure the public of their soundness, and the need for prudential strength was reinforced by the growing competition of the public-sector savings banks whose market share grew from 6 per cent in 1890 to over 30 per cent by 1928 (Merrett 1989: 84). The trading banks also tended to take fewer risks and give more emphasis to short-term self-liquidating investments in place of longer, more speculative ones (e.g. Merrett 1989: 83). The 'spirit of banking entrepreneurship was dead, cremated in the fire of 1893' (Schedvin 1989: 8). One other change was that the banks were now able to maintain agreements on deposit rates and foreign exchange rates and margins, and there was no longer any effective competition except for advances. Competitive banking had given way to a banking cartel operating in the government's shadow.

Section 51 of the Commonwealth Constitution gave the Common-wealth the power to legislate currency and banking, and Andrew

Fisher's Labour government used it to begin the process of capturing seigniorage revenues (Fane 1988: 5). The first stage in the process was a pair of Acts passed in 1910 to give the Commonwealth a monopoly of the note issue. The Australian Bank Notes Act authorized the Commonwealth Treasurer to issue notes which would be legal tender throughout the federation but would be redeemable in gold at the Commonwealth Treasury. The Act also specified that the government was to observe a minimum gold reserve ratio of 25 per cent for amounts less than £7 million and to observe a 100 per cent reserve ratio on amounts exceeding that value, but the 100 per cent reserve ratio was abolished in an amending Act the following year (Copland 1920: 490). (The bankers strongly resisted this amendment as they obviously feared – rightly, as it turned out – that it would pave the way for the government to inflate the currency, but they could not prevent it.) The other Act of 1910 was the Bank Notes Tax Act which imposed an annual tax of 10 per cent on all other note issues and effectively taxed them out of existence. These measures were followed by the establishment in 1911–12 of the Commonwealth Bank as a Commonwealth-owned trading and savings bank. It was to compete with the private banks and promote a national savings bank system, but it was also to assist the government by conducting the government account and managing the national debt.

More government interventions followed after the outbreak of war in 1914. In September 1914 the Associated Banks were 'persuaded' to supply the Commonwealth government with £10 million in gold, and the banks reluctantly consented in case the government passed an order to seize all their gold instead (Fane 1988: 6). Gold was replaced by notes in inter-bank clearings at the same time (Copland 1920: 491, n. 13) and private non-bank holdings of gold were mostly expropriated (Fane 1988: 6). Gresham's Law ensured that gold disappeared from circulation and the Australian pound note replaced the gold sovereign as the economy's basic unit of account. The government's augmented gold reserves enabled it to increase the note issue massively – from £9.6 million notes in June 1914 to £32.1 million notes a year later, and then grew to £55.6 million by June 1919 (Copland 1920: table VI). The resulting increase in monetary base represented a major contribution to the government's war finances (Fane 1988: 8), but it also fuelled a considerable increase in the broader money supply and a substantial rise in the price level (Copland 1920: table X). Though the nominal price of gold continued to be fixed at its old rate, the automatic discipline which the gold standard would have applied to this monetary expansion was aborted by the prohibition of gold exports effective in June 1915 and the government's refusal to redeem its notes even though they remained convertible *de jure* (Fane 1988: 5–6). This refusal provoked no legal challenge – presumably, no one wished to appear 'unpatriotic' by demanding redemption – and the gold standard was effectively suspended.

The First World War also saw the Commonwealth Bank develop further into the role of central bank. It

> greatly assisted the Government in financing the war, and was especially helpful in floating war loans and in establishing the enormous issue of Australian notes which the financial policy of the Government necessitated.
>
> (Copland 1920: 491)

The development of central banking continued in the 1920s. The note issue was transferred to a Notes Board by the Commonwealth Bank Act of 1920, but then transferred to the Commonwealth Bank itself by an amending Act of 1924. In addition, the amending Act reorganized the Bank and gave the Secretary of the Treasury a seat on its Board (Fane 1988: 9) as well as granting the Bank authority to publish a rediscount rate (Schedvin 1989: 10). Fane also notes, by the way, that this last section was never proclaimed because the banks adopted it 'freely' and made formal proclamation unnecessary. This episode illustrates how the trading banks were willing to comply with official wishes without waiting for formal orders to do so.

Australia did not return to the gold standard until 1925 when the ban on exporting gold was lifted and Australia joined Britain in restoring the convertibility of the currency into gold. The exchange rate between the Australian and British currencies was maintained by the

> trading banks, acting as a cartel. To a limited extent one can regard the behaviour of these banks as a manifestation of official monetary policy: any attempt blatantly to flout the government's wishes might have precipitated stringent controls or nationalisation. To a large extent, however, the banks appear to have voluntarily chosen to set the exchange rate at parity, or close to parity, and were able to do so because the government kept the growth of domestic credit within [suitable] limits.
>
> (Fane 1988: 10–11)

Apart from a brief episode in 1920–1, these arrangements managed to keep the exchange rate between the Australian and British

pounds reasonably stable until 1929 (Fane 1988: 10–11), but
the combination of heavy government borrowing overseas, a fall
in the overseas funds of the trading banks, and a 60 per cent fall
in export prices between 1928 and 1931 made the exchange rate
increasingly difficult to defend (Fane 1988: 15). The government's
response was the Commonwealth Bank Act of December 1929 which
provided for the control of gold exports and the requisitioning of
gold, and this Act 'marked Australia's effective departure from
the gold standard' (Fane 1988: 16). These measures prompted the
trading banks to agree in January 1930 to hand over two-thirds of
their gold reserves to the Commonwealth Bank, and they then sold
their remaining gold while they still could. The banks feared that
full-scale exchange controls would follow, so they tried to placate
the authorities and head-off more drastic measures by agreeing in
August 1930 to the 'Mobilization Agreement' by which they were
to hand over UK£3 million each month to the Commonwealth Bank
and restrict their overseas borrowing. The authorities had effectively
seized the bulk of the trading banks' foreign exchange reserves and
then left the banks to defend an exchange rate that was already
under considerable pressure because of Australia's large current
account deficit (see Fane 1988: 16–17). The banks responded
with a combination of rationing sterling and raising its price, but
sterling was at an even greater premium on the unofficial market
and the trading banks saw their foreign exchange market share fall
significantly. Their attempt at price fixing then broke down when
the Bank of New South Wales broke ranks in January 1931 and
the banks only recovered their market share once the price of
sterling had risen to A£1.3 (Schedvin 1970; Fane 1988: 18). The
price of sterling fell to A£1.25 following Britain's abandonment of
the gold standard in September 1931. The Commonwealth Bank then
maintained the exchange rate at this level and the price of sterling was
to remain unchanged until sterling was devalued in 1967 (Fane 1988:
18–19).

The Commonwealth Bank's role expanded further in the 1930s.
Apart from taking responsibility for the exchange rate, it also assumed
greater responsibility for setting interest rates and managing the
financing of the government deficit. It became a key player in the
determination of fiscal as well as monetary policy, and its influence
on fiscal policy 'politicized banking to a remarkable degree' and
created 'rising popular antagonism against the banking system as
a whole' (Schedvin 1989: 10–11). Governments, especially Labour
ones, were then able to portray banks

as uncompromising and unwilling to share in the general sacrifice, a perception that triggered underlying resentment about the use of oligopoly power and activated memories of . . . the 1890s. Even more important was the widespread belief that the banks in association with the international 'money power' were, somehow, responsible for the depression.

(Schedvin 1989: 11)

The controversy led to a Royal Commission whose Report in 1937 advocated increasing the Commonwealth Bank's central banking powers still further. It recommended that the private trading banks be required to maintain minimum deposits with the Commonwealth Bank and give it greater access to their London funds. The central bank was also to supervise banks and impose capital standards, and it was to have the power to take-over weak banks. The Report also recommended that the government consider controlling the banks' profits, and it proposed the public utility model of the banking system that provided the rational for later regulation (Schedvin 1989: 11–12). It is interesting to note how the resentment created by the central bank's own policies was channelled against the private banks and used to justify further increases in the central bank's powers, and the option of curtailing the Commonwealth Bank's powers instead does not appear to have been taken seriously.

Yet even this far-reaching regulatory regime was insufficient for the government, which used it to rationalize regulation but actually adopted far more drastic measures than the Report itself recommended. Comprehensive exchange controls were adopted in August 1939, and these were followed in November 1941 by the National Security (Banking) Regulations introduced under the Commonwealth's defence power. These gave the central bank the powers to direct banks' advances and impose interest rates. They also gave it the power to require banks to lodge funds in Special Accounts at the Commonwealth Bank, and the interest on these funds was manipulated to control the trading banks' profits (Schedvin 1989: 13). Government control was now effectively unlimited and the public interest model was imposed 'lock, stock and barrel' (Schedvin 1989: 14) as a kind of fig-leaf in order to rationalize that control. These regulations were only constitutionally valid under the defence power, but they were enshrined none the less in a modified form in the banking legislation of 1945 and this regulatory regime continued substantially intact until the mid-1980s (Fane 1988: 21).

Two factors were therefore decisive in the twentieth century transformation of the Australian banking system. The first was the Commonwealth government's craving for revenue. 'The history of Australian monetary policy from Federation to the Second World War can best be understood as a gradual process by which the new government established a monopoly on the ability to issue money and then expanded the revenue by inflationary finance' (Fane 1988: 1). The establishment of the currency monopoly, the establishment of the Commonwealth Bank and the use the government made of it, the expansion of the central Bank's powers, and the reluctance to set aside 'emergency' powers once emergencies had passed were all geared towards raising revenue for the government. The other decisive factor was ideological. The climate of opinion in Australia was hostile in the extreme to *laissez-faire*, and prevailing mythology blamed the banks for much of the misery of the 1890s and 1930s. The banking system was therefore an easy target for demagogues looking for convenient scapegoats. Governments stirred up anti-bank feeling and made good use of it to promote their own interests while masquerading as defenders of the broader social good. In the process they undermined the banking system further and lent additional credence to the view that the banks were letting the economy down. Government self-interest and the prevailing ideology thus reinforced each other and there was relatively little to resist them. Australian free banking had thus given way to its opposite – central planning – after just forty years.

ACKNOWLEDGEMENTS

I should like to thank Mervyn Lewis, David Merrett and Ray Evans for comments on an earlier draft; and the Durell Foundation for financial support. The usual caveat applies.

NOTES

1 These warnings were by no means isolated. Further examples are given in Boehm (1971: 246–7) and Merrett (1989: 67).
2 These were an association of the larger Melbourne-based banks.
3 These two institutions had only recently converted from being building societies, and the Metropolitan had only started to issue notes in January (Butlin 1961: 285). These institutions were two among a number that had commenced as building societies but transformed themselves into conventional banks.
4 The politicians themselves were also heavily criticized. In Victoria 'one of the worst features of the mounting disclosures of mismanagement, chicanery, falsified accounts, and fraud, was the extent to which leading

members of Parliament were involved' (Butlin 1961: 286). Boehm (1971: 266) also refers to the 'corruptness and incompetence within the Victorian Legislature' which were revealed in the passage of the Voluntary Liquidation Act.

5 There was some controversy over whether the Federal should have been rescued, but an inquiry by the Victoria Supreme Court concluded later that it was already beyond rescue (Boehm 1971: 288).

6 Some depositors did object, however, and the 'inconvenience' caused by the suspensions was in some cases a cause of considerable distress (see Gollan 1968: 37–40).

7 For what the comparison is worth, one might add that 12.5 per cent would be considered very sound in the USA today, and American banks now, like Australian banks then, have a large number of problem loans on their books. The assets of US banks now are also probably no more diversified than the assets of Australian banks a century ago, so the comparison is perhaps not as far-fetched as it might otherwise appear.

8 One might also note, by the way, that the claim that banks' risks were becoming more concentrated only receives very weak support. Pope's figure 8 indicates only a barely perceptible increase in the suspended banks' risk-concentration, and the fact that the risk-pooling variable always has an insignificant coefficient in Pope's estimates (1989: 20) indicates that it had little effect on the bank failures anyway.

9 Gollan (1968) has a good account of the controversy over banking and the political background to the banking legislation.

4 Free banking in Canada

Kurt Schuler

THE BEGINNINGS OF FREE BANKING, 1817-67

Canada had experience with note issue long before the first banks opened. From 1685 to 1713 and from 1729 to 1760, the government of the French colony of Quebec issued makeshift promissory notes by cutting up and signing playing cards. For the first several years of both periods of playing-card money, the government redeemed the cards promptly when the next ship with gold and silver coin came from France. Later, though, it used forced-tender issue as a means of inflationary finance. Both periods ended with the playing-card money depreciating by one-half or more (Shortt 1986: 105-99). British colonial governments in Quebec, Nova Scotia, New Brunswick and Prince Edward Island also issued paper money in the 1700s and early 1800s, which likewise depreciated. Merchants' promissory notes, though widely used for small sums, were generally disliked, because redemption was often in goods rather than in money. There was a need for a more reliable, widely acceptable medium of exchange.

After abortive attempts as far back as 1792 to found banks in the larger towns in Canada, the Bank of Montreal opened in 1817. It modelled itself on the Bank of the United States, though with the vital difference that it had no official sanction. To be chartered as a limited liability corporation required a special act of the legislature, but the Bank of Montreal and two other banks that opened soon afterwards in Quebec (then called Lower Canada) operated as self-declared corporations until they secured charters from the legislature in 1824 (Shortt 1986: 72-6).

Banking in Lower Canada was competitive from the start. Banks there accepted each other's notes and regularly cleared notes and cheques with their rivals. The Bank of Montreal established a few branches soon after opening its main office. By 1822, Ontario (then called Upper Canada), New Brunswick and Nova Scotia also had banks, but all were monopolies owned by politically privileged groups.[1] (Prince Edward Island and Newfoundland, the other provinces existing at the time, did not have banks until decades later.) The legislatures of the provinces with monopoly banking refused to grant charters to potential rivals. Bank promoters were reluctant to proceed without charters because the partnership form of organization was awkward and riskier to stockholders than the corporation, and possibly illegal for banks in some provinces. Geographical barriers and local laws stymied interprovincial branch banking, which could have brought competition.

The fight to gain additional bank charters became a leading political issue in the provinces with monopoly banks. Would-be rival banks appealed to local pride and to disgruntlement with the monopoly banks' lending practices, which gave political opponents of the existing ruling parties less than a fair share of loans. As the population grew and as democratic ideas made headway, agitation for more banks broke the banking monopolies. In 1832, legislators supporting the Bank of Upper Canada agreed to grant a charter for the Commercial Bank, to break an impasse in which the Commercial Bank's supporters had refused to grant the Bank of Upper Canada a much-needed increase in authorized capital. The same year, the Nova Scotia legislature granted a charter to the Bank of Nova Scotia, giving Halifax's less wealthy citizens a convenient means of challenging the unchartered Halifax Banking Company, a partnership of the town's richest merchants. In 1834, the governor of New Brunswick exercised his power to grant a charter independently of the legislature, allowing the City Bank to open in St John in rivalry with the Bank of New Brunswick (Shortt 1986: 289–91; Breckenridge 1894: 156, 159).

Once the door to competition opened, it could not be shut. Provincial legislatures embraced competition mainly out of political expediency, not out of devotion to *laissez-faire*. Legislators who opposed new bank charters incurred the wrath of organized, vocal groups of voters. By the middle 1830s, an unwritten rule had emerged in the provinces with banks that almost all parties able to raise a certain minimum of capital would be granted a charter. Canadian bank charters did not prohibit branching, as many American charters did, so branch networks became common.

Bank promoters who lacked the capital for a charter started unchartered banks in Ontario and Quebec in the middle 1830s, and in Prince Edward Island and British Columbia in later decades. They were 'joint-stock' banks whose organization imitated that of British banks of the time. Joint-stock banks had unlimited liability but, unlike partnerships, their stock could be freely traded. In other respects the joint-stock banks operated on nearly the same legal footing as the chartered banks. Unlimited liability was apparently not a great deterrent to potential stockholders in that optimistic time, but none of the joint-stock banks ever became very large (Shortt 1986: 311–15; McIvor 1958: 58, 90). Unchartered banks ceased to exist after a federal law of 1870 made them illegal.

The British government in 1836 granted a royal charter to a group of investors who wanted to establish a Bank of British North America directed from London, but with all its branches overseas. The royal charter allowed the bank to establish branches in any Canadian province that consented. The bank soon had branches in every province then existing except Prince Edward Island. It was the first bank to come to Newfoundland. The Bank of British Columbia, founded in 1862 (no relation to the recent bank of the same name), was Canada's other royally chartered bank (Shortt 1986: 325–7; Rowe 1967: 506–7).

Branch banking was just one of the typical features of free banking that the Canadian system spontaneously evolved in its early years. Another was mutual note and cheque acceptance. Banks that refused to accept notes and cheques from rivals found such a policy self-defeating, because if the rivals accepted their notes, they had no offsetting claims to present when rivals demanded redemption in gold or silver. 'Note duelling' tactics also proved unfruitful, because they increased the reserves that all note duelling banks needed to hold without giving any particular bank a strong competitive advantage. Note duelling by rivals never made any Canadian bank fail. Routine acceptance and regular exchange of notes and cheques issued by rival banks in the same province quickly became the rule (Shortt 1986: 279, 312, 320; Shortt 1990: 11–12). Correspondent banking arrangements between banks in different provinces, plus the interprovincial network of the Bank of British North America, tied all the banks of Canada into a loose system by the late 1830s. Formal clearing-houses did not arise until 1887, because bilateral clearing was satisfactory until then. It was the opinion of the writer of a manual for Canadian bankers that economies of scale sufficient to justify establishing a clearing-house did not exist until there were at least seven banks in a city (Knight 1908: 137).

Competition also induced Canadian banks by the mid-1830s to offer interest on small time deposits and to experiment with Scottish 'cash credit' lending, which allowed borrowers to draw credit at will up to a fixed amount. Banks eventually ceased cash credit lending as unsuited to Canadian economic conditions, perhaps because of laws that prohibited banks from owning and lending on the security of land, the most important asset that many Canadians had (Breckenridge 1894: 62; Shortt 1986: 312).

Banks accepted locally issued notes and cheques of all banks at face value, but sometimes charged commissions on notes and cheques from distant areas of the same province, even those from their own branches. Discounts on notes and cheques issued elsewhere within a province seem not to have exceeded 1 per cent (cf. Denison 1966: vol. 1, 150; Shortt 1986: 304). The discounts reflected transportation costs and interlocal exchange rates, much as today's foreign exchange rates do. For instance, bank drafts on Quebec City were frequently at a slight premium in Montreal because certain provincial taxes could only be paid in Quebec City. Some large banks that redeemed notes and cheques at more than one branch had separately marked notes for each branch. Other banks only redeemed notes and cheques at their headquarters. Improved transportation apparently eliminated note and cheque discounts within provinces by the 1840s.

Discounts on notes and cheques from other provinces were much larger. Note discounts continued until 1889, four years after railroads linked Canada from coast to coast. Cheque discounts continued into this century, as in the United States. Prohibitions on branching across provincial lines kept Canadian banks, except the Bank of British North America, from developing nation-wide branch networks until the 1870s, which delayed the advent of the lowest-cost clearing methods. Also, until the provinces federated in 1867, although all provinces used the dollar as the unit of account, each province defined the dollar differently. Canada minted no gold and silver coins of its own at the time, so it used foreign coins. Instead of allowing the free interplay of market forces to determine the relative values of the various coins, most provinces established statutory ratings that overvalued some coins relative to their metallic content. Around 1837, for instance, the actual basis of the currency was the American gold $20 coin in New Brunswick, the British silver shilling in Upper Canada, the French silver crown in Lower Canada, and depreciated government paper issues in Nova Scotia and Prince Edward Island.[2] Newfoundland had no legal tender ratings. Undervalued coins vanished from circulation, giving rise to frequent complaints about shortages of them, and, less often, gluts of overvalued coins (Chalmers 1893: 402–12; Ross 1920: vol. 1, 458; Redish 1984).

During its first twenty years, Canada's banking system grew rapidly with few interruptions. Canadian banks suffered not at all during the US financial panic of 1819. The English panic of 1825 caused one small, frail Canadian bank to fail and imposed foreign-exchange losses on other banks, but it did not shake the banking system as a whole. However, the panic of 1837 caused a system-wide banking crisis. The panic was clearly of foreign origin: it began in England in late 1836. The Bank of England's refusal to lend at any price to firms importing cotton from the United States led to failures in the cotton trade on both sides of the Atlantic early in 1837. An internal drain on gold and silver by apprehensive customers made New York City banks suspend gold and silver payments on 10 May in that year. Banks elsewhere in the United States and in Canadian provinces except Upper Canada followed suit as soon as news of New York banks' action reached them, and Canadian bank notes were at a 6 per cent discount against gold within a week (Shortt 1986: 335–6).

The banks suspended payments in violation of their contracts with noteholders and depositors and without government approval. Even so, suspension was popular and officially tolerated because it seemed the least painful course of action. Suspension gave banks a breathing space to liquidate assets in an orderly fashion, avoiding 'fire-sale' losses. The exception occurred in Upper Canada, where the governor threatened to close down banks that suspended. Banks there suffered severe reserve drains, and had to contract loans more than banks in other provinces. The effect of the panic was said to be worse in Upper Canada than anywhere else in North America, and all banks there except the tiny Bank of the People eventually suspended payments with government approval in March 1838 (Shortt 1986: 344–50).

In the Maritime provinces, banks resumed gold and silver payments at the end of the summer of 1837. Banks in Lower Canada resumed payments in May 1838, a few days after the US banks, but suspended again in December when a rebellion against British rule broke out. They resumed payments in June 1839. Banks in Upper Canada resumed in November 1839 (Shortt 1986: 358–9; Gibson and Schull 1982: 35). The panic of 1837 was the only system-wide peacetime banking crisis that Canada ever suffered. Comparing it with later years of stress on Canadian banks, the difference seems to have been that prohibitions on interprovincial branch banking kept the banks from being as large and as solid in 1837 as they later became.

As part of its strategy to quell the discontent that had caused the recent rebellions, the British government in 1841 united Upper Canada and Lower Canada into the Province of Canada. The united province established a uniform coinage and allowed unrestricted branching anywhere within its boundaries. Banks that previously had been confined to Upper Canada or Lower Canada now expanded into each other's home territory.

The new province's first governor, Lord Sydenham (Charles Poulett Thompson), was a follower of the British Currency School, and tried to introduce its principles into Canadian banking. The Currency School wished to make note currency behave in the same way as a purely metallic currency. It advocated monopolizing note issue and subjecting the issuer to 100 per cent gold or silver reserve requirements beyond a certain ceiling. Sydenham proposed to establish a government-owned bank to issue notes, and to use its profits to finance public works. He justified his scheme with explicit reference to a sophisticated, though incorrect, theory of banking, which contrasts with the crude ideas that dominated later debates over banking regulation. Vigorous bank lobbying convinced the legislature to reject Sydenham's scheme, although it imposed a 1 per cent tax on bank note circulation as an alternative revenue-raising measure (Shortt 1986: 401–7, 413–14).

Canadian banks suffered losses in the depression years 1847 and 1857, but avoided the large-scale bank failures and suspensions or near-suspensions of convertibility payments that occurred in England and the United States, Canada's largest trading partners.

In 1850, the Province of Canada imported bond-collateral banking, inappropriately called 'free banking', from the United States. Bond-collateral banks had to buy specified government bonds as a requirement for issuing notes. Their note issues could not exceed their holdings of the bonds. The provincial government hoped that bond-collateral banking would increase demand for its bonds, which were a drug on the market. Only five bond-collateral banks were ever founded, and none achieved prominence. The bond-collateral and chartered banking systems existed side by side. No chartered bank joined the bond-collateral system because the bond-collateral requirement and the prohibition (later eliminated) on establishing branches did not nearly offset the advantages of a lower minimum capital requirement.[3] The bond-collateral banks all failed or became chartered banks by the end of the decade, and the legislature repealed the bond-collateral law in 1866 (Breckenridge 1894: 103–17).

The Province of Canada's finances had been troubled almost from the beginning because of deficit spending on unprofitable canals and railroads. By the 1860s, the government's credit was so bad that it could not sell bonds in the London market. To raise money, it proposed government legal-tender note issue, with incentives for banks to give up their own note issues. The Bank of Montreal favoured the plan, which would enable the bank to convert its huge government bond holdings to legal-tender notes. Many other banks, especially those heavily dependent on their note circulation for profits, vehemently opposed the plan. When the proposal came into effect in 1866, the Bank of Montreal was the only bank to give up its own note issue for a time, and even it later resumed note issue (Shortt 1986: 541, 560–9).

In 1866 there also occurred the first of three important bank failures. The Bank of Upper Canada, which had a favoured relation with the government of the Province of Canada, had been ailing for some years. Had stockholders been held to the double liability for the bank's debts that its charter specified, noteholders and depositors would probably have lost nothing. However, the government wanted to hide its dealings with the bank, and it did not enforce double liability. The provincial government ultimately lost $1 million of the deposits it kept with the bank, while other creditors lost $310,000 (Shortt 1986: 584–9; Breckenridge 1894: 134). The Commercial Bank failed in 1867 after its largest borrower defaulted, and the Gore Bank failed the following year. Both were bought by other banks, and noteholders and depositors lost nothing. No general runs on the banking system occurred during the failures of the three banks. Their passing left the Bank of Montreal with an unchallenged pre-eminence within Canada's banking system for the rest of the century.

THE HEYDAY OF FREE BANKING, 1867–1914

The Province of Canada, Nova Scotia and New Brunswick united to form the Dominion of Canada in July 1867. Ontario and Quebec were carved out of the former Province of Canada, and corresponded to the old provinces of Upper and Lower Canada. Other provinces joined the federation later, with the last, Newfoundland, joining only in 1949. The federation charter gave exclusive jurisdiction over banking and currency to the federal government. Almost immediately after confederation, banks were allowed to establish branches across provincial borders, and some quickly did so.

The new nation faced three problems in currency legislation. The first was to establish a uniform coinage. That was easily solved by extending the coinage standards of the former Province of Canada to the whole nation, and in particular by redenominating the currency of Nova Scotia, whose dollar was worth 2.67 cents less than the Canadian dollar. The Canadian dollar was a gold currency equal to the US gold dollar (not to the US 'greenback' of 1861 to 1879).

Canada's second problem in currency legislation was to establish a uniform banking law. Before confederation, minimum capital requirements, the number of years charters lasted, stockholder liability, and other details of bank charters differed among provinces and sometimes even among banks within each province. A federal Bank Act (Statutes of Canada 1870: c. 11, slightly revised as Statutes of Canada 1871: c. 5) replaced the system of provincial charters with a federal chartering system. Bank charters were granted to coincide with the ten-year life of the Bank Act, so that every time the Bank Act was revised, bank charters would be revised as well. The Bank Act's main provisions were: every bank was to have a government charter; at least $100,000 of paid-in capital was required; note issue was not to exceed the amount of paid-in capital; stockholders bore double liability for a bank's debts if it should fail; banks could not engage in non-banking business or mortgage lending; they were to accept their own notes at face value at all branches; and they had to hold an average of half of their total reserves in government legal-tender notes (to force a demand for government notes), although there was no minimum reserve ratio. Similar provisions had previously existed in most provinces.

Government note issue was the third and most difficult currency problem. The federal government agreed to assume liability for the note issues of the Province of Canada and Nova Scotia, and later of Prince Edward Island. Most banks wanted the government to stop issuing notes (the Bank of Montreal again being the chief exception). Many politicians, on the other hand, favoured a government monopoly of note issue or a bond-collateral system. The banks and their allies buried a government bill of 1869 that would have established bond-collateral banking (Shortt 1986: 576–81). The government would not give up note issue, however, because it wanted the taxing power that note issue provided. The Dominion Notes Act (Statutes of Canada 1870, c. 46) was therefore passed to permit the government to issue up to $9 million in legal-tender notes against a gold reserve of at least 25 per cent. Any issue in excess of $9 million had to be covered dollar for dollar by extra gold reserves. To force a demand for Dominion notes in retail trade, banks were forbidden from issuing notes for under $5. (At the time, bank note circulation was about $15 million and Dominion note circulation was about $7 million). Beginning in 1892, successive governments increased gold reserves held against the Dominion note issue, which reduced the possibility that inadequate reserves would cause the government to take itself and the nation off the gold standard. The reserve ratio exceed 80 per cent by 1911 (Curtis 1931: 20, 92–3).

During the 1870s and 1880s, Canadian banks spread from coast to coast. New banks crowded in alongside old ones, and the number of banks rose from 37 in 1867 to a peak of 51 in 1874. Thereafter, it steadily fell as failures and mergers thinned the field to a small number of banks, most of which had large nation-wide branch networks. There were only 24 banks by 1914 (Neufeld 1972: 78–9). The number of bank branches, however, increased from about 150 in 1869 to over 4,000 in 1919, surpassing the United States in branches per capita during the Canadian economy's great growth spurt around the turn of the century (Chapman and Westerfield 1942: 277, 340).

American prohibitions on branch banking and restrictions on note issue were responsible for several financial panics that beset the United States in the late nineteenth century but had little effect on Canada's banking system. Almost every autumn, the demand for notes and coins rose because many farmers were paid in cash for crops. Bond-collateral requirements prevented bank note circulation from accommodating the increase in demand, because they made the profitability of note issue dependent on bond prices, and not just on demand for notes. In Canada, note circulation was usually about 20 per cent higher in the autumn than at the seasonal low of note demand in mid-winter, whereas in the United States, it showed no seasonal variation. Interest rates, on the other hand, had no seasonal pattern in Canada and a strong seasonal pattern in the United States. American banks could not easily expand their note issues to meet the increased seasonal demand for notes, and the effect spilled over into interest rates.

The United States suffered minor credit stringencies almost every autumn from the 1870s until 1908, and major shortages in 1873, 1893 and 1907. During the major shortages, notes and coins went to a premium over bank deposits, and regular hand-to-hand currency virtually disappeared from circulation. To fill the gap, bank clearing-house associations and some corporations issued emergency currency. While technically illegal, emergency currency was useful and quite safe, and the American authorities turned a blind eye towards it because they understood that it was essential to trade (Timberlake 1984).

Canada suffered no note famines, no interest rate 'spikes', and few extraordinary business failures during the US panics. In 1893 and

1907, Canadian bank notes circulated extensively in the United States as substitutes for American currency (Denison 1966: vol: 2: 260, 284–5), and in general, Canadian banks provided liquidity to the New York money market during times of severe financial stress (Rich 1989: 158–9), because short-term interest rates were so much higher in New York during such times than they were in Canada. The only notable adverse events for Canadian banks in this period were limited runs on some small banks in Montreal in 1879, local banks in Prince Edward Island in 1881, and both local banks in Newfoundland in 1894. All the runs had readily identifiable causes and did not spread to large banks or to other small banks with dissimilar loan portfolios. Only in Newfoundland did a run on one bank cause another bank to fail.

However, legal restrictions on note issue threatened to make almost all of Canada's banks somewhat unstable by the early 1900s. In 1907, some Canadian banks took extraordinary measures to economize their customers' use of bank notes, and the government issued $5 million of its own notes over the legal ceiling (Johnson 1910: 144–8). Since 1867, bank-note issue had increased more rapidly than bank capital, and the legal limit on note issue finally threatened to become binding. The most logical remedy would have been to abolish the requirement that note issue should not exceed the amount of paid-in capital. Instead, the government offered only partial relaxations, but they were adequate until the basis of note issue changed completely during the First World War. In 1908 the note issue ceiling was raised to 115 per cent of paid-in capital for the months of peak demand (Statutes of Canada 1908, c. 7). The Bank Act revision of 1913 (Statutes of Canada 1913, c. 9) allowed banks to issue notes in excess of the previously established ceilings, provided the excess was backed dollar for dollar by gold deposited in a government vault.

Many American economists and bankers admired Canada's relatively unregulated banking system. The American Bankers' Association's 'Baltimore plan' of 1894 and a national business convention's 'Indianapolis plan' of 1897 referred to Canada's happy experience without American-style bond collateral requirements. The Aldrich-Vreeland Act of 1908, which legalized clearing-house emergency currency, was a step towards note issue along Canadian lines. The US National Monetary Commission, formed after the panic of 1907, investigated Canada's system as a possible model, but rejected it in favour of central banking.

The one respect in which Canada imitated American note issue arrangements to some degree was in establishing a bank note guarantee fund by the Bank Act revision of 1890. There was a widespread sentiment that noteholders needed special protection from bank failures, because noteholders tended to be poorer than depositors and less able to withstand the consequences of a bank failure. The Minister of Finance proposed that banks be required to hold a minimum reserve ratio of 10 per cent against liabilities. The bankers' counterproposal was for a bank note guarantee fund, raised by taxing bank note circulation and available to pay noteholders of any failed bank. Like present-day deposit insurance, the bank note guarantee fund had moral hazard risks and would have been exhausted by any large bank failure, but by 1890 notes were a small proportion of total bank liabilities, so the moral hazard risk was small, and the fund stayed solvent because the largest loss to depositors from any single bank failure from the beginning of Canadian banking (1817) to 1914 was just $3.3 million, in the 1908 failure of the Sovereign Bank.

CENTRAL BANKING COMES TO CANADA, 1914–35

Canada took a step towards central banking when it entered the First World War. For the next two decades, Canada had a curious system under which the government could have controlled the money supply like a central bank but usually it did not.

At the beginning of August 1914, Canadian bank customers began redeeming large amounts of notes and deposits for gold, apparently fearing that the country would enter the recently begun war and suspend the gold standard. On 3 August, the government issued an emergency decree suspending the convertibility into gold of its own notes and permitting banks to do likewise with their notes and deposits. The emergency decree was regularized in the Finance Act (Statutes of Canada 1914, 2nd session, c. 3), which then became the basis of Canada's monetary system until 1935.

Inconvertible forced-tender government notes replaced gold as the basis of the monetary system. (Banks held the bulk of government notes as reserves, in special large denominations that did not circulate among the public.) To finance war expenditures, the government relied in part on inflation. Government note issue rose from $131 million in 1913 to $327 million in 1918. Bank liabilities in the same period rose from $1.147 billion to $2.340 billion, and the wholesale price index more than doubled (McIvor 1958: 112–13).

Under the Finance Act, the government set a discount rate at which it would lend government notes to the banks in return for their i.o.u.'s. The banks decided how much, if any, they wished to borrow at that rate. The Finance Act rate was often below the market interest rate, but the government made no attempt to limit the total amount of Finance Act borrowing. The banks, on the other hand, appear not to have taken full advantage of the opportunity that the Finance Act offered for credit expansion, perhaps because other banks may have interpreted Finance Act borrowing as a sign of weakness (McIvor 1958: 123).

Bankers, economists and politicians were generally happy with the Finance Act. They especially praised the emergency 'liquidity' that it offered the banking system. They evidently did not understand that the price of such liquidity was a potential for great inflation. Nor did they appreciate that the Finance Act system was markedly different from the pre-war free banking system. The bankers were a decidedly unphilosophical group: during hearings about the 1923 revisions of the Bank Act and the Finance Act, the general manager of the Canadian Bank of Commerce and vice-president of the Canadian Bankers' Association testified that he had never heard of the quantity theory of money, and remarked further that 'we do not want theories introduced into banking. If you get into theories, you are on dangerous ground' (HBC 1923: 379). The few dissatisfied parties at the hearings indicated that they favoured a complete shift to central banking, not a return to free banking.

The government informally restored the Canadian dollar's convertibility into gold for banks in 1922, and officially re-established convertibility in July 1926. The Finance Act system had neither the automatic incentives for convertibility that had existed under the pre-war free banking system nor the conscious control of reserves or discount rates that exist under central banking. It was nobody's job to maintain convertibility, and the government unofficially suspended it in January 1929, following a drop in gold reserves from $109 million to $59 million in the preceding two months (McIvor 1958: 122). (The government officially acknowledged suspension in 1931.) Following the unofficial suspension, Finance Act borrowings rose a further 50 per cent from their already record post-war levels before the Great Depression set in at the end of 1929.

The Great Depression gripped Canada as tightly as it did the United States. GNP statistics show similar percentage declines for both countries. (A floating exchange rate did not insulate Canada's economy, which depended heavily on trade with the United States, from real declines in American demand for Canadian products.) The number of banking offices also fell by roughly the same proportion in both countries. However, Canadian banks weathered the Great Depression much better than American banks. No Canadian banks failed, nor did Canada suffer bank runs or impose 'bank holidays'. The extensive branch networks of Canadian banks had enabled them to spread lending risks across regions and types of borrowers (Chapman and Westerfield 1942: 108, 122, 357–8). Total losses to depositors and noteholders during the whole period up to the establishment of a central bank in 1935 were probably less than $30 million (cf. Beckhart 1929: 337), far less per capita than in the United States. No Canadian banks failed from 1923 to 1985, while the United States suffered thousands of failures during the 1920s and 1930s.

As the Great Depression deepened, a clamour arose for the government do something to pull Canada out of it. Attempts to increase the money supply by forcing Finance Act borrowing on the banks in 1932 were unsuccessful (McIvor 1958: 133). Political opinion increasingly favoured establishing a central bank as an attempted cure for the Depression. Left-wing political parties had favoured a central bank since the 1920s on the grounds that it would subject the banking system to democratic control. The Liberal Party, which had previously opposed central banking, began advocating it in 1933, more from a perception of political advantage than from ideological conviction. The ruling Conservative Party would have been pilloried for inaction had it not taken measures that seemed to fight the Depression, and by 1934 it too advocated central banking. A bill to establish a Bank of Canada was passed in July 1934, and the bank opened in March 1935.

Economic debate about the merits or defects of central banking was generally carried on at a very low level. Advocates of central banking had extravagant hopes for it; some saw it as the first step towards nationalizing the whole banking sector. Advocates did not explain what a central bank could do that the chartered banks were unable to do, and especially, how a central bank would get Canada out of the Depression. Opponents of central banking put forward an even weaker case. Most defended the existing system because they were comfortable with it and apprehensive about the changes that central banking might bring. Only a few tried to point out real defects in the idea of central banking (Stokes 1939: 64–123), and even they saw the existing system as the only alternative to central banking; there was no thought of returning to the pre-war free banking system, because very few people understood how it had differed from the Finance Act system.

The Bank of Canada had no noticeable effect in ending the Great Depression. Canada did not recover from the Depression until British demand for Canadian products during the Second World War stimulated the economy. Since the Second World War, the Bank of

Canada's record in managing the Canadian money supply has been mediocre: inflation has been high both by historical standards and compared to the contemporary United States.

CONCLUSION

Canada's free banking system was among the most impressive on record. It offered customers a wide range of services through convenient nation-wide branch networks, caused few losses to depositors and noteholders, and maintained convertibility into gold or silver almost uninterrupted for about a century. Its efficiency and stability impressed many outside observers, especially in the United States.

The qualities for which the Canadian free banking system gained renown were the result of vigorous competition under a political regime that interfered little in the banking business. The few defects of the system were mainly caused by needless regulations, such as the prohibition on mortgage lending (not completely lifted until 1967), legal constraints on bank-note issue that began to bind around 1900, and early prohibitions (later dropped) against interprovincial branch banking. Central banking came to Canada mainly for political reasons, not for economic ones. Its record compares poorly with the record of free banking.

NOTES

The best summary of Canadian banking history is McIvor (1958). Shortt (1986), which originally appeared as articles in the *Journal of the Canadian Bankers' Association* from 1896 to 1925, remains the standard work on the period up to 1880. Breckenridge (1894) has the keenest appreciation of how freedom from much regulation enabled the Canadian banking system to become stable and efficient.

1. The Bank of Upper Canada's monopoly was not secure until 1823, when a rival unchartered bank failed because of inept management. New Brunswick chartered a small-town bank on the understanding that it would not expand to compete with the Bank of New Brunswick (Breckenridge 1894: 47, 155).
2. Nova Scotia's banks maintained a dual currency system, paying a premium over provincial notes for customers who dealt in gold and silver, despite a law forbidding it. After 1833, the government did not even accept its own notes for payment of customs duties; it would take only specie (Ross 1920: vol. 1, 420). Prince Edward Island had no banks yet.
3. The Bank of British North America used certain provisions of the bond-collateral law to issue notes for less than $5, which its British charter prohibited, but it remained a branch bank.

5 Free banking in Colombia

Adolfo Meisel

This chapter summarizes the development of the Colombian banking system from 1871, when the first successful commercial bank was established, to the foundation of the central bank, Banco de la República, in 1923. These years are rich in events for the students of monetary and banking history: there was a period of free banking (1871–86); a near hyperinflation (1899–1902); a monopoly of note issue (1887–1909); and a period in which there was no institution which could issue bank notes (1910–22).[1] Each period is now considered in turn.

THE FREE BANKING ERA, 1871–86

The first successful commercial bank in Colombia was the Banco de Bogotá, established in 1871. The credit system had been controlled until the 1860s by the Roman Catholic Church through the *censos*, which were mortage loans extended on the guarantee of rural or urban property, generally at an annual interest rate of 5 per cent (Colmenares 1974). During the reforms of the 1860s, the Liberal Party put an end to this pre-capitalist credit system, and in the process created the conditions for the establishment of commercial banks.

The economic prosperity of the 1870s produced by the booming export sector helped the newly established Banco de Bogotá to prosper. The notes issued by the bank increased rapidly from 132,165 pesos in June of 1871 to 606,898 pesos by June 1874.[2] In the next few years banks were established all across the country. Although the period under consideration (1871–1922) was characterized by the creation of banks, the number established in the era of free banking (1871–86) was larger than in subsequent subperiods (see Table 5.1).

Banks were first allowed to operate under a law of 1865 that had originally been passed to permit a foreign bank in Bogotá (Meisel 1990: 138). This bank quickly failed, apparently because of its directors' lack of familiarity with local conditions. However, the door was open to other banks.[3] This law allowed banks to issue notes that were to be accepted by the government as payment for taxes and other contributions (Meisel 1990a: 138).

Table 5.1 The establishment of commercial banks in Colombia 1871–1922

Region	1871–86	1887–1909	1910–22	Total
Bogotá	9	7	5	21
Antioquia	12	16	5	33
Atlantic coast	9	3	5	17
Other regions	9	6	8	23
Total	39	32	23	94

Source: A. Meisel (1990a)

From 1863 to 1886, the Colombian state was organized under a rather extreme federalist constitution, the Constitution of Rionegro, which adhered to the principles of Manchesterian liberalism. This constitution made each regional state – and Colombia had nine – responsible for the regulation of economic activity, including banking. A good example of the spirit of *laissez-faire* that predominated in Colombian legislation of the time is provided by the banking laws of the State of Bolívar. This legislation gave ample space to private initiative and permitted only a minimum of government intervention. As the basic banking law of the State of Bolívar declared in its first article, 'The establishment of banks of issue, deposit, and discount and mortage banks is free in the state and their activity is only subject to those duties that the laws impose on commercial companies and merchants'.[4] Equally there were no barriers to the entry into the banking business. No charters were necessary and there were no minimum capital requirements.

When the Banco de Bogotá was established in 1871, the Secretary of the Treasury granted it the same privileges that had been granted in 1865 to the foreign bank that had earlier operated for several months in Bogotá (Villamarin 1972: 271). The main privilege was the right 'To issue notes admissible as currency in the payment of taxes and in general in all the transactions of the National government, with the obligation on the part of the government, of receiving them at par'

(Meisel 1990a: 138). The government also granted other privileges to the Banco de Bogotá, the main one being the deposit of all of its revenues.[5]

In many respects, the history of the Banco de Antioquia is similar to that of the Banco de Bogotá. The former was a privately owned bank established in 1872 by a group of merchants from Medellín, and it obtained important privileges through Law 194 of 1871, issued by the State of Antioquia (Botero 1989: 31). The regional government guaranteed the bank's notes and accepted them in all of its own transactions (as in the payment of taxes). The bank's notes circulated widely in the region at par with gold pesos (Botero 1989: 53), and it made clearing agreements with other banks for the mutual acceptance of their notes.

Perhaps the most difficult crisis faced by Colombian banks during the experience of free banking occurred in 1876 as a result of the civil war of 1875. The largest bank of the country, the Banco de Bogotá, suspended the convertibility of its notes from November 1876 until May 1877, because of problems involved during the civil war in transferring funds from one town to another. In Medellín, for instance, the civil war led to a local bank panic. A Swedish traveller in Antioquia at the time, Fr Von Schenck, described these events:

> A very natural panic occurred as result of the war and all the notes returned to Medellín, where the banks were faced with the obligation of converting more than a million pesos, at a time when metallic currency had disappeared as by magic, as it [sic] always occurs in Colombia in times of revolution. In this emergency all the merchants of Medellín agreed to accept the notes as credit to the banks. This agreement was observed rigorously and the convertibility of all notes was maintained.
>
> (Von Schenck 1953: 46)

One of the main characterictics of the Colombian banking system up until 1923 was the co-existence of many regional banks and the virtual absence of branch banking. Although branch banking was allowed, it did not develop, possibly due to the enormous difficulties of communication as a result of Colombia's rugged topography and rudimentary transport system.[6]

While the regional banks were quite small, two large banks – the Banco de Bogotá and the Banco de Colombia – played an important role in Colombian banking from the very beginning. (In 1912 they were also joined by the Banco Alemán Antioqueño.) These banks were managed in a very conservative and prudent manner, maintaining a diversified portfolio and avoiding speculative activities. They were uncharacteristic in not being family banks nor directly involved or associated with firms in the export business, and their ownership was quite dispersed.[7]

There is no information available for this period that permits a comparison of the relative size of the different banks in existence. However, a government report of 1888 calculated the metallic currency available in each bank. This variable can be used as a proxy for their relative size. The two main banks, Bogotá and Colombia, had between them 53.1 per cent of the metallic currency in the banking system.[8] Two other banks, had another 18.8 per cent which meant that just four banks had 71.9 per cent of the currency. The remaining 28.1 per cent was shared among the remaining twenty-three banks.

In 1880, President Rafael Nuñez established a government bank of issue, the Banco Nacional, to be its fiscal agent and granted it, by law, the right to a monopoly of the note issue.[9] However, the same law also permitted the Banco Nacional to authorize note issues by private commercial banks which accepted its own notes. The newly created government bank initially issued relatively moderate amounts of notes – only 2,831,000 pesos in the period 1881–1885 (see Table 5.2) – but the war of 1885 led to a large fiscal deficit which the government

Table 5.2 Annual issue of Banco Nacional Notes (1885–99) in pesos

Year	Annual increase in issue	Accumulated issue	Increase %
1885	2,831,000	2,831,000	0
1886	2,516,725	5,347,725	88.9
1887	2,956,722	8,304,447	55.3
1888	3,695,553	12,000,000	45.5
1889	2,970,903	14,970,903	24.8
1890	831,098	15,802,001	5.6
1891	4,243,298	20,045,299	26.9
1892	1,226,732	21,272,031	6.1
1893	2,500,000	23,772,031	11.8
1894	2,363,575	26,135,606	9.9
1895	5,000,000	30,862,350	18.1
1896	–	30,862,350	0
1897	–	30,862,350	0
1898	7,440,000	38,302,000	24.1
1899	14,559,000	52,861,000	38.0

Source: Meisel and López (1990: 76).

financed by borrowing from the bank. The note issue consequently grew by almost 90 per cent in 1886, and the government responded to the subsequent inflation by suspending the convertibility of its notes later that year. Simultaneously, it suspended the right of commercial banks to issue notes, and some banks responded by liquidating themselves and going out of business.[10]

It is very important to stress that the government's monopoly of note issue arose in 1886 from its desire to obtain resources through seigniorage. The pressing fiscal demands of the government led it to suspend the convertibility of its notes, and consequently to abolish, supposedly temporarily, the right of other banks to issue notes. The government's note monopoly did *not* arise form any dissatisfaction with the way free banking had operated, and there had been no panics or abuses that had led people to question the principle of free banking.

TOWARDS CENTRAL BANKING, 1887–1922

The Banco Nacional was liquidated in 1896 after the discovery of illegal issues of its notes,[11] although the Treasury continued printing the Banco's notes until 1904. From the late 1880s until 1898, the note circulation of the Banco Nacional was (relatively) moderate (see Table 5.2), but a civil war begun in October 1849 between the governing Conservative Party, and the opposition Liberal Party, and the resulting fiscal pressure led to increases in the monetary base of 118, 108 and 117 per cent in 1900, 1901 and 1902, respectively. Prices consequently rose, and the peso devalued against the pound sterling by 142.5, 158 and 165.8 per cent in each of these years.[12] The increase in the monetary base slowed down again when the war ended and the fiscal pressure relaxed, and prices began to stabilize again.[13]

In 1905, the government of Rafael Reyes instituted a series of reforms in the monetary and banking sector. The objective of these reforms was to return to the gold standard which had been abandoned in 1886. Among the reforms, one of the most important was the devaluation in the legal value of the peso in terms of gold: one hundred paper pesos were to be legally valued for one gold peso, a rate of exchange that correspond to their market value (Torres Garcia 1980: 248). Another measure in the government's reform package gave a group of Colombian capitalists a concession for the establishment of a private bank, the Banco Central, which would have a monopoly over the right to issue notes and act as fiscal agent of the government, but the Banco's privileges were taken away in 1909 and it became a regular commercial bank.[14]

Also in 1909, the constitution was amended to prohibit the issue of notes altogether, in an effort to eliminate any future resort to inflationary finance. From that date until 1923 no institution in Colombia was allowed to issue any notes at all, and increases in monetary base could only come about through the minting of gold and silver coins by the Treasury or through the introduction of foreign currency (which ocurred in several years in the 1910s).[15]

In the early 1910s there was an ongoing debate in the Colombian Congress over the relative merits of free banking and central banking. There was an increasing perception of the need for an orderly and elastic provision of notes to put an end to the heterogeneity prevailing in the monetary base.[16] Between 1904 and 1919 a total of fourteen projects to establish free banking were presented to the Congress (Ibañez 1990: 165). The controversy was particularly intense after 1910 because of the ban on issuing notes.

Since the earlier experience with free banking (1871–86) had been reasonably successful but the later monopoly issue (1887–1909) had produced considerable instability, it was quite natural that most Colombian policymakers seemed to favour free banking. The tendency towards free banking is reflected in the fact that eleven out of eighteen banking reform bills presented to Congress in the period from 1911 to 1916 favoured some form of free banking (Ibañez 1990: 176–7). However, one free banking sentiment began to dissipate towards the end of the decade. As a result of international influences Colombian policymakers started to favour the establishment of a single bank of issue. The examples of France, England and Germany were cited as cases where free banking had been abandoned, but perhaps the biggest impact was caused by the establishment of the Federal Reserve System in the USA in 1914 (Meisel 1988: 100).

The 'charisma of success', made it very difficult to contradict a project such as the one that Esteban Jaramillo presented to the Congress in 1918 for the organization of a central bank inspired by the Federal Reserve System (Jaramillo 1918), and there a consensus among Colombian policymakers in favour of a monopoly of issue by 1921. Three bills presented in that year for the creation of a central bank proposed the monopoly of issue (Ibañez 1990), and an Act was passed the following year – Law 30 of 1922 – to establish a central bank.

On 10 March 1923, a group of US financial advisers arrived in Bogotá, at the invitation of the Columbian government. The mission's head was Edwin W. Kemmerer, a Princeton professor of economics. He was one of the foremost members of an 'informal colonial service' that reformed the monetary and banking systems of numerous Latin American and Asian countries in the second two decades of the century. Kemmerer's task was made much easier by the fact that the Act authorizing the central bank had already been passed when he arrived. He then proposed a number of additional measures to reform the Colombian banking and fiscal systems, and eight of these – the most important ones – were readily passed by Congress with almost no changes.[17] Kemmerer's reforms completed the new Colombian system of central banking.

In 1923, Colombia became the second country in Latin America to have a central bank. Why did Colombia acquire a central bank before countries such as Argentina and Canada that were much more developed, and despite the fact that the Colombian banking system had been quite stable since it had been founded, and had never experienced a national bank panic?

The Columbian central bank was not created as part of a gradual evolutionary process in the Columbian banking system.[18] Rather, it conforms better to the argument formulated by Vera Smith (1990 [1936]: 148) that a central bank is often not the result of the natural evolution of the banking system, but the outcome of historical and political circumstances. The main motivation that the Colombian government had for setting up a central bank and inviting the mission of US financial advisers was ensure access to American loans.[19] As Kemmerer noted in his Presidential Address to the American Economic Association, one of the main reasons that a country had to arrange a mission of foreign financial advisers was to cause a good impression on US investors and banks (Kemmerer 1927: 4).

At the beginning of the century Colombia had some of the lowest investment in Latin America.[20] In the early 1920s Colombian officials tried to interest US bankers in the country but they repeatedly failed. 'When their representatives searched for the necessary funds from investment bankers of New York, most were not interested. . . . When they asked what they had to do to be elegible they were informed of the work of Doctor Kemmerer' (Kemmerer 1987: 59). Paul Drake's research on the financial missions of the so-called Money Doctor to the Andean countries (Colombia, Peru, Bolivia, Chile, Ecuador) in the 1920s and 1930s also shows that 'the main objective for many Andean leaders [for inviting E. W. Kemmerer], was to inspire confidence on the part of foreign investors' (Drake 1984: 25).

The 'medicine' offered by Kemmerer for the Colombian banking system included a gold standard and a central bank. He proposed exactly the same institution he had defended for his own country only a few years before, although the Colombian conditions were quite different.

Aside from the interest on the part of Colombian authorities in obtaining loans from US bankers, the Kemmerer reforms were readily accepted because there was already a growing consensus among Colombian policymakers in favour of the creation of a bank of issue along the lines of the Federal Reserve System. Why the Federal Reserve System? Because it was the regime established in the country to imitate. It appears therefore, that it was the 'charisma of success' that explains the shift away from free banking and in favour of monopoly issue.

CONCLUSIONS

The history of Colombia's banking system from 1871 to 1923 shows that the establishment of a central bank in the later year was not the result of some gradual evolutionary process. Instead it was the outcome of a deliberate policy on the part of the Colombian government to set up a central bank in order to obtain funds from US banks.

Free banking in Colombia (1871–86) was not characterized by overissues of bank notes nor by bank panics. It was abolished because of the fiscal difficulties of the government resulting from the civil war of 1885. Although free banking was never re-established, many banks survived the unstable years of monopoly issue on the part of the government (1887–1904), and the banking system was actually quite stable throughout the period of transition from free banking to central banking (1887–1922). During those years the country *never* experienced a national bank panic. Thus, political considerations and the *international demonstration effect* of the most successful countries were behind the creation of a lender of last resort with monopoly issue in 1923: the Banco de la República.

ACKNOWLEDGEMENTS

I wish to thank Kevin Dowd, Jorge Garcia Garcia and Humberto Mora for valuable comments on earlier drafts of this paper.

NOTES

1 The definition of free banking used throughout this article is the standard one: it refers to a banking system in which there are no barriers to entry, all banks have the right to issue notes, there is competition in the banking business, and there is no central bank. By the term central bank, we understand an institution which is the lender of last resort, holds the reserves of the banking system, and has a monopoly over the supply of currency.

2 *Memoria del Tesoro*, Bogotá, Colombia, 1875: xx.

3 *Memoria del Tesoro*, Bogotá, Colombia, 1874: 45.

4 *Recopilación de las Leyes del Estado Soberano de Bolívar, 1857–1875*, Cartagena: Tipografia de Antonio Araujo, 1976: 151.

5 *Memoria del Tesoro*, Bogotá, Colombia, 1875, xx.

6 For a discussion of the development of Colombia's transport system in this period, see William Paul McGreevey, *Historia Economica de Colombia, 1845–1930*, Bogotá: Tercer Mundo, 1982: 262.

7 The export business was particularly risky due to the sharp fluctuations of international prices that were usual in the principal export products, for example, coffee.

8 *Memoria del Tesoro*, Bogotá, Colombia, 1888: 55.

9 Law 39, 1880. See Diez (1989: 42).

10 This was the case of the first Banco de Bolívar in Cartagena. See Meisel (forthcoming).

11 Romero (1987: 147–8). The scandal that was generated in 1883 over the discovery in 1889 that the Banco Nacional had issued $2,206,319 pesos that had not been legally authorized created an adverse climate of opinion towards this bank. The sum in question was used by the government to buy, through the Banco de Bogotá, outstanding public debt at a discount. See Torres Garcia (1980: 207–10).

12 *Crédito, Moneda y Cambio Exterior*, Bogotá, 1909: 66–7.

13 *Memoria del Tesoro*, Bogotá, Colombia, 1904: 66–9.

14 These privileges ceased because the Banco Central was accused of increasing the amount of inconvertible paper money in circulation (to finance the fiscal deficit) and of not having helped in the re-establishment of the gold standard. See Avella (1987: 43).

15 However, from 1918 the constitutional prohibition to issue inconvertible paper currency was partially side-stepped through the issue of Treasury bonds that were accepted as currency.

16 *Informe Anual del Gerente del Banco de la República a la Junta Directiva*, Banco de la República 1924: 10.

17 The two bills not passed in Congress were one regulating income taxes and another on travel taxes. Meisel (1990b: 221).

18 Charles Goodhart in *the Evolution of Central Banks, a Natural Development* (LSE, October 1985) argues that in several European countries central banks evolved from commercial banks that were granted special privileges, including being the fiscal agents of the government.

19 The historian Carlos Marichal argues that in the 1920s, 'To facilitate the acquisition of foreign loans, numerous Latin American countries invited U.S. financial experts to reorganize their public finances in

order to obtain the approval of New York banks' (Marichal 1988: 215–16).

20 In 1913, Colombia was the country with the least amount of US investment. Of a total of almost US$1,242 million invested in Latin America, Colombia received only US$2 million from the USA. *Investment of United States Capital in Latin America*, Boston: World Peace Foundation Pamphlets, 1928: 1031–4.

6 Free banking in Foochow

George A. Selgin

INTRODUCTION

> Prior to 1900, China never had anything resembling government regulation of banks, and since that time its banking ordinances have mostly provided regulation without inspection – merest paper. Until recently there were no banking laws at all. A man might start even a savings bank or a bank of issue with no more ado than is necessary to start a grocery store.
>
> (Hall 1922: 3)

Until the 1980s nearly all economists believed that free trade in money and banking must lead to unlimited inflation or general monetary chaos or both. Recent studies, however, dispute this traditional view. They include the studies by Rockoff (1975a) and Rolnick and Weber (1983, 1986) of decentralized banking in the US prior to the Civil War, White's (1984b) study of free banking in Scotland, Jonung's (1989 [1985]) study of plural, private note issue in Sweden and Weber's study of Swiss currency competition (1988). The new research shows that some decentralized banking systems free from extensive regulation actually worked rather well.[1]

Though they cast doubt on conventional views the new studies are not conclusive. For one thing, the decentralized banking systems they discuss were not *entirely* free from regulatory interference, though Scotland's came very close.[2] Also, all of them were based on the gold standard and on western legal arrangements for the enforcement of contract and for punishment of default. These arrangements may have been special sources of stability. Finally, the examples are simply too few in number to warrant any reliable generalizations.

This chapter adds to the small set of studies of decentralized banking systems by examining – through the use of secondary sources[3] – the banking system of Foochow (Pin-yin romanization *Fuzhou*), capital and largest city of the south-eastern province of Fukien (*Fujian*), in mainland China. From the beginning of the nineteenth century until the second quarter of the twentieth, Foochow's banking and currency system was entirely private and free from all legal restrictions: whereas much of the west in the nineteenth century adopted a *laissez-faire* economic policy for everything except currency and banking, China chose to let currency and banking alone. Although free banking in China was based on dramatically different monetary and legal arrangements from those in the west, its consequences were similar in many ways to those of free banking in Scotland and Sweden: bank notes circulated at par and were widely preferred to coin; banking failures were restricted to very small banks; noteholder losses were minimal; free banks were an important and relatively low-cost source of loanable funds; there were no serious outbreaks of inflation or deflation; and counterfeiting was rare. Thus Foochow offers a further example of a decentralized and unregulated banking system that worked well.

GENERAL MONETARY ARRANGEMENTS

China's monetary system in the nineteenth century included three different units of account, each with its own exchange-media representatives. The *tael* (of which there were many varieties – Foochow's contained 532.5 grains of silver (Anti-Cobweb Club 1925: 70) was used in interprovincial trade and for some local, wholesale trade. The dollar, originally based on the full-weight Mexican dollar coin, was employed in foreign trade. Finally, the copper *ch'ien* or 'cash' was used in local, retail exchange. It was represented by round copper coins (*wen*) with square holes in their centre. The coins were used in 'strings' (*ch'uan*) of 100 units or more. A string of 100 coins worth 10 *ch'ien* each was once standard. However, the presence of many worn and debased coins (some of which were minted centuries before) made inclusion of more than 100 10-cash coins typical for a string valued at 1,000 'standard' cash.[4]

Though exchange-media representing 1,000 standard copper cash were sometimes called *tael* units, their value fluctuated freely against that of silver monies: despite appearances to the contrary China did not have a bimetallic, copper–silver standard, but, rather, parallel standards.[5] Copper–silver exchange rates varied continually both over time and across localities due to changing market conditions.

The bulkiness and weight of copper coin – a mule cart was needed to move sums exceeding 10,000 cash (Wilkinson 1980: 17 fn.) – together with its uneven and fluctuating quality, created great opportunities for issuers of paper money. Indeed, as Tullock (1957) observes, the Chinese, having invented paper, ink and printing, were also the earliest users of paper money. Imperial governments resorted frequently to paper money finance, and paper issued by them typically depreciated until it became worthless. This practice finally came to an end during the Ming dynasty, mid-way through the fifteenth century. Except for two brief, unsuccessful issues during the 1650s and 1850s, the Ch'ing dynasty (1644–1911) also refrained entirely from issuing paper money. The Manchus did not, however, interfere with private banks issuing paper notes on their own. Thus China by 1644 had entered into an era of official *laissez-faire* in money and banking. In Foochow and elsewhere this policy gave rise to a well-developed and fascinating private currency industry.

KINDS OF BANK

During the free-banking era two groups of banks operated in Foochow: old-style or 'native' banks and modern or 'foreign' and 'foreign-style' banks. Modern banks, which first appeared after the opening of the Treaty Ports in 1842, included all foreign-owned commercial banks and their Chinese imitators. Native banks (which were of much older origin) included 'Shansi' banks (named after the province where banks of this type first opened) and 'local' banks. Shansi banks were large branch banks mainly involved in interprovincial trade, including the handling of payments to and from the central government. Local banks were usually single-office firms involved in local lending and exchange only. Some, however, belonged to a distinct class – they were the 'big' local banks or *tso piao tien*. These issued the bulk of Foochow's monetary assets, including demand notes current throughout the city. They were also members of the local bankers' guild and clearing association. The remaining, 'small' local banks issued notes current only within their immediate vicinity and trading elsewhere at varying discounts. Small banks did little lending, concentrating on the exchange of different kinds of money. Consequently they were also known as 'money shops,' 'cash shops' or 'exchange shops' (*chien yang tien*). Some small banks reissued notes of larger banks, and many operated as sidelines of other businesses.

Notes issued by the *tso piao tien* included 'cash' notes and, beginning in the second half of the nineteenth century, 'Dai-Fook' dollar notes (*tai fu piao*). Cash notes were issued in denominations ranging from 400 to several thousand cash, 400 standard cash being the rough equivalent of eighteen pence or three-fortieths of an English pound around 1850 (Fortune 1847: 373). Dai-Fook notes were issued in denominations of one to fifty 'dollars', where $1 Dai-Fook was equal to 1,000 'standard' copper cash.[6] Foreign banks established after 1845 issued notes representing 'big' (Mexican) silver dollars. In 1928 the Dai-Fook dollar unit was abolished, and native banks were required to denominate their notes in Chinese dollars or *yuan*. These were officially equivalent to 'big' silver dollars, though actual government coins were of somewhat lower metallic content.

Native bank notes, and copper-backed notes especially, were widely preferred to coin in local transactions; as early as 1853 the Governor-general of Fukien could report that 80–90 per cent of all transactions in Foochow were being settled with them (Wang 1977: 13). Sir Harry Parkes, interpreter for the British consul at Foochow from March 1845 to August 1846, observed that paper notes were 'adopted by everybody, high or low, to the almost entire rejection of their bulky coins, which they seldom continue to carry on their persons' (Parkes 1852: 180). This contributed savings both in transactions costs and in opportunity costs associated with the production of commodity money. Because of the overwhelming popularity of the notes, prices were expressed in amounts of standard cash, with actual, worn coin circulating at a discount. This appears to confirm White's (1984a) view that competitive forces encourage the linking-up of the unit of account with the preferred means of payment.

GROWTH OF THE INDUSTRY

Local banks were already present in Foochow in the eighteenth century. Most began as money exchange shops, which first undertook the issue of non-circulating promissory notes ('native orders') to well-known merchants. Promissory notes of more reputable firms were often assigned and circulated. This led to banks issuing bearer notes, which were often cashed on demand. Some local banks may also have been set-up by Shansi bankers to supplement their parent firms by specializing in local transactions (Chang 1938a: 36).

Local banking grew rapidly at the beginning of the nineteenth century, and by 1815 local bank notes were widely used in larger local transactions. The opening of Foochow to foreign trade following the end of the Opium War gave the industry a further boost, both by increasing the demand for convenient and reliable currency and by introducing 'modern' foreign banks. The modern banks issued silver-dollar-denominated demand notes, encouraging more local banks to make their copper-based notes redeemable on demand. Foreign banks also accepted local bank notes in payment, thereby directly enhancing their market.

By the mid-nineteenth century there were thirty local banks in Foochow with over $500,000 (silver) in capital each, together with hundreds of smaller cash shops (Parkes 1852: 182). By 1922 the number of *tso piao tien* had risen to forty-six; their average size had become much smaller, however, reflecting the general decline of Foochow as a commercial centre. This suggests that note issue was neither a natural monopoly nor subject to significant external economies of scale, though this result may also have hinged on the fact that banks were also unlimited liability firms (see Rockoff 1986: 627). By this time native banks issued Dai-Fook notes exclusively, cash notes having passed out of use by the end of the nineteenth century.

Foochow's most serious banking crisis occurred in 1922. In that year Cantonese (Nationalist) troops occupied Fukien, causing many local banks temporarily to close their doors and suspend payments as a precaution against having forced loans exacted from them by the occupying forces (Tamagna 1942: 21). Though most of the banks recovered, four of them, including the large Bank of Fukien (banker to the provincial government and therefore a special target of invading warlords) failed, leaving $1,200,000 (Dai-Fook) of unredeemed notes (*Chinese Economic Bulletin*, 27 June 1925: 145).[7] Responsibility for these notes was taken by the remaining *tso piao* through a new agency formed by them expressly for the purpose called the Association for the Maintenance of the Money Market, which replaced notes issued by the Bank of Fukien with its own, redeemable, notes. Also in response to the crisis the bankers' guild of Foochow, called the Native Bankers' Association, froze its membership. This fixed the number of *tso piao* at forty-five, permitting new entry into the guild only in the event of the failure or voluntary closure of an existing member-bank. Overhead costs for existing *tso piao* were also increased: these now included a fee of $600, payable to the Chamber of Commerce, and a $3,000 contribution to the common pool established by the Association for Maintenance of the Money Market to support its notes issued in exchange for the unredeemed notes of the Bank of Fukien.

In 1927 forty-five banks, plus the Association for the Maintenance of the Money Market, still had 10,000,000 Dai-Fook dollars outstanding. That winter nearly half of the *tso piao* either suspended or declared *hou chi* (a promise to redeem their notes without undertaking any further issues) in response to a threat of occupation by the Southern Revolutionary Army (*Chinese Economic Bulletin*, 2 April 1927: 180;

and 9 June 1927: 19). Then, in 1928 (after most of the banks had recovered from the winter crisis) the Nationalist government abolished the popular copper-based Dai-Fook unit, requiring all notes to be denominated in *yuan* (*Chinese Economic Bulletin*, 17 March 1928: 135; Kann 1936: 42). This reform – which was aimed at combating the depreciation of the *yuan* – was strongly opposed by the banks, to the point of provoking them to go on strike. Its successful implementation would have eliminated the principal remaining advantage of native bank notes in local exchange, where many prices were still expressed in terms of copper units (cash or Dai-Fook dollars). Although the banks were forcefully compelled to resume business (*Chinese Economic Bulletin*, 30 June 1928: 45–53) it appears that they were able to escape the law's potentially adverse consequences by adhering to it in a token manner only: although the Dai-Fook dollars were withdrawn and new notes were issued in denominations of between 1 and 200 *yuan* this Foochow *yuan* ('*hua piao*') actually differed from the official *yuan*, by being in effect a continuation of the copper-based Dai-Fook dollar (Wong 1936: 399). The reprieve was short-lived, however, as a new set of regulations enacted by the provincial government of Fukien in 1933 abolished the *hua piao* unit and required native banks to redeem their notes at par in official, silver *yuan* (pp. 400–1).

Sources differ as regards the fate of the large note-issuing banks after the 1928 and subsequent reforms. According to Kann (1936), only twenty of them remained in business in 1931; two other sources, however (*Chinese Economic Journal*, 2 May 1932: 441 and Tamagna 1942: 68–9) claim all forty-five banks to have continued in operation at least until 1932, with $4 million (*hua piao*) (or roughly $10 per capita) in outstanding notes. After 1932, however, all sources agree that note issue was given up at a rapid rate. By 1934, according to Tamagna (1942: 68–9), only twenty-seven note-issuing banks remained in business; and according to Young (1935: 66) and Wong (1936: 402) all but five of these had discontinued their issues by 1935, when the government passed legislation intended to give the Central Bank of China a monopoly in note issue.

ORGANIZATION AND OPERATION OF LOCAL BANKS

Local banks were unlimited-liability firms, usually of two to ten partners, though some were individual proprietorships (Anonymous 1932: 441; Chang 1938b: 27). Prior to 1933 they could be set up by anyone with the necessary capital without a charter or any kind of permission from the government. To become a *tso piao*, however,

Table 6.1 Note-issuing native banks in Foochow, 1932

Bank	Location	Date of establishment	Outstanding Notes (hua piao)	Capital (hua piao)
Gee Chun	Chung Tin Street	1928	100,000	?
Tin Cut	Ha Po Street	1922	150,000	?
Sun Cheung	Chung Tin Street	1931	150,000	?
Sing Yu	Tai Kiu Tow	1877	60,000	?
Sung Yee	Han Yuan Lui	1926	120,000	?
Foo Yu	Tai Lin Street	1928	150,000	?
Hsin Chun	Kun Yin Chang	1925	100,000* 70,000	100,000*
Wan Yuan Yip Kee	Nam Tai Street	1931	100,000	?
Heng I	Nam Tai Street	1889	140,000* 60,000	100,000*
Tien Chuen	Nam Tai Street	1877	70,000* 100,000	100,000*
Lung Shen	?	?	100,000*	100,000*
Chuen Yu	Shan Han Street	1917	250,000* 150,000	200,000*
Hou Yu	Tai Lin Street	1892	180,000* 150,000	100,000*
Chi Fung	Koo Lau Chien	1931	100,000	?
Kow Ho	Nam Tai Street	1913	100,000	?
Hsiang Kang	Ha Han Street	1918	156,000* 150,000	100,000*
Shen Ho	Tai Lin Street	1907	150,000* 200,000	200,000*
Him Yu Hing Kee	Chung Tin Street	1929	155,000	?
Fu Yu	Chung Tin Street	1928	140,000	?

Sources: * Anonymous (1932: 441); otherwise Wong (1936: 399)

a bank had to gain admission to the clearing-house and bankers' guild. This required that the new bank throw an elaborate feast for the directors, staff and brokers of its established rivals, to establish goodwill. The new bank also had to pay a membership fee of $300 to the guild (Anonymous 1927: 139). Upon joining both the bankers' guild and the clearing-house a bank was said to have 'entered the garden' (Chang 1938b: 310) – an achievement which appears to have added substantially to its brand-name capital, allowing its notes to pass current throughout the city.

Local banks' revenues came from speculating on exchange-rate movements (especially silver-cash exchange rates), from issuing demand notes (which sold at a premium of 0.5 per cent) in exchange for copper cash, from cashing notes of other banks for a fee, and from making loans. Loans included call loans (*fu-chiuh*), usually settled at the end of the year; fixed-term loans (*chang-chiuh*) of three, six or twelve months; call ('chop') loans to other banks; and commercial loans involving the issue of promissory notes or 'native orders' (*chuang-piao*) (Chang 1938b: 313; McEldery 1976: 39). Native orders could be either time notes (*yuan-ch'i*), typically maturing in ten days, or demand notes (*chi-ch'i*). In granting loans local banks emphasized the creditworthiness of borrowers rather than documentary formalities – which was precisely the opposite of the practice of foreign and foreign-style Chinese banks (Anonymous 1932: 443; 1938a: 29; Chang 1938b: 310). In later years extensive use was also made of overdrafts. Borrowers' backgrounds were carefully investigated by street-runners – a practice that underlined the banks' role as information-gathering intermediaries. Often a borrower had to be recommended by a reputable third party, who also served as a guarantor (Chang 1938b: 310). Family ties were very important.[8]

Loans based on personal credit were not completely unsecured. Borrowers sometimes had to keep unborrowed accounts at the lending bank, like contemporary 'compensating balances'. Banks could also confiscate the goods of a defaulting borrower. The security here was the borrower's general property rather than specific collateral (McEldery 1976: 38). Loan rates ranged over time from 12 per cent to 22 per cent per year (*Chinese Economic Bulletin* 3 January 1924: 4; Anonymous 1927: 136; Anonymous 1932: 443; King 1965: 105), and were therefore comparable to rates charged by modern banks.

Of the two kinds of native orders only demand notes issued by *tso piao* circulated widely, the rest being sometimes limited to their *street* of issue. This suggests that the public did discriminate among various note-brands, as hypothesized in Selgin (1988: 42–7). Demand notes appear, moreover, to have been the only kind of promissory notes commonly in use in Foochow, and the only kind issued by *tso piao*:[9] the local banks had discovered that refusing to cash their notes on demand (even when the notes were immature time-notes) could seriously erode public confidence in them (Wagel 1915: 136). Eventually this led to abandonment of formal time-clauses. Local banks may also in some cases have been encouraged by the example set by foreign banks (pp.167–8). Local bank notes prior to 1928 were usually payable in copper cash, or in silver at the request of the noteholder. In emergencies, though, banks could exercise discretion in redeeming notes in gold or silver (at the current rate of exchange) or even, in the case of smaller banks, in current notes of the *tso piao tien* (Parkes 1852: 184; Doolittle 1865: 141). This implies a form of contingent-convertibility contract akin to those discussed by Gorton (1985), Dowd (1988) and Postlewaite and Vives (1987).

Compared to notes, demand deposits at first played a minor role. Reporting on conditions in the 1840s Parkes (1852: 181) noted that local bankers had 'a decided aversion toward extending such liabilities' except in a few instances involving friends who were also reputable merchants (though chequing accounts were routinely available at foreign and foreign-style banks). Of much greater importance were time deposits, which were withdrawable only in whole, and never by cheque, and which accounted for the bulk of native bank liabilities. These deposits paid interest at rates typically around 9 per cent per annum for the larger banks, which was comparable to rates paid by foreign banks. Rates offered on deposits by smaller banks were higher, reflecting a higher risk of insolvency (Parkes 1852: 181; *Chinese Economic Bulletin* 3 January 1925: 4; Anonymous 1927: 136). No interest was paid on demand notes. This contradicts the view of legal-restrictions theorists such as Wallace (1983), that bank notes would pay interest, or else give way to interest-bearing, small denomination bearer bonds, in an unregulated setting.[10] It suggests at the same time a possible source of inefficiency in the form of sub-optimal holdings of real money balances.

Unlike foreign and foreign-style banks, local banks observed traditional Chinese business customs (Anonymous 1932: 447; Wong 1936: 398–9; Chang 1938a: 29). They closed only on Chinese holidays, remained open on Sundays, and had no midday closing hours. They were also known for their courteous accommodation and convenient procedure in the withdrawal of funds, which on some occasions included delivering funds by special messenger to customers in urgent need (Chang 1938a: 30). Such service, together with more widespread offices and thorough knowledge of local enterprises, made local banks more successful than modern banks in lending to small businesses. It also allowed them to do an exclusive business in interior regions, so that modern banks had to use them as agents for lending there.

NOTE EXCHANGE AND CLEARING

Although small banks sometimes paid out notes of larger banks, or used them to redeem their own notes, large banks issued only their own notes, returning all others immediately on receipt in exchange for their own notes collected by rival banks or for cash. Thus, bank notes played only a limited role as high-powered money, with specie being the most important bank reserve medium. This was an important reason accounting for the inability of local banks to overissue independently of their rivals or to engage rivals in a system-wide overissue. It is in sharp contrast to the situation faced by a privileged monopoly bank of issue, the liabilities of which generally come to be treated as a reserve asset by less privileged banks (Selgin 1988: 47–9). Daily note exchange had already become standard practice by 1847 (Parkes 1852: 184). Large banks accepted one another's notes at par, which further served to expand the market for notes (p. 182). Parkes was greatly impressed by the 'mutual support' local banks derived from 'constantly exchanging and continually cashing each other's notes'.[11]

Though no details are available concerning early clearing arrangements, by 1927 there were no fewer than five different note-clearing centres, consisting of a central clearing-house at Shang Hang Chieh and its four branch units (Anonymous 1927: 134). Clearings were held every morning at 11 o'clock. Balances were settled in the afternoon, usually in cash. Clearing-house members forced to delay payment were required to pay an interest fee ('*tieh fan shui*') to creditor banks at a rate of $1.10 to $1.20 cents per diem for every $1,000 owed (Anonymous 1932: 441; Wong 1936: 399). This charge was set daily by the Native Bankers' Association. Banks did not, however, often take advantage of emergency borrowing privileges: the rates involved were punitive, and any bank habitually unable to pay its clearing balances was likely to face a loss in public confidence, possibly resulting in a run.

Perhaps the most important consequence of daily note clearings was that no bank could afford to be overgenerous with its issues. Thus Wagel (1915: 177) observed that 'while there was no lawful check on the issue of paper by the banks, the evil of the unrestricted issue was to a large extent minimized.' Certainly it was less than the 'evil' which had occurred in previous centuries when paper money was issued by the Chinese government rather than by competing, private banks.[12] This supports the claim of, for example, Selgin (1987a, 1988) and White (1984b, chapter 1), that competition in the issue of redeemable notes places strict limits on note issue.

FAILURES AND PANICS

Prior to the twentieth century, local-bank failures were infrequent and generally confined to small banks or cash shops (Jernigan 1904: 100). Sir Harry Parkes reported that only four small banks had failed from

1844 to 1848, and that 'a general crash, seriously affecting the public interest, is a thing unheard of' (Parkes 1852: 181). Banks that failed usually did so just before the Chinese New Year, when many debts had to be settled, causing exceptional withdrawals of cash and bullion and bringing to light the existence of bad loans. This put a heavy strain on weaker, poorly managed banks.

Premeditated fraud was rare, though it occurred in isolated cases. Defaulting banks usually paid off between 50 and 60 per cent of their outstanding liabilities (Parkes 1852: 185; see also *Chinese Economic Bulletin*, 29 March 1924: 1–2 and 3 January 1925: 3–4). This suggests that most failed bankers were not fraudulently absconding with assets.

Though the public had no reason to suspect foul play on the part of bankers, this did not prevent bank runs (known in Foochow as *kun piao*). The insolvency of a single bank (especially at the end of the year, when other banks were also at greatest risk of default) often triggered runs on other banks suspected of being low on cash or specie (King 1965: 103). Thus the native banking industry appears to have been exposed to confidence or information externalities, which were, however, limited to small banks. On the other hand the clustering of runs around the New Year suggests that panics, rather than being random events as suggested by Diamond and Dybvig (1983), Waldo (1985), and others, were instead based on a kind of prior, real 'shock' with predictable adverse repercussions on bank earnings (cf. Gorton 1986). Ironically, banks' unlimited liability, which might have discouraged bank runs, seems actually to have encouraged them because of China's special, help-yourself version of unlimited liability. According to Justus Doolittle (1865: 142), if a bank could not redeem its notes in copper cash (or some preferred medium) on the spot, the noteholder could 'seize hold of anything in the bank and take it off, to the full amount of his demands' without being liable 'for prosecution for theft or misdemeanor'. Consequently the disappointment of a single noteholder could provoke his immediate confiscation of bank property, which would in turn draw other bank customers (who might not originally have been after cash) into a frenzied round of 'bank gutting'.

Until 1855 noteholders engaged in bank gutting would quickly be joined by other persons who had no legitimate claims against the run-upon banks. 'Beggars and idlers' were 'only too happy to assist in such an exciting and profitable hobby as robbing a bank'. Once this happened, a run would degenerate into a full-scale riot: 'When an excited and interested crowd has begun such a work,' Doolittle observed, 'it is exceedingly difficult to prevent the completion of the undertaking.' It was not unusual for a bank, once run upon, to be robbed 'of every portable thing worth carrying off, even to the sleepers and the rafters' (1865: 142).

Such inadequate protection of bank property made bank runs more severe and frequent than they would have been otherwise. It also added to the losses suffered by legitimate claimants, because many bank gutters were 'nothing but thieves and robbers'. At last, in 1855, in the wake of a particularly severe run on several small banks (including one that had not even been guilty of defaulting on any of its notes before it was looted), the provincial authorities decided to put a stop to unwarranted bank gutting. They arrested several rioters ranging from a poor coolie to a respected rice-dealer. After determining that the arrested were guilty of robbery (having held no claims against the victimized banks), the viceroy – at the risk of provoking an uprising – beheaded them, without trial, before a large crowd of other looters. According to Doolittle, this 'summary act at once quelled the disorderly rabble, and no such disposition to rob a bank was manifested . . . for a considerable time' (1865: 142).[13] Following the 1911 revolution the bankruptcy law was revised and bank gutting became illegal.

Even prior to 1911 larger banks had been able to protect themselves against runs. They would assist each other with emergency loans of cash, and it was not unusual for friends of a bank to rally around it during a run to maintain order and to keep looters away (Doolittle 1865: 143; Jernigan 1904: 97). In the early days more reputable banks, if threatened by a run, could secure permission from a local mandarin to suspend payment. A bank that secured such permission would be closed, its doors sealed by two long strips of paper in the form of an X (Doolittle 1865: 144). The strips bore, along with other notices, the name of the responsible mandarin, who might even pledge his personal assets as security for the bank's liabilities (Parkes 1852: 185). After being officially sealed the bank could settle its accounts with greater leisure than would otherwise have been available to it. Eventually this practice evolved into the custom of having insolvent banks post signs and publish notices declaring that they would 'hereafter pay' (*huo chi*), i.e., redeem all their outstanding notes and not undertake any further issues. Once a bank formerly announced its plans to liquidate its assets and pay off its notes, its property could not be confiscated even prior to the reform of 1911 (Doolittle 1865: 144; see also *Chinese Economic Bulletin*, 3 January 1925: 3–4).[14] This was one means by which large banks were able to protect themselves from information externalities.

Thanks to such emergency measures and to their long-standing reputation for trustworthiness the *tso piao* were practically immune to runs and to failure due to runs. Their record appears to have been unblemished until the crisis of 1922.

COUNTERFEITING

Counterfeiting of local bank notes was discouraged through an ingenious technique known as the 'proof-slip' system for identifying legitimate notes. Notes were printed with extra-wide right-hand margins on which various words, phrases or even complete sentences would be stamped or written. Then the margins of a stack of freshly printed and marked notes would be trimmed with a sharp knife. The trimmed-off slips of paper, bearing half of the marginal identification markings, would then be kept in a reference book after having the value and date of issue of the formerly attached notes recorded on them. If a bank had any doubt concerning the authenticity of a note presented to it for payment, it could check the proof-slip to see if the identification markings matched. Thus forgeries, unless executed with such skill that their authenticity was never questioned (an unlikely possibility, considering the elaborate system of special inks and markings used in preparing legitimate notes), would be detected rapidly. This greatly increased the odds of tracing them to their source.

Thanks to such precautions counterfeiting was seldom practised in the earlier days of Foochow's free-banking system, despite relatively lenient penalties typically applied to forgers (Williams 1851: 292; Parkes 1852: 185; Doolittle 1865: 138). When it did occur it was on a very small scale, involving notes of small denominations (which were less scrutinized). In an exceptional case local bankers put a stop to a particularly intransigent forger by *hiring* him as an expert detector of other forgeries! (Parkes 1852: 185–6).

Following the Nationalist take-over – when former cash notes had been entirely replaced by Dai-Fook dollars – counterfeiting for a time became more frequent (Anonymous 1927: 130–1). This was due partly to the declining quality of local notes in the twentieth century: the paper was poor, and the printing was less intricate and less well executed than before. This probably reflected the general decline in prosperity suffered throughout Fukien since the 1850s, due to the collapse of the tea trade and continuing political instability. The proliferation of counterfeits made local bank notes less convenient, as they would sometimes be refused unless declared authentic by an expert or endorsed by their tenderer (if his credit was good) (cf. Cagan 1963: 19–21). Many notes were blackened by multiple endorsements. Yet even this did not guarantee their authenticity, for counterfeiters soon learned to add fake endorsements to their issues, which gave them the appearance of having circulated for a long time. Eventually experts were employed by all banks to scrutinize all notes received, and the counterfeiting problem diminished. Thus even by the early 1930s native bank notes continued to be the main circulating medium in Foochow, being preferred even to notes issued by the modern banks (Anonymous 1932: 440). They continued to circulate at par and to command a premium over cash until they were suppressed by provincial and central government reforms (Tamagna 1942: 68).

THE END OF THE FREE BANKING ERA

Despite counterfeiting, mounting political instability (including periodic military occupations and the continued threat of forced loans brought by them) and economic depression, the local banks of Foochow and their note issue business in particular remained profitable and commanded high public confidence well into the twentieth century. They had carved a niche for themselves which modern banks, both domestic and foreign, were not able to fill.[15]

Unlike the Shansi banks, which relied on the Imperial government as their main source of funds, local banks survived the Republican revolution, even benefiting from it by taking over some of the business formerly given to the larger native banks. The revolution also ended the Imperial banking regulations of 1907–9, intended to restrict private note issues by imposing a stiff 60 per cent cash and specie reserve requirement, but never enforced in the south (Young 1939: 225).[16]

Ironically, the same lack of involvement with central government affairs that saved local banks from the fate suffered by Shansi banks also hastened their ultimate decline. While many local bankers were inclined to support the revolutionaries, they had relatively little to offer them in the way of funds. In contrast, several modern Chinese banks lent heavily to the Republican (and later Nationalist) government. This eventually cost local banks their right of note issue, as 'a connection' developed 'between the right to note issue and the loaning of funds to the government' (McEldery 1976:

144). The connection first became evident under the Republican government, which between 1913 and 1926 borrowed $600,000,000, (*yuan*), almost all of it from modern banks. In 1926, their last year in power, the Republicans borrowed another $80,090,000, less than 8 per cent of which was lent by local banks. As a sop in return for these loans the government renewed the Imperial regulatory agenda, modified to include provisions favourable to the modern banks. Besides re-implementing the 60 per cent reserve requirement on note issue the Republican reforms of 1915 and 1920 marked a victory for modern banks by making their notes alone receivable in payments to the government (McEldery 1976: 144–145).

Fortunately for local banks in Foochow and elsewhere in the south the Republican government, like the Imperial government before it, was unable to enforce its regulations in that part of the country. Only following the Nationalist take-over did regulations favouring modern banks take their toll on local banking in Foochow. Like the Republicans the Nationalists borrowed heavily from the modern banks, especially to finance military expenditures: by 1935 they had an outstanding debt of over $1 billion – exceeding the estimated value of $800 million for the aggregate value of native bank assets (Tamagna 1942: 62) – with native bank loans accounting for less than 5 per cent of the government's borrowings (McEldery 1976: 163). As the Nationalist government grew, so did its financial demands from modern banks. It therefore continued Republican reforms that favoured the modern banks, simultaneously pressurizing them to absorb large amounts of government debt while placing additional restraints on note issues by local banks. An example of such restraints was the suppression of the popular Dai-Fook dollar-unit in Foochow in 1928, which was aimed at eliminating the main advantage (for local exchange) possessed by native bank notes over modern, silver-dollar-denominated notes. Although the 1928 reform was for a time evaded, it was effectively enforced by the provincial reform of 15 March 1933, which abolished the *hua piao* (copper *yuan*) unit while also requiring native banks to back their fiduciary note issues with real-estate collateral valued at 30 per cent below its market value (Wong 1936: 400). This reform also for the first time made note issue a privilege, subject to the approval of the Finance Department of the provincial government.

Other reforms directly enhanced the privileged status of modern banks while at the same time forcing them to employ their resources to finance China's deficits. In March 1935 the government took control of the Bank of China and Bank of Communications by forcing them to issue more shares in exchange for government bonds. The capital of the Central Bank of China was also augmented by the same means (Coble 1980: 180–1). The power of private bankers was correspondingly eroded. This action was followed by the reform of 3 November 1935, which made the notes of the three government banks – the Central Bank of China, the Bank of China and the Bank of Communications[17] – full legal tender or *fa-pi* currency. The Central Bank of China, which had been the main fiscal agent to the Nationalist government since being rechartered in Shanghai by that government in 1928, was given the sole right of unrestricted legal-tender issue. The authority given to the other modern banks to issue legal tender notes could be rescinded at any time by the Ministry of Finance.

While notes of modern banks were made legal tender, the use of silver as money was declared an act of treason. Silver coin and bullion had to be turned in to the Currency Reserve Board of the Ministry of Finance, or to one of the legal-tender issuing ('official') banks, in exchange for legal tender notes. The former 60 per cent specie-reserve requirement became *de facto* 60 per cent legal-tender reserve requirement. This meant that the government banks could expand their issues without confronting any sort of liquidity constraint.

The immediate circumstance provoking these reforms was the continuing loss of silver reserves by modern banks and by the Central Bank of China in particular. This was largely due to the American Silver Purchase Act of 1934. But the government also had another motive for abandoning the silver standard, which was its desire to use *fa-pi* currency to monetize its growing deficits (Tamagna 1942: 4; Coble 1980: 202–3; cf. Brandt and Sargent 1989). In just over eighteen months the combined note issues of the government banks increased almost four-fold, from $427, 414, 917 to $1,607, 202, 334, less than half of which represented notes issued in exchange for silver. Prices expressed in *yuan*, which had fallen 21 per cent in the three years before the reform, afterwards rose 43 per cent (Shen 1939: 224). China was on its way to experiencing yet another instance of government paper money becoming utterly worthless.

It is significant that local banks, had they been allowed to adhere to a copper standard, would have been immune to fluctuations in the value of silver that threatened modern banks. Bloch observed that while silver slumped heavily in 1930 and 1931, coppers rose in terms of the standard silver dollar. On the other hand, when silver rose from 1931 to 1935, coppers depreciated considerably. Thus, China's copper currency has been more closely related to the general international movement of prices than China's silver currency.[18]

Though actual copper currency was phased out in many parts of China, copper–silver exchange quotations continued to be used to make cost-of-living adjustments in contracts specifying payment in silver.

A final provision in the new reform prohibited local banks from extending their note issues. Their outstanding notes were to be gradually retired and replaced by notes of the Central Bank of China. The Ministry of Finance planned to give the Central Bank of China a monopoly in note issue (Shen 1939: 223; Young 1939: 229). But this goal was set aside with the outbreak of the Sino–Japanese War in 1937, and it became a dead letter when the Communists gained power in 1949. From then on the Communist People's Bank became the focus of monetary reforms, gradually taking over the branches of the Central Bank of China as well as local bank offices. By the mid-1960s local banks had been completely phased out (Ecklund 1973: 580). Private notes disappeared along with them.

Or did they? According to a report in the *Far Eastern Economic Review* of 11 April 1957, Communist financial experts were perturbed by their discovery in the late 1950s that Agricultural People's Cooperatives (APCs) throughout the country were illegally issuing large quantities of small-denomination bearer notes (to make up for insufficient issues of small-notes by the People's Bank). Government officials were reluctant to take steps against the APCs, for fear that the publicity would inspire more of them 'to adopt the expedient to solve their own difficulties'. The government did, however, issue a statement in the *People's Daily* denouncing the unauthorized note issues as a 'Capitalist crime'.

CONCLUSION

Though not free from shortcomings Foochow's free banking system – an example of complete *laissez-faire* in paper currency and banking – can be judged to have been largely beneficial. True, it was based on an archaic copper-cash system, with a confusing array of units of account. But the local banks themselves were mainly a source of order, convenience, efficiency and stability. Their currency was widely preferred to cash, and it provided a superior unit of account. Native banks were an important source of loanable funds, and there is no evidence that they behaved recklessly. On the contrary: by all accounts the local banks of Foochow were among the most reputable ever to have operated in all of Chinese history (e.g., Fortune 1847: 372–3; Parkes 1852; Williams 1863: 271; Doolittle 1865: 138ff; Imperial Maritime Customs 1922; Anonymous 1927; Tamagna 1942: 68). There were few losses to noteholders from local bank failures, and only smaller banks were vulnerable to runs (which were in any case encouraged by a peculiar approach to unlimited liability). Finally, although the record of local banking was in later years marred by counterfeiting and by serious banking crises, the source of this was political unrest and not any instability inherent in the banking system. On the whole, local banks performed better than Chinese government banks either before or after the free-banking era. In China as elsewhere, decentralized currency supply was abandoned, not because of any inherent shortcomings of competitive note issue, but largely because the government wanted to improve its ability to borrow from particular banks.

In brief, the shortcomings of Foochow's monetary system existed despite, and not because of, its freely evolved banking institutions. The case of Foochow supplies further evidence that free banking is neither inherently unstable nor inferior in practice to centralized banking. It was, moreover, only one of numerous instances of free banking in China – of which many were more important and quite possibly more successful.[19] A comprehensive study of free banking in China should prove a most worthwhile undertaking.

ACKNOWLEDGEMENTS

I wish to thank Steven Cheung, John Hsu, Kerry Macpherson, Gary Shiu, John Blundell, John Greenwood, Y.C. Jao, Isabella Ling, Sheldon Richman, Kurt Schuler, Gordon Tullock and Lawrence White for their help. Remaining errors will be mine.

NOTES

1 As Rockoff (1975a) and Rolnick and Weber (1983, 1986) show, the shortcomings of pre-Civil War banking in the US may be attributed to regulatory interference, including bond-collateral requirements for note issue.
2 For critical assessments of the Scottish system as a model of free banking see Rothband (1987), Sechrest (1988) and Cowen and Krozner (1989).

3 Regrettably I have been unable to uncover primary source material – newspaper accounts, bank records, etc. – much of which was destroyed in the course of the Japanese occupation and, later the Cultural Revolution. Though the secondary sources cited are mainly in English, Chinese materials were examined by an assistant, who was, however, unable to uncover very much new information.

4 Although they allowed private issues of paper currency the Manchus also maintained an official, and highly unsatisfactory, monopoly of coinage. Unauthorized mints did, however, operate at various times. See Ch'en (1980: 12–15, 33–8, and 120–3).

5 On this see Bloch (1935).

6 The Dai-Fook dollar had the advantage of avoiding any confusion over differences between 'market' and 'standard' cash, because a Dai-Fook dollar always represented 1,000 standard or full-weight cash, rather than a nominal quantity of actual, debased or worn coin.

7 All but $200,000 of these unredeemed notes belonged to the Bank of Fukien.

8 On this see McEldery (1976: 45–53).

9 Doolittle, however, (1865: 141–2) states that in Foochow even prior to 1865 *all* bank notes were payable on demand. This would seem to include notes issued by smaller banks.

10 For further evidence contradicting the legal-restrictions view see Makinen and Woodward (1986) and White (1987).

11 For an account of how mutual acceptance of notes emerges in conditions of competitive note issue see Selgin and White (1987) or Selgin (1988: chapter 2).

12 Compare Williams (1851: 292–5). For references on inflation prior to the Ch'ing Dynasty see Tullock (1957).

13 The provincial authorities had to intervene again to protect small banks in 1887, when the failure of the Chi'un Feng Bank provoked runs on several other cash shops (The *Peking Gazette*, as quoted in the *North China Herald* of 29 April. Cited in King 1965: 103 fn.). In later years the provincial authorities also tried to limit failures of cash shops by prohibiting them from issuing small-denomination notes (Imperial Maritime Customs 1891: 415). However, since such prohibitions had to be issued on several occasions, it is doubtful that they were ever heeded.

In recent times bank runs have once again become a problem in Fukien province – a consequence of the outbreak of inflation in response to the relaxation of price controls combined with low rates of interest paid on deposits.

14 On the economic rationale of bank suspension of payments see Gorton (1985a).

15 On the competitive advantages possessed by local banks see the *Chinese Economic Bulletin* for 13 March 1926 and Wong (1936: 398).

16 A law passed by the Imperial government in 1908 actually awarded a monopoly of note issue to the Ta Ching Bank (established in 1905 as the Hupu Bank), but was not enforced. The Ta Ching Bank collapsed with the downfall of the dynasty (Tamagna 1942: 35).

17 Notes of the Farmer's Bank of China were included upon its establishment in 1937.

18 This had also been true during the quarter century prior to 1851, when silver appreciated markedly and the purchasing power of cash remained stable (Wang 1977: 19). According to an anonymous referee, however, copper currency depreciated twice as rapidly as silver between 1918 and 1927.

19 In 1927 Canton had over 500 native banks, Swatow over 200, Ningpo over 100, and Shanghai 80 (compared to Foochow's 45). Although Canton's banks were on average twice as small as Foochow's, those of Swatow and Ningpo were about the same size, and Shanghai's were typically much larger (Tamagna 1942: 59–61). On native banking in Canton see Ou (1932); on Shanghai see McEldery (1976); and on Ningpo see Jones (1972).

7 Free banking in France (1796–1803)

Philippe Nataf

INTRODUCTION

The economists of the eighteenth century regarded free banking as the natural banking system, and they believed that the most efficient, stable and just way of organizing it was to allow it to grow spontaneously. As early as 1735 Richard Cantillon in his famous book *Essai sur la nature du commerce en général* criticized the monopolistic privileges granted to banks by European governments. The first physiocrat, Vincent de Gournay, using for the first time the maxim '*Laissez-faire, laissez-passer*', advocated the abolition of all restrictions on agriculture, commerce, industry and credit. He also advocated the freedom of interest rates, against the prejudices of his time, in favour of usury.

His disciple, Jacques Turgot, managed to open the field of corporate banking in France. He arranged for the Caisse d'Escompte to begin operations in 1776 and he regarded the opening of this bank as the first step in the creation of a free banking system along the lines of the Scottish system described by Adam Smith in *The Wealth of Nations*, in 1776. This free banking system served as an ideal for the French economists. Freedom in banking became for them the model of a natural and efficient organization. It was justified in theory and confirmed by the economic progress demonstrated in Scottish history.

Turgot's reform programme was halted when he left the government, and the Caisse d'Escompte found itself with an unintended monopoly in the field of banking. Its exclusive privileges generated monetary crises of a kind unknown since the collapse of John Law's Bank in the beginning of the eighteenth century. The Count of Mirabeau analysed in his book *De la Caisse d'Escompte* (1785, tome I: 141) the annoying consequences of this monopoly. Noticing the link between the 1783 financial crises and 'the troublesome and difficult periods that afflict commerce almost periodically', Mirabeau endorsed equal treatment for borrowers, opposed bank privileges, and cited the British systems as examples. His opinion was based on the observation that as banks in 'the three British Kingdoms' spread, commerce and manufacturing flourished, creating prosperity for all classes of citizens. This situation, he wrote, 'thus facilitated long-term credits which give the English merchants a marked superiority over those of all other nations' (Mirabeau 1785: 34).

The opposition to all privileges, including those for banks, became, in the 1750s, the dominant attitude among French economists. Four translations of Adam Smith's famous book had already appeared by the start of the French Revolution[1] and Smith reinforced the physiocratic influence on the members of the Constitutional National Assembly.[2] The *laissez-faire* ideas of the physiocrats were so widespread that when the economist Du Pont de Nemours proposed total freedom in banking he got the backing of a clear majority. 'Banks should be submitted to the laws of free trade', he said, 'if this privilege includes some exclusivity, you should refuse it. You came here to abolish exclusive privileges and not to create new ones' and, concluding his speech, he advocated that 'the establishment of banks should be free like any other commercial enterprise' (Du Pont de Nemours 1789: 38,40).

This programme was endorsed by Laborde and Lecouteulx de Canteleu as well as Du Pont de Nemours whose speech favouring free banking was immediately published as a booklet which was much acclaimed by the public. However, several factors prevented the development of a true free banking system. The *caisses patriotiques*, recently studied by Eugene White (1989) can hardly be considered free banks. Most, and probably all of them, lacked the legal status of large-scale associations of individuals. The corporate framework of joint stock banks organized by freely contracted by-laws did not exist. The rapidly changing legislative situation, political instability and the assignats inflation most likely account for this state of affairs. As far as we know, the *caisses*, although numerous, did not issue a significant portion of the money supply. Finally, sound free banks cannot be based on a rapidly depreciating fiat paper money like the assignats. These historical considerations explain an important fact: not a single member of the French Free Banking School considered this experiment as a free banking system. None the less the multiplication of the *caisses patriotiques* shows the existence of a demand for a full-scale corporate banking organization as it appeared a few years later. In any case, price controls destroyed even the embryonic credit system of the *caisses patriotiques* until the end of the Reign of Terror. When domestic peace and monetary stability came back in 1796 the time was ripe for the spontaneous emergence of what could truly be called free banking system.

As soon as the freedom of speech reappeared, the economist Camille Saint-Aubin published a small book entitled *Des Banques particulières* (1795), advocating free competition for banks.[3] In 1796 ideas favouring economic freedom, including for the management of all banking operations, were widely spread.

COMPETITIVE BANKING: SPONTANEOUS EXPANSION AND MONETARY STABILITY

The free banking period in France (1796–1803) is relatively well known to historians (e.g Smith 1990 [1936]: 29–30). From F. Buisson (1805) to Edmond Servais (1960) and Louis Lair (1967), this era has been described with accuracy and fairness.[4] Economists Paul Coq (1850), Charles Coquelin (1852), and Edouard Horn (1866) provided revealing interpretations of this period's banking system. Interestingly no historians of this topic have complained that this credit organization did not work or even that it contained important defects. On the contrary, Coq, Coquelin, Horn, Courtois (1881) and their disciples pointed out the efficiency and the stability of this period's banking under free competition.

'When the peace of Amiens was signed (March 1802), six institutions existed in Paris for discounting and issuing claims ("effets"), (Banque de France, Caisse d'Escompte du Commerce, Comptoir Commercial, Banque Territoriale, Factorerie du Commerce, Caisse d'Echange des Monnaies) and six *caisses* for receiving funds or granting credit to the public without issuing claims.' These remarks by Gabriel Ramon in his well-documented *Histoire de la Banque de France* (1929) show the existence of several banks of issue in Paris at the beginning of the nineteenth century.

In order to understand the rapid extension of free banks and their operations one must recall certain characteristics of the old regime. If private bankers operated in large numbers in continental Europe before the French Revolution, discounting banks managing under the status of commercial corporations were relatively rare. Only Scotland, soon followed by England, escaped this apparently general rule. Notwithstanding the important need for large credit institutions, France had authorized only one bank to operate as a commercial corporation. Although not conceived as a central bank the Caisse d'Escompte had issued bank notes without competition since 1776. Banks, like other corporations, needed legal authorization to begin their activities and in spite of a large demand for credit, as shown in France at the turn of the century (1796–1803) or in Great Britain, the administrative authorities refused to grant the right to create new credit institutions. Government restrictions thus prevented the development of banks to compete with the Caisse d'Escompte.

The reason for French backwardness in banking was pointed out by Charles Coquelin in his famous *Dictionnaire de l'economie politique* (1874) and in *Le Crédit et les Banques* (1876). He wrote:

> it is too easy to recognize this cause in the brutal resistance from laws which opposed very strong obstacles to the multiplication [of banks]. . . . In old France [before 1789] no bank institution could have been founded without the direct intervention of government. Furthermore, it was not even permitted to open a stockholders' corporation without its permission; corporations of this kind being forbidden by law. Consequently there have been no public banks (joint stock banks) under this regime other than those instituted by the government. The mind of the French nation and the particular character of its industry has nothing to do with this question. . . . Only two experiments with banks have been made by the old government, one in 1716 with the bank of John Law; the other, in 1776 with the Caisse d'Escompte.
>
> (Coquelin 1874: 135)

Given such obstacles, banking in France was reduced to the activities of individual bankers using funds of a relatively limited scope.

The French Revolution is a complex event. However, the understanding of the free banking era in France requires the examination of certain pieces of legislation. On 4 August 1789 all privileges were repealed by the Constitutional National Assembly. This Assembly passed in 1791 a specific law favouring freedom of work and domestic free trade. Without the assignats inflation and political instability, free banking probably would have appeared at that time in the form of large-scale corporations as they did later on. But two new obstacles to banking then appeared: first, a decree of 8 November 1792 prohibited all claims like bills of exchange or bank notes and later, in April 1794, all business corporations including banks were banned. These factors explain, in large part, the postponement of free competition in banking.

After the fall of the Robespierre dictatorship, an entire book, *Des banques en France*, published by Camille Saint-Aubin in 1795, advocated free competition in banking along Scottish lines, while the spokesman for the Finance Commission of the Conseil des Cinq Cents (a legislative body), Monsieur Eschasseriaux, recommended immediate repeal of the anti-bank laws of 1792–4. He advocated 'the establishment of free banks . . . which would serve to expand our commercial relations, to rejuvenate credit, to increase the progress of trade, agriculture and arts, and which would become as in England and Holland, the source of national prosperity'.[5] This advice led to the abolition of all restrictions on banks and to the end of inflation. Immediately banks began to spring up and grow.

In his *Dictionnaire*, Charles Coquelin made the revealing comment that

> at the end of our great revolution, when the terrorist regime had just ceased and the memory of the assignats was still recent, several corporations opened in Paris to discount and issue bank notes. As laws on that matter were either abolished, or had fallen into obsolescence, these institutions opened spontaneously without other rules than their by-laws. In spite of the confusion still reigning at this time, and the prejudice supposedly rooted in the minds against any kind of credit paper (bills and notes), they did not have too much trouble finding their way; this proves anew this truth, that in spite of so many bad memories, banks would have spread in France as easily as elsewhere, if obstacles had not been put intentionally to bar their progress.
>
> (Coquelin, 1874: 137)

This sentiment was echoed by Jean-Gustave Courcelle-Seneuil, who wrote that

> the Revolution had left France under the regime of freedom for banks, and, at the end of the XVIIIth century, no legislation hampered the issue of redeemable notes. So, as soon as the catastrophe of the assignats and of the mandats territoriaux was over and government stopped issuing paper money, private credit reappeared . . . several corporations settled in successively, all of them issuing redeemable bank notes.
>
> (Courcelle-Seneuil 1920: 35)

In 1881, Alphonse Courtois, in his *Histoire des banques en France* summarized the development of the French banks of issue. On 29 June 1796 a group of bankers created a bank of issue to facilitate their activities. It was the Caisse des Comptes Courants, located in the centre of Paris. Its resources consisted of FF5 million of equity and bank notes to the value of FF20 million. It is worth noting that its own resources amounted to 20 per cent of its assets. Financed by such an equity, the bank enjoyed great strength. With 20 per cent of its assets financed by its own funds, the bank was well sheltered against normal business risks. However, an unusual disaster befell the Caisse on 17 November 1797 when thieves stole FF2.5 million – representing 10 per cent of the bank's assets. Today, such a loss would destroy almost any bank.[6] But its strong equity position and its liquidity enabled the Caisse des Comptes Courants to avoid failure and successfully to face the run that followed.

If solvency avoided total failure, the liquidity of its assets permitted immediate redemption when the run began. Du Pont de Nemours, in his book *Sur la Banque de France* (1806), explained the situation as follows. When this 'loss' occurred, bank notes in circulation amounted to FF16.5 million. These notes were backed by a very liquid portfolio of bills of exchange for a net value of FF13 million, by cash of over FF4 million, and by cash from surplus capital of FF940,000. Total liquidity amounted to FF18 million, and consequently Du Pont commented that the Caisse 'could pay.' He added that

> several of its stockholders and managers were men of intelligence and common sense. They showed that . . . [notes] were backed and that therefore one should remain calm. With their corporation lacking the protection of special legislation, the responsibility of the stockholders would be pronounced under general common law, and it would be more honourable for them, and viewed more favourably by public opinion, to assume it [their responsibility] themselves, like a spontaneous movement of their loyalty and of their will.
>
> (Du Pont de Nemours 1806: 33–6)

After only one day of suspension of payments, the stockholders pledged to reimburse every note, the bank reopened its doors and confidence was rapidly restored. The run stopped and no failure occurred. For Edouard Horn this strength in difficult times stems from the characteristics of a free bank of issue. Its managing corporation 'has no legal privilege and is submitted to general common laws, which means that all stockholders are responsible for their social commitment' (Horn 1866: 321).

To analyse further the nature of this bank it is necessary to add that its capital was divided into a thousand shares, each worth FF5,000 each. The Caisse circulation of FF20 million consisted of notes with face values of FF500 and FF1,000. Such face values were high for the time. The stockholders established a 6 per cent discount rate on a ninety-day basis and all discounted bills were required to bear three signatures. The requirement for three signatures excluded merchants and industrialists. As a result the borrower had to seek a private banker's signature, further increasing the discounting cost. Coq and Horn thus concluded that this bank was reserved for bankers and was bound to face competition from newcomers in the field.

In *La Liberté des banques*, Edouard Horn commented on the rapid evolution of the banking situation.

> Created by bankers and for bankers, the Caisse des Comptes Courants only benefits commerce and industry in an indirect manner, and it sometimes hurts them: the agreement born from this association diminishes competition or lessens it between banks, to the great disadvantage of people requesting loans or discounts. To escape the exploitation, large businesses and manufacturers enter into partnerships.
>
> (Duverneuil and de la Tynna 1800: 596)

The Caisse d'Escompte du Commerce was founded on 24 November, 1797. At this time the forty-seven stockholders owned a capital of FF470,000 and as early as 1802 its resources increased to a nominal capital of FF24 million, of which only FF6 million was advanced, and to a circulation FF20 million in bank notes. This institution discounted, according to the *Dictionnaire universel de commerce*, the associates' bills 'not exceeding sixty days and bearing (only) two signatures if they had a solid reputation' (Buisson 1805: 340).[7] Apparently this bank also received time deposits bearing high interest as a result of its use of short-term loans and was very stable. Its strength, noticed by Du Pont de Nemours stems also from its high solvency and liquidity. He wrote that in June/July 1802, 'one of the managers of the Caisse d'Escompte stole FF800,000; but it still held, in addition to its portfolio, more than sufficient assets in écus [metallic money] and other assets in buildings . . . Its payments have been neither suspended nor slowed down. Its notes did not lose any value' (Du Pont de Nemours 1806: 36). Its developing resources and discounts

> considerable for the time and for the group that used them attest to a real success. It provokes imitation. The retailers did not wait long to follow the example of the merchants and the industrialists. They created in 1800 the Comptoir Commercial, also known as the Caisse Jabach.
>
> (Horn 1866: 323)

This third banking institution, also located in the centre of Paris, discounted Parisian bills and issued notes with face values of FF250,

FF500 and FF1,000 (Duverneuil and de la Tynna 1800).

Other banks of issue began to operate (although on a smaller scale) in the same central business quarter of Paris. Such institutions included the Factorerie du Commerce, la Banque Territoriale and the Caisse d'Echange des Monnaies, which operated also in Rouen. It issued redeemable bank notes with a face value of at least FF20. In this city another bank of issue functioned, the Banque de Rouen, also called Société Générale du Commerce and was founded on 20 April 1798. This bank discounted bills with only two signatures and paid interest on its deposits.[8]

The documents of the period show that, in spite of difficult times (wars, theft, embezzlement), banks suffered no failures. They functioned 'freely, smoothly and to the high satisfaction of the public' (Courcelle-Seneuil 1867). The importance of their own funds (equity financing 20 per cent or more of the assets) and the responsibility of their stockholders explain in large part the capacity of these banks to meet several demands for the redemption of notes. Prosperity, liquidity, solvency and stability characterized the credit institutions of the Directory and the Consulate. The free banking system of France worked remarkably well.[9]

NAPOLEON'S DESTRUCTION OF FREE BANKING

The idea – so widespread today – that free banking would be and has been very unstable, never entered the minds even of its opponents in early nineteenth century France. If the adversaries of free banking recognized its prosperity, solvency and stability, then why was it destroyed? Enigmatic as this question seems today, historians of the era devoted considerable attention to this paradoxical issue. Edouard Horn and Paul Coq expanded Charles Coquelin's explanation. In the twentieth century Gabriel Ramon and Achille Dauphin-Meunier brought more light through extended research on the topic. Horn's analysis enlightens the problem with surprising views when he wrote that

> the alleged reason in favour of the monopolized issue [of bank notes] in the preamble to the law of Germinal 24 an XI [destroying free banking] is the exact opposite of that used now by the monopoly. Here is the major argument articulated by M. Crêtet: 'the divided action of banks on circulation and credit runs against any central combination and no bank could ever manage its operations on the needs of business and the situation of money in circulation. . . . This rivalry induces in competing banks prudent

behaviour which prevents them from using their means with confidence and which obliges them to refuse loans to commerce in proportion to their needs.' In other words, hampered by their mutual competition, competing banks use the power of fiduciary issue only with timidity and circumscription and in narrow limits; they do not use all the benefits which it provides. Yet, today the principal justification of the opponents to free issue [of notes] is abuse, overissue, with which competing banks would be led, pushed and fatally carried away! Reconcile who can such clearly contradictory arguments! For me, if in this purely negative part of my chapter I dared to reason and to judge, I would side without hesitation with M. Crêtet's opinion against his rival opponents. Yes, the author of the law of Germinal 24 [ending the free banking era] is right: competition, jealously watching over and controlling, is an embarrassment, a brake; no free and multiple banks ever pushed or could push fiduciary issue to the excess that, under the regime of privilege and monopoly, we say it reached in England during the 'restriction', in Russia or in Austria. However, this embarrassment, this forced prudence, far from being a defect, is one of the big advantages of free and diversified issue; the reverse [overissue] is one of the large wounds; one of the serious dangers of monopoly.

(Horn 1866: 333–4)

If free banking was abolished in France by an 'arbitrary act of authority' as Courcelle-Seneuil terms it (1867: 38), with the only justification being the under-issue of bank notes and its correlative limitation of artificial credit expansion, it means that free competition in banking, including notes creation, is the best remedy for our age of inflation ridden with business fluctuations.

The legal destruction of the free banking system did not spring only from an intellectual error; it has other sources which must now be described.

To give a rapid summation of French history at the end of the eighteenth century: a few bankers, afraid of political instability, associated themselves with a successful and popular general, Napoleon Bonaparte, who soon took over power through a *coup d'état*. This general installed an authoritarian dictatorship which immediately began 'banking reforms' jointly with the group of bankers just mentioned. This co-operation of interested bankers and the military-minded Napoleon reintroduced the old and backward corporativist organization into banking.

By the end of the century two bankers, Jean Barthelemy Le Coulteux de Canteleu and Jean-Frédéric Perrégaux, who had earlier supported classical liberal principles, became increasingly concerned about a return of the terrorist dictatorship of the Jacobins or of an eventual reaction of the royalist party. They had become closely associated with the newly created Caisse des Comptes Courants which by then had to endure the tough competition of newcomers, mainly the Caisse d'Escompte du Commerce and the Comptoir Commercial. Moved by political and economic insecurity, they contacted Napoleon Bonaparte, and initiated him into business life.[10] The young student rapidly became a master. In 1799, before an imminent Jacobinist danger, Le Coulteux and Perrégaux sent a Greek emissary to Egypt to reach Bonaparte. 'Bourbaki', wrote the historian Dauphin-Meunier, 'informed Bonaparte that two million French Francs were at his disposal for a coup d'Etat' (1936: 19). Bonaparte came back to Paris to 'save the Republic'. His successful *coup d'etat* on 10 November 1799 brought him to the position of First Consul the following day. This political event sealed 'the alliance of Bonaparte and the bankers' (Dauphin-Meunier 1936: 20). Wanting his own bank, Bonaparte asked Le Coulteux and Perrégaux to help him with the creation of the Bank of France. In that process, the two previous advocates of economic freedom were led slowly, and reluctantly perhaps, to renounce their former stance. Although he was First Consul, Bonaparte became a stockholder of the newly created bank in January 1800. He was the first subscriber, with thirty shares.[11]

Dauphin-Meunier indicates that although the equity of the Bank of France was FF30 million, divided into shares of FF1,000 each, the founders could subscribe to only FF2 million. He states that 'the Bank had no resources, no location, no personnel, no customers'. The situation required a merger with an operative commercial bank. Bonaparte used the imprisonment of the renowned banker, Ouvrard, to pressurize the Caisse des Comptes Courants. With enforced compliance, the Bank of France began operating on 20 February 1800 in the Caisse's headquarters office in Paris. Its management, a 'Conseil de Regence', of fourteen members, included nine bankers and five merchants (Dauphin-Meunier 1936: 21–3).[12] Since the Board of Directors was elected by a General Shareholders' Meeting, limited to the first 200 stockholders, the Bank had an oligarchic nature, which led Paul Coq (1850) to use the pejorative expression 'Haute Banque' to characterize its management.

Under those circumstances, Perrégaux, who had been named Bank President, thought it necessary to remind the General Shareholders' Meeting on 17 September 1800 that

> free by its creation, which belongs only to individuals, independent by its by-laws, free of privately contracted conditions with government or legislative acts, the Bank of France exists under the protection of general laws and only through the will of its stockholders.

(Ramon 1929: 24)

Alphonse Courtois exposed the underlying hypocrisy of this statement: 'The Bank of France', he wrote, 'felt that, thanks to government support, it had created unfair competition and it tried to dissimulate to the public the harm that this state of affairs caused' (Courtois 1881: 113–14). He added 'Alas it did not keep for long this blessed freedom of which it was so proud' (p. 48). In spite of the absorption of the Caisse des Comptes Courants, the Bank of France had not been able to place all its stocks. Its subscribed equity was still small and, in the 'absence of depositors, the volume of its borrowing resources, of its current accounts (i.e. demand deposits) was insufficient to allow normal activity' (Dauphin-Meunier 1936: 24–5). In order to increase equity and external resources, the Directors requested Treasury funds and deposits from other government agencies. With this artificially increased funding, discount operations expanded from FF100 million to FF320 million in the first year (Dauphin-Meunier 1936: 25).

Other Paris banks were still a serious threat. With government support, the Bank of France attempted several manoeuvres to eliminate competition. First, FF3 million was presented for reimbursement at the Caisse d'Escompte du Commerce. The Caisse stockholders honoured their debt immediately. A few days later, a further FF4 million was presented for redemption and the Caisse paid in full (Dauphin-Meunier 1936: 26). In the light of the Caisse's strength and stability (based on liquidity and solvency), the state authorized the use of brute force to close down this persistent competitor. 'A group of soldiers invaded the building of the Caisse d'Escompte du Commerce, took over all books and papers, threw everybody out and closed the offices.'[13]

At the same time, the management of the Bank of France acted to suppress the freedom to use bank notes. Even Bonaparte's personal adviser, Mollien, was 'not very favourable to the Bank of France' (Marion 1914–28: 209). Mollien explained that the Bank of France was only a Paris bank, not a national one.[14] Bonaparte, however, was determined to have 'his' bank and, to the satisfaction of the stockholders, the law of 24 September 1803 granted the Bank of France the exclusive privilege to issue bank notes in Paris for fifteen years (Wolowski 1864).

On top of its exclusive privilege of note issuance, the Bank of France, Courtois repeated, counted its assets at FF100 million in 1805 with FF80 million in the form of government bonds and only FF20 million in bills of exchange. He specified that the Bank's cash reserves consisted of FF2 million to cover FF70 million in bank notes and FF20 million in deposits (Courtois 1881: 117–20). In addition to all of the Bank's commercial credit, half the government bonds were also financed by fiduciary means. Given such heavy government borrowing and low cash reserves, a run on the Bank became inevitable (Nataf 1984b). On 7 November 1805, 4,000 people lined up at 3 a.m. to demand the redemption of their notes and deposits. Before banking hours began, they were already fighting amongst themselves. In Napoleon's absence, Police Chief Foucher dispersed the crowds by announcing that special documents would be required for withdrawals (Sedillot 1979). This amounted to a *de facto* suspension of payment.

The financial crisis affected commerce first. Interest rates climbed to 18 per cent. In only two years the monopoly regime had engineered the sharpest depression since the Bank of Law disaster of 1720 (Courtois 1881). Attempting to reverse the effects of his first banking interventions and government borrowing, Napoleon I acted to increase state control over the Bank of France.

As a result, the law of 22 April 1806 established a triumvirate of a governor and two vice-governors, nominated by the chief of state (Emperor Napoleon I) to manage the Bank. This legislation extended bank note-issuance privileges for twenty-five years and doubled the Bank's equity to FF90 million (Sedillot 1979). As Courtois remarked, it was at this point that the Bank became a government institution supported by private individuals (Courtois 1881: 120). Mainly interested in conquest, Napoleon I had found an excuse to take-over the Bank's management and grant precedence to 'war needs' over domestic trade. Courtois noted that the 'Emperor, who was stopped by no consideration when it came to supporting war, did not always take into account the caution needed for trade and the Bank itself'.[15] Napoleon's 1806 legislation paved the way for recurring business fluctuations and a new depression in 1811. The business cycle's institutional foundations had been laid for the next two centuries. Adding to financial instability, administrative obstacles prevented the creation of new banks for almost six decades (Nataf 1990). Commenting on this situation, Charles Coquelin wrote

> Two equally fatal principles prevailed in France from the beginning of the empire [of Napoleon I]; the first, that no bank can issue redeemable bank notes, that is to say, engage in banking activity on a large scale without prior government authorization; the second, that each of these authorized institutions benefits from an exclusive privilege covering its area of operations. These two principles probably were enough to condemn France to eternal inferiority. Under such a system, it was impossible for credit to develop widely. . . . Unfortunately, the French government used its discretionary power with rare parsimony. [Before 1848] only nine banking institutions existed in our departments . . . ten banks for all of France! This is the fruit of fifty years of study and thirty-three years of peace. Is this not a reason to groan over such a result? . . . To obtain the authorization to establish a bank, even for the largest and best located cities, was an arduous task, a Herculean effort . . . We think we are prudent in France and we are wrong; we are just meticulous and restrictive.
>
> (Coquelin 1876:)

In Coquelin's view, these faults explain business fluctuations in France and its delayed economic development. He added 'Just as credit is rare in France, it is widespread in England. . . . [Due to the multiplicity of credit institutions] productive capital there [in England] abounds'. Coquelin explained that credit financed capital goods, thus increasing English productivity. He concludes that 'one need not look elsewhere for the cause of the great industrial superiority of this country' (Coquelin 1876: 292–3). France's backward banking restrictions explain, to a large extent, its increasing economic lag behind Great Britain in the first half of the nineteenth century.[16]

NOTES

Translations from the French are by the author.

1 See Homer Vanderblue (1939) *The Vanderblue Memorial Collection of Smithiana*, pp. 24–6.
2 See Henry Higgs (1963) *The Physiocrats*, p. 4, and Joseph Garnier (1874) *Dictionnaire de l'economie politique*, p. 367.
3 Camille Saint-Aubin (1795) *Des Banques particulières*. This book is presented as a translation: noting that it is 'a notorious fact' that Scottish

banks 'produced advantages for all', Saint-Aubin concluded that 'there is no reason why their establishment would not produce the same advantages in France' (p. 76).

4 F. Buisson (1805) *Dictionnaire universel du commerce*: 'Caisse d'Escompte du Commerce', pp. 340–1; 'Comptoir commercial', pp. 381–2; 'Banque de Rouen', pp. 237–41; 'Banque de France', pp. 212–20. E. Servais (1960) *La Banque de France* pp. 35–6 (1942 edn). L. Lair (1967) *La Banque de France*, pp. 56–60.

5 Cited in G. Ramon (1929) *Histoire de la Banque de France*, p. 13.

6 According to the statistics published by *Le Nouvel Economiste* (November 1986: 256–61), the average equity of French banks represents less than 2.5 per cent of bank assets.

7 Buisson, op. cit., p. 340. In the same entry we learn that the Caisse d'Escompte du Commerce opened not only demand deposits, but also time deposits bearing market rates of interest for important merchants. The Caisse was dedicated exclusively to commerce, and did not accept government bonds in its assets. Apparently the equity grew rapidly and reached FF24 million, which represented more than half the total liabilities. Consequently, and understandably, this entry concludes that 'such was the solidity of this institution, that after six years of existence, and during very stormy times [Revolution and wars], it suffered no losses' (p. 341).

8 After 1796, some 'banks' began to issue notes 'backed' by copper tokens. The renowned free-banking advocate, Michel Chevalier, did not recognize the authenticity of these issuances. 'Alleged banks', he wrote, 'were founded which isued notes redeemable in tokens made of copper', see Coquelin (1974) *Dictionnaire*, vol. 1: 180.

9 Eugene White (1989) concludes that the French free banking system worked only 'moderately' well. I prefer to stay in the company of Courcelle-Seneuil, Horn, Coquelin, Paul Coq and many others, judging that the system did work remarkably well.

10 See Dauphin-Meunier (1936) *La Banque de France*, pp. 15–30 and (1937) *La Banque à travers les ages*, pp. 13–92.

11 See Salin (1990) *La Vérité sur la monnaie*, pp. 115–26, and Ramon, op. cit., facsimile des signatures autographes, p. 20.

12 The bankers were Perregaux, Le Coulteux, Recamier, Mallet, Germain, Carie, Basterrèche, Sévène and Barillon. The merchants were Robillard, Perier, Perrée, Hugues Lagarde and Ricard.

13 *Courrier de Londres*, 9 October 1802, quoted by Dauphin-Meunier (1936), p. 27.

14 Quoted in Marion (1914–28) *Histoire financiere de la France depuis 1715*, tome IV, p. 209; and see also Marion (1934) 'La Fondation de la Banque de France', pp. 303–12.

15 Courtois is quoting Gautier (1839) *Des Banques et des institutions du credit en Amerique et en Europe*, Paris: Coulon, Mme Dondey-Dupre.

16 Coquelin (1849) 'The causes of commercial crises', pp. 371–89. To cure economic stagnation and business fluctuations, Coquelin explains 'that free banking would prove a certain remedy for all these evils' (p. 388).

8 Free banking in Ireland

Howard Bodenhorn

INTRODUCTION

This chapter examines Ireland's experience with free banking. While some historians have criticized the banks for causing economic chaos in a largely agricultural economy, the evidence presented here shows that such was not the case. Banks, more than most other market institutions, attract a great deal of government interest. Banks, therefore, are as much a prisoner of their political environment as the economic one. It was the legislative influences that differentiated the results of the two periods of free banking in Ireland. Lawrence White attributes the success of the Scottish free banking experience to minimal government interference and the presence of unlimited liability. If these are indeed the keys to success, it is not surprising that the second period of free banking in Ireland should rival the success of the Scottish. After 1824, restrictions on banking were repealed, except unlimited liability, and joint-stock banks were formed based on the Scottish mould. Failures were infrequent, losses were minimal – particularly when compared to the period 1797 to 1820 which was characterized by restrictions like those placed on English country banks – and the country was allowed to develop a system of nationally branched banks that was to form the core of the Irish banking industry until the 1960s.

FREE BANKING GONE AWRY?: THE IRISH EXPERIENCE 1797–1820

The Bank of Ireland was created by Act of the Irish Parliament in May 1783 and opened for business in June of that year. The wording of the Act followed that of the Act forming the Bank of England eighty-nine years earlier. The charter gave the Bank of Ireland a 'semi-monopoly' privilege in that no other body exceeding six partners could legally issue bank notes. In return for this privilege the full amount of the paid-up capital of £600,000 Irish was lodged with the government as a permanent loan with interest at 4 per cent annually (Barrow 1975a: 2–3). The Act also limited the amount of the bank's borrowing to the amount of its paid-up capital. Any judgement creditor of the bank could receive payment from the Exchequer with the amount deducted from the annual interest payment.[1] The lodgement with the government of its capital was then a security fund to meet creditors' demand should the bank default.[2]

Although the note issue privilege provided the ammunition for critics of the bank, it was not the legislation that most impeded the development of stable and competitive banking in Ireland. The provision did not forbid all banks; it only forbade those with more than six partners. This ultimately led to a multiplicity of poorly capitalized 'private' banks that were ill-prepared to meet their obligations when the frequent crises came.

An Act of 1721 made banking in Ireland an unlimited liability enterprise. It provided that, upon dissolution, a banker's real and personal estate be first liable for the debts of the bank, even if there was a prior encumbrance on those assets. The legislation appears to have been a response to bankers deeding their assets to family members or business partners just prior to the bank's dissolution. This did little to afford a bank's creditors any real security. Special Acts of Parliament were required for dissolution of a defaulting bank with the Irish House of Commons acting as the Bankruptcy Court (Hall 1949: 5). The winding up of one bank – Burton's Bank – lasted twenty-five years, and there are reports that another dissolution process lasted nearly fifty years (1949: 10). As a result any assets of the bank or its partners were generally eaten up by legal fees and left little, if any, indemnity for creditors. The terms of the charter of the Bank of Ireland were designed to avoid this problem.

Following a pattern of crisis-induced legislation, the next Act aimed specifically at banks was passed in 1755. The crisis of 1754–5 brought down three large and respected private banks in Dublin. The failures were due not so much to bad banking practices as to losses by their partners in trading ventures.[3] The deficit of one bank – Wilcox & Dawson – was £42,500 including what remained of the personal assets of the partners: and it is thought that the accounts of the other failed banks were similar. The Irish Parliament appointed a committee to investigate the causes of the failures and the committee concluded that the failures were due to inadequate capitalization (Hall 1949: 9–10). The Parliament, however, responded with an

Act that forbade the combination of merchant trade and banking (Simpson 1975: 2). All partners in a banking partnership were to be bankers only. By forbidding merchants from banking, the Parliament had effectively barred from the business the people who would most benefit from a stable banking system and the people with the wherewithal to form well-capitalized banks. That the Act was restrictive is demonstrated by the fact that only two new banks were formed in Dublin between 1760 and 1783 (Hall 1949: 13).

The first period of Irish free banking began in 1797. From about 1790 onwards the Bank of England had experienced a constant drain on its reserves. The harvests of the 1790s were generally poor, which forced importation of foodstuffs. At the same time, William Pitt pushed a bill through Parliament which allowed the Bank of England to advance, without limit, any sum required by the government. The Directors opposed the legislation but dared not refuse any government drafts, and by 1797 the Bank had made advances to the government of £8,075,400. During the same period, Britain had also been sending subsidies to its Continental allies. The effect of these actions was to turn the exchanges against London until the specie point was reached in May 1795 (Andréades 1966: 187–94). In August the drain was intensified when France restored the gold standard; and gold continued to flow out until the exchanges stabilized in the early months of 1796. But this did not ease the tension in the money market. With rumours of an imminent French invasion circulating, note-holders of all banks exchanged notes for specie. The country banks of England accelerated their withdrawals of specie from the Bank of England so that even with gold flowing into England with the favourable exchange, the country was quickly absorbing it. The Bank of England's reserves continued to decline. The final blows occurred in February 1797. A local rumour of French invasion caused a run on the banks in Newcastle on 18 February. This news reached London on the same day that news that the French fleet had been spotted off the south coast of England. Then, on 25 February, French forces landed on the Welsh coast (Hall 1949: 78–9). Although they were quickly captured and posed no real threat, the money markets collapsed, and 3 per cent Consols sold at 51.[4]

The Directors of the Bank of England asked the government for assistance. On 26 February, the Privy Council ordered the Bank of England to suspend cash payments.[5] Similar events were occurring in Ireland as the Bank of Ireland saw its reserves dwindle as the population hoarded specie. News of the suspension travelled quickly to Dublin, and on 2 March the Irish Privy Council ordered the Bank of Ireland likewise to suspend specie payments. Work on the Irish Restriction Act began immediately and on 3 May it received Royal Assent. The provisions of the Act allowed the Bank of Ireland to suspend specie payments for as long as the Bank of England was suspended, plus an additional three months following resumption by the Bank of England. It also stated that the Courts were to regard payment in Bank of Ireland notes as payment in cash. The Act stopped short, however, of giving the notes full legal tender status. If suit was brought by a party not willing to accept the notes, proceedings could be stayed until resumption, but under no circumstances was the Bank of Ireland to have costs imposed against it in such suits.

The result of the Act was that private bankers were given the same privilege, which was fully authorized by an Act of Parliament in 1799. This Act allowed private banks to issue notes of less than five guineas so long as such notes were payable in Bank of Ireland notes. In essence, Bank of Ireland notes were made legal reserves of the private banks. And the acquisition of these reserves became easier as the Bank of Ireland's circulation expanded. In March 1797, the Bank's circulation was £560,000. By March of 1798 the circulation had increased to £926,200, and by March 1802 it reached £2,263,400.

What followed was a proliferation of private banks. In 1797 there were eleven private banks distributed throughout the country, though not all issued their own notes. By January 1803 the number of private banks of issue stood at thirty; a year later the number had increased to a total of forty.[6]

Although exact circulation figures fail to survive for the private banks of this period we can piece together some idea of the increase in currency during the Restriction period. The 1804 Committee published the stamp duties paid on the various denomination notes from 1800 to 1804. Notes under three guineas required a tax stamp of 1½d per note, notes less than £10 required a 3d stamp, and notes less than £50 required a 4d stamp. The figures are reported in Tables 8.1 and 8.2. In interpreting these figures two considerations must be kept in mind. First, the values in the tables do not represent the value of the notes, they are simply the number of notes paying the stamp tax.[7] Second, the values may not be representative of the actual circulation of the banks. Since a bank could expect to have its notes returned for redemption or deposit, the total number of notes stamped were probably not in circulation at all times. Additionally, the banks were not required to pay the tax annually so that notes put into circulation in previous years may well have continued to circulate as new ones were issued.

Table 8.1 Number of notes paying duty by bank, year end March 1800

Bank Name	City	1½d	3d	4d
Finlay & Co.	Dublin	–	15,413	18,048
Lighton & Co.	Dublin	18,300	72,800	46,800
Beresford & Co.	Dublin	5,200	54,200	20,100
Roberts & Co.	Cork	42,100	10,900	8,900
Cotter & Co.	Cork	39,012	200	2,700
Newport & Co.	Waterford	9,100	12,000	3,650
Mansell & Co.	Limerick	16,000	9,500	3,300
Rial & Co.	Clonmel	2,500	6,500	–
Redmond & Co.	Wexford	2,000	1,598	–
Woodcock & Co.	Enniscorthy	400	1,200	200
O'Neile & Co.	Waterford	13,500	14,050	550
Totals		134,612	198,361	104,248

Source: 1804 Committee, Appendix D, p. 147.

If representative, these figures exhibit not only the proliferation of banks, but also the proliferation of 'small' notes. In 1804 the distribution between notes of less than three guineas, less than £10, and less than £50 showed a slight preference for the 'medium' denominations. By 1804, however, the preference for 'small' notes is apparent. Stamp taxes were paid on over a million new small-notes, while the number of large notes fell to 90,000. Fully three-quarters of these banks registered no new large notes. For later in the period, some scattered and sketchy circulation figures are available. A contemporary observer estimated the circulation of Malcomson's Bank in Lurgan at £170,000 in 1808; and the average circulation of the private banks in Belfast at £225,000 in 1810. Ollerenshaw, however, believes these to be underestimates. He found the circulation of a single bank was £354,000 in 1812; it reached its peak in 1819 at £412,000 (1987: 8).

The effect of this monetary expansion was inflation. Although no reliable price indices are available for Ireland in this period, the extent of the inflation can be seen by the movements in the Irish/English currency exchange rate. Until 1826 Ireland had a distinct currency. The official Irish/English exchange rate was I£108 6s 8d for £100 English – that is thirteen Irish pounds equalled twelve English pounds – but the rate was allowed to float. In March 1797 the exchange rate was £105–£106 Irish for £100 English. By April 1801 the exchange rate had risen to £111–£113 Irish for £100 English; and Dublin's condition

Table 8.2 Number of notes paying duty by bank, year end January 1804

Bank Name	City	1½d	3d	4d
Finlay & Co.	Dublin	5,000	36,500	26,200
Lighton & Co.	Dublin	43,455	60,500	23,100
Beresford & Co.	Dublin	42,500	117,300	29,500
Roberts & Co.	Cork	128,000	3,000	–
Cotter & Co.	Cork	146,800	1,200	–
Roach & Co.	Cork	35,004	2,075	–
Pike & Co.	Cork	64,400	–	100
Mansell & Co.	Limerick	7,453	–	–
Roach & Co.	Limerick	21,131	–	–
Rial & Co.	Clonmel	36,300	5,300	–
Watson & Co.	Clonmel	34,400	1,500	–
Redmond & Co.	Wexford	1,800	1,900	–
Codd & Co.	Wexford	4,000	–	–
Hatchell & Co.	Wexford	5,400	1,700	–
Sparrow & Co.	Enniscorthy	13,000	–	–
Redmond & Co.	Enniscorthy	5,400	–	–
Codd & Co.	Enniscorthy	22,500	–	–
Williams & Co.	Kilkenny	4,000	500	–
Loughlin & Co.	Kilkenny	1,000	1,000	–
Anderson & Co.	Fermoy	23,900	–	–
Rawson & Co.	Athy	6,000	–	–
Delacourt & Co.	Mallow	51,600	–	2,000
Bernard & Co.	Birr	41,500	2,496	1,800
Herron & Co.	Callan	15,825	–	–
Giles & Co.	Youghall	13,000	1,000	–
Scully & Co.	Tipperary	14,700	800	–
Manning & Co.	Rathdrum	800	–	–
Barrow & Co.	Dungarvan	1,800	–	–
Tallow & Co.	Dungarven	509	–	–
Joyce & Co.	Galway	68,632	–	–
Blacker & Co.	Loughlin Bridge	8,587	–	–
Rossister & Co.	Ross	3,400	–	–
Cliff & Co.	Ross	21,800	5,400	400
Talbot & Co.	Malahide	24,938	–	–
Foley & Co.	Lismore	1,200	–	–
Trench & Co.	Tuam	67,703	1,900	–
Perren & Co.	Wicklow	1,800	–	–
Evans & Co.	Charleville	32,221	400	1,500
Langrishe & Co.	Thomastown	24,240	630	115
Bennett & Co.	Carlow	26,219	5,000	2,030
Totals		1,110,217	256,801	90,265

Source: 1804 Committee, Appendix H, p. 149.

continued to deteriorate until in January 1804 when the rate reached £117–£118 Irish to £100 English (1804 Committee: 8).

The rising price level may not have been due to the proliferation of the private banks, though some contemporary observers placed the blame on them. In Lawrence White's model of free banking (1984b: 1–19), a bank in the short term may be able to issue an excessive quantity of notes, but it will find its circulation decision untenable in the long term. When individuals find themselves holding more of a bank's notes than they require, they will redeem their excess holdings directly at the bank of issue, by depositing the notes with their bank of choice, or by passing the notes to other individuals. The offending bank will sooner or later be forced to reduce its note issue as its gold reserves are depleted. But the Bank of Ireland had a monopoly in irredeemable reserves and was increasing the stock of those reserves. In even the simplest money multiplier model, an injection of reserves or high powered money will lead to a proportional money expansion, given a fractional reserve system. Such was the case with Ireland. The private banks were simply responding rationally to forces that were completely exogenous to them. The system reacted no differently than it would have had the injection been an inflow of gold.

Concern over the deteriorating exchange rate prompted the British Parliament to appoint a Committee to investigate its causes. The Committee placed the blame on the Irish Bank Restriction Act which had allowed the Bank of Ireland to increase its issues without a corresponding increase in its reserves. In fact the reserves had been continually falling. The reserve ratio in January 1808 was 31 per cent; by January 1814 it had fallen to 17 per cent.[8] In view of this the Committee's recommendations were that 'it is incumbent on the Directors of the Bank of Ireland . . . to limit their paper at all times . . . and it may be material also to assist their endeavours by a diminution of the issue of paper from private bankers'.[9] The Bank agreed to comply with the Committee's recommendations, but it failed to keep its promise. In March 1810 the circulation of the Bank was £2,291,300. It continued a slow increase until by March 1813 the circulation reached £3,185,400 (Hall 1949: 393).

A crash came when specie payments were resumed in 1820. In 1804 there were forty private banks of issue. Through failures and entry, thirty-one were in operation in 1819. Of the failures that occurred prior to 1820, some were quite spectacular. The failure of Cotter & Kellet & Co in Cork resulted in an estimated loss to the public of £210,000 in 1807. But the failure of Colcough's Bank in New Ross enjoyed the most public attention. Upon failure, it was found that the bank had liabilities of £200,000, with only £4,000 of invested capital. Despite these celebrated failures, most of the banks that failed before 1819–20 went quietly. Upon the voluntary liquidation of Beresford's Bank in 1810, the creditors were paid in full (Hall 1949: 124–6).

The years 1819–20 brought a severe recession to Ireland. The causes were threefold. With the end of the Napoleonic War, the government had decreased its spending – particularly as most of the British Army and Navy returned home. To this was added the decreased British demand for Irish foodstuffs at the war's end; and with it came the resumption of specie payments. Runs on banks immediately after resumption were widespread as the public wanted to convert its notes into gold. The Bank of Ireland could offer little help as it too was forced to import gold from England to fortify it own position as it saw its own notes being presented in large numbers for payment in specie.

Failures were widespread. Of the thirty-one private banks operating in 1819, only fifteen survived at the end of 1820, and of those that did survive, all – except for those in Dublin and Belfast – were forced to suspend for various periods. The exact degree of losses to the public from these failures is impossible to determine. One contemporary observer, however, estimated the total losses due to failures from the whole of the Restriction era at £20 million (Hardcastle 1843: 367).

THE SECOND FREE BANKING PERIOD, 1824–45

The crisis of 1820 sparked agitation for reform. Critics of Anglo-Irish banking concentrated their efforts on the repeal of the Act of 1756 and the abolition of the Bank of Ireland's note issue privilege. These reformers were impressed with the stability of the Scottish banks which popular belief attributed to a lack of restrictive legislation, particularly a lack of anything resembling the six-partner rule.

There was strong pressure for reform in both England and Ireland, but there was also strong pressure, primarily from the Bank of England, not to alter the existing machinery. The authorities determined that something needed to be done and decided to experiment first with Ireland.[10] In February 1821 discussions were opened with the Bank of Ireland regarding the abrogation of their note issue privilege. The current and ex-governor of the Bank negotiated for the Bank, during which they established and maintained close contact with officials from the Bank of England who took a keen interest in the negotiations as this would set a precedent for the restriction of their own privileges (Hall 1949: 134–5). In May of 1821 agreement was reached whereby the Bank of Ireland's monopoly as a bank of issue with more than six partners was restricted to a radius of 50 Irish miles (65 English miles) from Dublin. In return the Bank was authorized to increase its capital by £500,000. This brought the total paid-up capital to I£3 million. However, the government again required that the increase in capital be lodged with the Treasury as a loan at the rate of 4 per cent annually (Barrow 1975a: 62). The Act was passed and received Royal Assent in July of 1821.

Pathbreaking as the 1821 Act was, it was to rcmain a dead letter until the restrictive Act of 1754 was lifted. Further, wording of the 1821 act was ambiguous. It allowed any number of persons 'in Ireland' to form themselves into a partnership for the business of banking. When pushed by the potential entry of the first 'joint-stock' bank – the Provincial – whose share subscription opened in 1824, primarily in London, the Bank of Ireland interpreted this provision to mean that shareholders must be residents of Ireland *and* reside outside the 50-mile limit (Barrow 1975a: 64, 76). Not only did this disallow any bank capital to flow from England to Ireland, but it also pre-empted potential banks from soliciting capital from the most prosperous part of Ireland, around Dublin.

For three years no new banks were formed under the law. The cause for repealing the offending clauses was taken up in the House of Commons by Sir Henry Parnell on behalf of several merchants and bankers in Belfast.[11] The result was the Irish Banking Act passed in 1824. This Act repealed the residency requirement of the 1821 Act and allowed any citizen of the United Kingdom to be a shareholder; it repealed the ban on merchants being partners or shareholders; and it allowed the names of shareholders to be registered in the Court of Chancery instead of appearing on all notes.[12]

A week after the Act of 1824 became law, it was announced in Belfast that a joint-stock bank was to be formed as quickly as possible. This new bank – the Northern – was to take over the business of Montgomery's, a private bank, as a going concern. Soon afterwards, the Provincial Bank, whose capital was raised in London, also entered the alliance. There was not, however, a headlong rush into the business of banking following the passage of the 1824 Act (see Table 8.3).

Table 8.3 Chartered and joint-stock banks in Ireland: dates of commencement and closure

Bank	Commencement	Closure	Cause
Bank of Ireland	1783		
Hibernian	1825		
Provincial Bank	1825		
Northern Banking Co.	1825		
Belfast Banking Co.	1827		
Agricultural and Commercial	1834	1836	Failed
National Bank	1835		
Limerick National Bank	1835	1839 (?)	
Clonmel National Bank	1836	1856	Merged with National
Carrick-on-Suir National	1836	1856	Merged with National
Waterford National Bank	1836	1839 (?)	
Wexford and Enniscorthy	1836	1839 (?)	
Tipperary National Bank	1836	1856	Failed
Tralee National Bank	1836	1839 (?)	
Ulster Banking Co.	1836		
Royal Bank of Ireland	1836		
Southern Bank of Ireland	1837	1839 (?)	
London & Dublin	1842	1857	

Note: The question mark designates some doubt on the actual date of closure. The Committee Report of 1857 shows six joint-stock banks closing in 1839 without naming them. The five here seem the most likely as they do not appear in any intervening or later reports.

Sources: Commencement dates, 1837 Committee; Closure dates, 1857 Committee, Barrow (1975a); Cause, Ollerenshaw (1987: 32).

The opening of the Northern provoked little response from the Bank of Ireland. The Northern's affairs were primarily tied up with the developing linen trade of Ulster, an area and a business with which the Bank of Ireland seemed little concerned. The entry of the Provincial, however, evoked quite a different response. The prospectus for the Irish Provincial Bank Company stated its purpose to open 'establishments for business in the principal towns of Ireland which are distant over fifty miles from Dublin' (Barrow 1975a: 75). The Provincial was to be set up along Scottish lines with the bank developing an extensive network of branches each of which would issue notes, open cash credit accounts (overdraft accounts), and pay interest on deposits received. To implement the plan the Provincial imported its branch managers and accountants from Scotland. However, since these Scots would initially know little of local business conditions each branch was to have a board of supervisors consisting of between three and five local merchants who would pass initial judgement on the extent of discounts appropriate for merchants presenting their bills.[13] The branch managers were allowed their discretion in the discounting of bills and advancing of credits up to £1,000 per individual, but any amount beyond this was to be first approved by the Board in London.[14]

The opening of the Provincial was to change radically the face of Irish banking. It meant that the Bank of Ireland had to face true competitive pressure for the first time. The announcement of the Provincial's intention to open branches throughout the country prompted the Old Bank into action. For forty years, the Bank of Ireland had refused to open branches despite numerous petitions to do so. They had claimed that branches were difficult to control and that the country was well served by the system of private banks. But just eleven days after the announcement by the Provincial that its first branch would be opened in Cork, the Directors of the Bank of Ireland met to discuss the expediency of opening country agents (Barrow 1975a: 85).

A fierce rivalry developed between the two banks from the day the Provincial announced its intentions. The Bank of Ireland quickly formed agencies in the same towns the Provincial had selected for its branch operations. In two cases, the Bank of Ireland's agencies were opened prior to the opening of the Provincial's branches. The Bank of Ireland had good reason for insistence that its branches maintained the title of 'agency'. According to law, notes were redeemable in the place where they had been issued. The Bank of Ireland printed its notes in such a way that they were redeemable only in Dublin. The Provincial received many of these notes in the course of its business, and by this device, it was forced to transport the notes to Dublin for redemption, then transport the gold back to the respective branches. Alternatively, the Bank of Ireland could present the Provincial's notes at the branch of issue. The Provincial experienced several runs on its notes in its early days and attributed some of them to practices by the Bank of Ireland.

The Provincial responded to this by petitioning Parliament for a law requiring that notes be redeemable at the branch of issue. The law was passed in 1829 causing some inconvenience to the Old Bank as it was now forced to bear the cost of holding and insuring reserves at each of its agencies. It had little effect on the Provincial as this had been its practice throughout. The law did, however, adversely effect the Northern Bank as it too had made all its notes payable at its main office in Belfast (see Simpson 1975: 34–7).

Despite this political setback and all its protestations, the Old Bank seems not to have suffered inordinately from the new competition. Its dividends remained at 10 per cent annually through 1829 after which they were decreased to 9 per cent until 1834 (see Table 8.4). Its profitability, however, had been diminished slightly. The Old Bank's rate of return on net worth in 1824 fell below 7 per cent for the first time. It recovered to slightly more than 7 per cent in 1825, but then again fell to between 6.5 and 7 per cent where it stabilized throughout the 1830s. As Table 8.4 shows, despite the loss of some of its monopoly privileges, the Bank of Ireland continued to out-perform the interlopers who paid annual dividends of only 4 or 5 per cent until the mid-1830s.

Table 8.4 Irish bank dividends, 1820–40 (dividends as a percentage of paid-up capital)

Year	Bank of Ireland	Northern Bank	Ulster Bank	Belfast Bank	Provincial Bank	Hibernian Bank
1820	10					
1821	10					
1822	10					
1823	10					
1824	10					
1825	10	5				
1826	10	5			4	4
1827	10	10		5	4	4
1828	10	5		5	4	4
1829	10	5		5	4	4
1830	9	5		5	4	4
1831	9	5		5	5	4
1832	9	9		5	5	4
1833	9	5		5	6	4
1834	9	5		5	7	4
1835	9	6		5	8	4
1836	8.5	7		6	8	4
1837	8	8	5	7	8	4
1838	8	9	6	7	8	4
1839	8	10	6.5	7	8	4
1840	8	10	7	7	8	4

Sources: 1837 Committee, Appendix; Hardcastle (1843); Hall (1949) Appendix G, p. 399.

The real wave of bank expansion in Ireland was not to begin, however, until the late 1830s. As Table 8.3 shows, only four new 'joint-stock' banks were formed between 1824 and 1827.[15] The rapid growth of banking did not occur until the mid 1830s with the entry of twelve new banking companies. This slow growth of joint-stock banks cannot be attributed to the growth of private banks in their place. Barrow (1975a: 106–8) believes that only five 'private' banks were opened during the period 1829 to 1833. Simpson (1957: 33) argues, as well, that the rise of well-branched joint-stock banks spelled the end to private banking in the countryside of Ireland. In 1835 the only private banks still in operation were located in Dublin.

One of the arguments against free banking is that competitive pressure induces bankers to issue notes beyond their capacity to redeem them. A cursory glance at Table 8.3 might give the impression that such was the case with banking expansion in the 1830s. Twelve banks entered between 1834 and 1837, but only six of them continued to operate in 1845. Most of the banks closed with a whimper. Of the five that closed in 1839, they dissolved for reasons other than 'failure'.[16] But such do not make the stories of legend. It seems that all countries that have experimented with free banking have experienced a celebrated failure or series of failures on which critics can focus their attention. Scotland had the infamous collapse of the Ayr Bank (see chapter 9). Ireland had the Agricultural and Commercial.

The Agricultural and Commercial was doomed from its inception. The promoter of the bank was one Thomas Mooney, who happened to have a prominent and wealthy namesake in Dublin. The prospectus also carried the name James Chambers, but it was not the respected Director of the Bank of Ireland (Simpson 1975: 48). The prospectus did not carry with it the addresses of the promoters and made no attempt to distinguish these men from their better known namesakes.[17]

Thomas Mooney's idea was different from most other bankers of his day. With unlimited liability, the reputation of a bank lay primarily in the reputation and public trust of its shareholders. Most banks, therefore, wished to be selective in who held their shares – a privilege granted to them since most share offerings were oversubscribed. Besides, most shares sold for £100, which typically pre-empted 'widows and orphans' from ownership. The Agricultural's prospectus, however, proposed one million shares of £1 each. With the success of previous joint-stock banks, the possibility of owning shares in a bank invited a plethora of small shareholders.

It should have been obvious from the outset that the Agricultural Bank was not long for this world. Banking expertise was scarce in the 1830s, while for the Agricultural it was almost non-existent. Only one member of the consulting committee had any bank experience, and that was for the Hibernian, which was not a bank of issue. No general manager was ever appointed, and the branch supervisor was a Scot with a chequered career (Barrow 1975a: 113). The necessary qualification for becoming a branch manager was that you owned more shares than anyone else in town (Simpson 1975: 49). The practices of the bank were also less than sound. The bank paid a premium on Bank of Ireland notes to obtain specie and get their own notes into circulation, and it discounted liberally. Its time came quickly as it could not redeem its notes and stopped payment in 1836.

With the collapse of the Agricultural came a run on the other banks. Though the majority were well managed, their reserves were soon depleted and most turned to the Bank of Ireland for help. The Old Bank appears to have softened its stance toward the joint-stock banks by this time as it rediscounted applicable commercial paper for all but one of the applicants. The Provincial and the Northern never applied for assistance. The Belfast Bank received £103,000, the Ulster received £60,000, and the National received £42,600 and although it was granted a further allowance of £70,000, it was never used (Barrow 1975a: 142–3). This was the beginning of the Bank of Ireland's recognition as its role as a lender of last resort.

Though much celebrated, the collapse of the Agricultural Bank did not produce devastation throughout the economy. The Auditors' Report on the Agricultural is included in the minutes of the 1857 Committee (pp. 116–17). Although they were unable to decipher completely the poorly kept records, they estimated that liabilities exceeded assets by only £33,638. Add to this the losses from the Provident Bank – a bank Mooney built on the ruins of the Agricultural that also quickly collapsed – which on dissolution was in deficit of only £14,000, and it is easily seen that the losses to creditors were small when compared to the losses sustained during the crisis of 1820.

By 1840, Ireland had developed a stable system of well-capitalized, broadly based branch banks. Ireland, then, like Scotland provides evidence that freely competitive banking need not be thought of as inherently unstable. Granted, failures did occur but failures are as much a part of the competitive process as entry. Schumpeter argued that the problem of capitalism is not how the system administers existing structures, rather how it creates and destroys them. The small and under-capitalized private banks were replaced by better capitalized joint-stock banks. Table 8.5 shows that the Irish joint-stock system compared favourably with both the prior system of private banks that were allowed at most six partners, and often had as few as two; and with the much-praised system prevailing in Scotland.[18] Competitive pressure forced, and superior capital enabled, the banks to establish a system of branch networks that allowed for geographic portfolio diversification which was impossible under a system of locally based private banks.

Table 8.5 Banks of Ireland: number of shareholders, paid-up capital, branches

Bank	Number of shareholders	Paid-up capital (£)	Number of branches
Bank of Ireland	N/A	3,000,000	22
Northern Bank	186	122,275	10
Provincial Bank	813	500,000	23
Hibernian Bank	N/A	250,000	0
Belfast Bank	270	125,000	20
Agricultural & Commercial	4,114	352,789	46
National Bank	1,140	245,575	14
Ulster Bank	590	204,325	11
Royal Bank	360	199,275	0

Sources: Column 2: Ollerenshaw (1987: 32); Columns 3–4: 1837 Committee, Appendix I.

When the Bank of Ireland had held its semi-monopoly privileges, the popular criticism was that it served the government and conferred little benefit on the commercial and merchant classes. Evidence from the semi-annual balance sheets of the Bank of Ireland suggests that these accusations were not groundless. In the accounts of the Bank of Ireland, private debt is defined as bills discounted and loans to individuals and firms; public debt is holdings of government securities. If one looks at the ratio of private to total debt held by the Bank of Ireland, the trend is decidedly downward during the Restriction period. In 1808 the ratio stood at 85 per cent (meaning that 85 per cent of all debt was issued to individuals or firms), but by 1822 the ratio had reached its trough at 15 per cent.[19] This means that the bank was discounting ever fewer commercial bills. However, with the advent of the joint-stock banks in 1824, the trend is quickly upward with a rough levelling off through the remainder of the period at about 40 to 50 per cent.[20] Much the same story can be told from looking at the denomination of note issues of the Bank of Ireland. Records of the Bank classify notes issued into those less than £5 and those £5 and greater. The ratio of small-notes (less than £5) to total note issue during the Restriction period was variable but averaged about 25 per cent. But with the advent of the joint-stock banks, it increased from 28 per cent in 1824 to 39 per cent in 1828; thereafter following a slow increase until it reached 48 per cent in 1844. Small denomination notes were important for merchants and linen exporters who often travelled from town-to-town buying small webs of linen or small quantities of produce from local weavers or growers. Most of these transactions were in small amounts, usually £5 and less, and since notes were more easily carried than specie most of these purchases were made with bank notes.[21] Therefore, as competitive pressures forced the Bank of Ireland to deal more with the public and less in government securities, it found it increasingly necessary to supply smaller denomination notes.

These small notes had come under attack in 1826. In England the bank crisis of 1820, culminating in the failure of many of the small country banks was blamed on the overissue of small notes instead of the restrictions on capital. The House of Commons proposed to outlaw the issue of such notes not only in England, but in Ireland and Scotland as well. A committee was formed to investigate the proposal. The banks of Ireland and Scotland banded together to oppose the measure. Their common front was effective as the eventual Act included only England and Wales, and left Scotland and Ireland free to continue with the issue of small notes. The most common note issues of the joint-stock banks were those of £1, £1 5s, £1 10s, £1 15s, £2 and very few over.[22] These issues were appropriate when transactions were small, as they were in the market towns of Ireland. Table 8.6 shows the proportion of small notes in circulation in Ireland and Scotland from 1845 to 1856. While this period is after the years under consideration here, it is doubtful whether a drastic change of regime would have taken place given the testimony of the officials.[23] What is striking is the exceedingly high proportion of small notes in Scotland. This is further evidence that the issue of small notes and bank stability are not mutually exclusive.

The final positive aspect of competitive banking to be considered is that of interest rates. Evidence from the 1837 Committee shows that competition had narrowed the difference between lending and borrowing rates. Throughout its history, the Bank of Ireland had

Table 8.6 Small notes as a percentage of all notes in circulation: Scotland and Ireland 1845–56

Year	Scotland	Ireland
1845	73	58
1846	68	58
1847	71	52
1848	68	51
1849	69	53
1850	68	55
1851	68	56
1852	65	58
1853	66	56
1854	64	55
1855	65	56
1856	66	54

Source: 1857 Committee

cited an ancient and obscure statute to defend its practice of not paying interest on deposits. The joint-stock banks, however, believed that statute inapplicable to deposits.[24] Table 8.7 shows the rates paid on deposits by the banks in 1837. The average rate was 2 to 3 per cent depending on the term of the deposit. In testimony given before the 1826 Committee, the head accountant of the Provincial testified that his bank charged 5 per cent on discounts and on credit balances in overdraft accounts but the rate moved with movements in the Bank of Ireland and Bank of England rates.[25] In March 1837, the Bank of Ireland's rate on Irish bills was 5 per cent, and 4 per cent on English bills. With deposits being paid 2 or 3 per cent, this gave the banks a narrow margin. Yet they found operation profitable as evidenced by increasing dividends through the late 1830s (see Table 8.4).

Free banking ended in Ireland, as it did in Scotland, in 1845. In 1844 Parliament passed an Act which restricted the issue of Bank of England notes to the amount of their holdings of government securities and specie not to exceed £14 million. Any amount over this limit was to be secured pound-for-pound by holdings of specie. The Bank Charter Act did not apply directly to Ireland, but it set the stage for the passage of the Irish Banking Act of 1845. This Act restricted the circulation of notes to only those banks that were presently banks of issue. It also stipulated that future circulations of each bank was not to exceed the average circulation of the twelve weeks preceding passage of the Act. Any amount of circulation above that average had to be secured by equal holdings of specie. In reality, the Act had little effect on the money supply of Ireland, as the banks typically circulated less than their allotted amount. It effectively froze, however, the size distribution of the banks for the remainder of the century.

Table 8.7 Rates paid on deposits – 1837

Bank	%
Bank of Ireland	0
Northern Bank	2–3
Provincial	1½–2
Hibernian	N/A
Belfast Bank	2½–3
Agricultural	2–3
National Bank	2–3
Ulster Bank	3
Royal Bank	2½–3

Source: 1837 Committee, Appendix I.

CONCLUSIONS

In summarizing the Scottish system of free banking, Lawrence White claimed the system succeeded because 'there were many competing banks; most of them were well capitalized . . . none were disproportionately large; all but a few were extensively branched . . . [and] all offered a narrow spread between deposit and discount rates of interest' (White 1984b: 34). The second period of free banking in Ireland produced much the same results. It can be argued that the Bank of Ireland held a degree of influence by reason of its size, but the other banks were able to compete effectively. By abolishing the six partner rule, Ireland was allowed to develop a system of stable, nationally branched banks. Although failures did occur in this period, they were in no way as disastrous as those that came before. Ireland thus provides additional evidence that free banking is a tenable system when it operates free of restrictions and government interference.

NOTES

This chapter draws its historical facts primarily from the works of Hall (1949), Barrow (1975a), Simpson (1975) and Ollerenshaw (1987).

1   Barrow (1975a: 3). A judgement creditor is one who has obtained the relief of the courts through suit in securing payment of a debt.

2 This feature is similar in form to the type of security used by banking authorities to secure the debts of 'free' banks in several of the United States during the period 1838–63. See Rockoff (1974).
3 See, for example, Simpson (1975: 1). Alternatively, Hall (1949) attributes two of the failures to the partners absconding with whatever assets that remained.
4 Andréades (1966: 197). For a more complete account of the events leading up to the suspension see Part IV, chapters II and III.
5 The full text of the Order is reprinted in Hall (1949: 79). The details in this section rely on Hall – especially pp. 79–82; see also his Appendix E.
6 1804 Committee: 8. Barrow (1975a: 14) reports the total number of private banks (both issuing and non-issuing) in 1803 at forty-one; Hall (1949: 126) gives the total in 1804 as forty-nine.
7 For example, a £1 note would bear the same stamp as a £3 note.
8 See Bodenhorn (1989: 8). Concern over the reserve ratio seems incongruous in a period of inconvertibility. But the Committee felt that the Bank should maintain some semblance of 'good' banking principles during the suspension so that resumption could take place without severe shocks or complications.
9 1810 Committee, quoted in Simpson (1975: 5).
10 Barrow (1975a: 61). This is Barrow's impression from the course of events, though it is not based on direct evidence.
11 See Ollerenshaw (1987: 10). Parnell's book *Observations on Paper Money, Banking, and Overtrading* (1827) is considered a classic defence of free banking, particularly that in the Scottish tradition.
12 See Ollerenshaw (1987: 10), Barrow (1975a: 65–6). Before this Act the names of all partners or shareholders had to appear on all evidences of debt, including bank notes. During the period of the six-partner rule this posed few problems, but with joint stock companies with several hundred partners this rule would have made the use of bank notes impossible.
13 1826 Committee, evidence of James Marshall, p. 90.
14 Ibid, p. 90.
15 Barrow points out that the term 'joint-stock' is a misnomer for the type of banks formed during this period. The banks were still little more than common law partnerships with the stockholders still having unlimited liability. The only resemblance they had to a modern corporation was that they could sue and be sued in the name of their officers instead of having to name all the partners in a suit.
16 The 1857 Committee listed banks as 'Relinquished from Failure' and 'Relinquished from Other Causes'. None of the 1839 closings was from failure in the sense of insolvent, but the Committee Report does not define precisely the meanings of the terms.
17 Barrow (1975a: 111–12) argues that there was no deliberate attempt to confuse the subscribers, but the coincidence seems a little too remarkable to dismiss the possibility.
18 For a comparison with Scotland see Lawrence White (1984b: 34–7).
19 For a more detailed discussion of this see Bodenhorn (1989), especially p. 20 and Figure 3.
20 An alternative explanation may be that with the end of the Napoleonic

Wars the government was offering fewer securities to fund its purchases, and the bank had to look to other sources for employment of its funds.

21 1826 Committee, testimony of James Marshall, Appendix 17, p. 92.
22 ibid.
23 Unfortunately the joint-stock banks did not have to make public their issues until the Acts of 1844 and 1845 required them to do so. Therefore, we have little information before that period.
24 Apparently government prosecutors felt the same as no suits were ever brought against the banks that paid interest.
25 1826 Committee, testimony of James Marshall, p. 91.

9 Free banking in Scotland before 1844

Lawrence H. White

INTRODUCTION

Scotland, a relatively industrialized nation with highly developed monetary, credit and banking institutions, enjoyed remarkable monetary stability throughout the eighteenth and early nineteenth centuries. During this time Scotland had no monetary policy, no central bank and very few legal restrictions on the banking industry. Entry was free and the right of note issue universal.[1] If the conjunction of these facts seems curious by today's lights, it is because central banking has come to be taken for granted in this century, while the theory of competitive banking and note issue on a specie standard has fallen into disrepair.

The Scottish success with near-*laissez-faire* in banking caused consternation to many of the monetary theorists of the nineteenth century as well. Sir Walter Scott, ably pamphleteering in defence of Scottish banking, noted the incongruity of Scotland's 'practical System successful for upwards of a century' with 'the opinion of a professor of Economics, that in such circumstances she ought not by true principles to have prospered at all' (1826: 38–9). The Scottish banking system enjoyed widespread popular support from practical men. It had its theoretically minded supporters as well. The record of free banking in Scotland figured prominently in British and American monetary debates of the 1820s, 1830s and 1840s (White 1984b: chs 3–4; White and Selgin 1990).

Scotland's free banking experience subsequently faded from the common knowledge of monetary economists. American economists, at least, have been prone to the misconception that 'free banking' was an experiment limited to several of the United States between the Jacksonian era and the Civil War. It has been commonly believed that English monetary and banking institutions, despite their imperfections, were the most enlightened that the nineteenth-century world had to offer. An account of the Scottish experience, and especially the contrast of Scottish with English institutions, is therefore informative. The success of Scottish free banking, as the result of self-regulating competitive mechanisms, suggests that England would have benefited from emulation of its northern neighbour. At the root of England's monetary difficulties was not too little central banking, as is sometimes suggested, but too much.

This chapter proceeds in the next section to trace the evolution of the banking industry in Scotland during the free banking period, emphasizing competitive entry and innovation. The third section then contrasts the arrangement and legal framework of Scottish banking in its heyday with those of English banking during the same period. Some limited evidence on the macroeconomic records of England and Scotland is examined in the final section.

The period of Scottish free banking coincided with a period of impressive industrial development in the Scottish economy. The growth of Scotland's economy in the century prior to 1844 was more rapid even than England's. Rondo Cameron (1967: 94), while acknowledging the lack of separate national income statistics for Scotland in this era, offers it as a reasonable estimate that Scotland's per capita income was no more than half England's in 1750 but nearly equal by 1845. Out of a backward agricultural and household economy with an active tobacco trade there developed an advanced (for its day) industrial economy. The leading industries became cotton cloth production, iron production, engineering and shipbuilding. Given Scotland's poor natural resource endowment and lack of other advantages, its ability to reach high income levels was remarkable. There is good reason to believe, as several historians have followed Adam Smith (1937 [1776]: 314–15) in suggesting, that Scotland's banking system played a major role in promoting the economy's growth.

EVOLUTION OF SCOTTISH BANKING, 1695–1845

The Bank of Scotland was created by Act of the Scottish Parliament in 1695, one year after the creation of the Bank of England.[2] The Act provided a legal monopoly on banking and the right of note issue for twenty-one years. Apparently thinking one bank was the most the country could accommodate, the bank made no effort to renew its monopoly upon its lapse in 1716.

Its founders intended the Bank of Scotland to be purely a commercial bank, to provide secured loans to merchants and noblemen and to discount commercial bills. Bank notes were to be placed in circulation by way of these advances. The issue of bank notes enabled the bank, just as the demand deposit account enables a modern-day bank, to create credit. By issuing notes the bank could lend far more than its paid-up capital. The bank was able to earn a handsome profit from the interest and commissions charged.

Despite its official-sounding title, the Bank of Scotland was – uniquely among European banks at that time – not a state institution. The government neither did business with the bank nor regulated it. In fact, the act creating the bank prohibited its lending to the government, under heavy penalty. This freedom was largely the result of the peculiar historical circumstances under which the bank was chartered. The crown of Scotland had been joined to that of England since 1603, and union of the parliaments was soon to come in 1707. There was no Scottish government with which to become entangled. In London the Bank of Scotland was commonly suspected of Jacobite leanings throughout the early eighteenth century. The British Parliament therefore turned a deaf ear to the bank's petitions against the chartering of its first rival, the Royal Bank of Scotland, in 1727.

An acrimonious rivalry between the two banks arose the day the new bank opened its doors. Both banks were housed in Edinburgh. As the Royal Bank's historian Munro puts it, 'at close quarters [there] opened a brisk duel in which the combatants used each other's notes as missiles' (1928: 55). The Royal Bank allegedly dispatched agents to trade its new notes for Bank of Scotland notes and to present the latter in large quantities at the Old Bank's office for coin. The Old Bank responded in kind, but lost the 'duel'. Within three months it was forced to suspend payments, call in its loans, make a 10 per cent call upon its shareholders, and even close its doors for several weeks in 1728. This was already the third suspension in the bank's history. A run on the Bank of Scotland in 1704, sparked by rumours of imminent upward revaluation of coin, had forced it to suspend payments for four months.[3] Its solvency was not threatened, but its assets were illiquid. The bank set an important precedent by announcing at the time of suspension that all notes would be granted 5 per cent annual interest for the period of the delay, payable when convertibility was resumed. The same policy was adopted for the eight-month suspension following a run during the civil unrest of 1715, and again for the eight-month suspension of 1728. We may think of these interest payments as part of the penalty cost of a shortfall of specie reserves, necessary to maintain the demand to hold the suspended notes.

Part of the Royal Bank's advantage in this contest came from the sums of cash lodged with it by government agencies. The Old Bank was of course bound to be confronted with an unusually great reflux of its notes upon the opening of a new note-issuing institution, regardless of that institution's tactics. The demand to hold Bank of Scotland notes had suddenly declined as the Royal Bank began to satisfy a large portion of the total demand for notes. The presentation of one bank's notes for payment by agents of the other bank provided the first step toward a regular and more amicable system of note exchanges that still later evolved into a central clearing-house for cheques.

The Royal Bank took advantage of the opportunity to put its own notes into wider circulation during the suspension, for a while offering them or specie in exchange for notes of the Old Bank. The Bank of Scotland's notes continued to trade at face value during the suspension. During the suspension a merger of the two banks was proposed by the Royal Bank's directors. Nothing came of the proposal, testifying to the difficulty of arranging cartelization of an industry even with only two firms. At the same time a private individual brought suit against the Bank of Scotland for its failure to honour the promise to pay given on the face of its notes. After much legal wrangling the note holder's right of 'summary diligence' or immediate payment on Bank of Scotland notes – a right stipulated in the bank's charter – was upheld. To lower expected liquidity costs, by protecting themselves against resumption of duelling tactics, the Bank of Scotland's directors in 1730 began inserting an 'option clause' into the obligation printed on its notes. The bank's pound note now promised to the bearer 'one pound sterling on demand, or in the option of the Directors one pound and sixpence sterling at the end of six months after the day of demand'. The implicit annual interest rate in case of delay was 5 per cent. Having finally learned from experience the proper specie reserve to maintain, the bank did not have to exercise the option until the 1760s. Its notes continued *de facto* to be convertible into specie on demand, much as thrift institutions today seldom invoke notice-of-withdrawal clauses in their deposit contracts. (For more on option classes see Dowd 1988.)

Competitive innovation by the two banks soon began to benefit the public. In 1728 the Royal Bank introduced the cash credit account, a form of overdraft account. An individual applying for a cash credit account had to provide evidence of sound character and two or more trustworthy co-signatories, who were jointly liable in case of the individual's insolvency. Once the account was opened, he could draw out the whole amount or any fraction for personal or business transactions. Interest was charged only on the outstanding daily balance. The cash credit system evidently lowered the cost of maintaining a note circulation by introducing more of the public to the use of bank notes. It proved an advantageous way for the bank to increase its note circulation while expanding its earning assets. The account allowed an individual to borrow against his human capital at lower transaction costs and so enabled him to undertake productive projects that otherwise would have been unprofitable. David Hume praised the system as 'one of the most ingenious ideas that has been executed in commerce' (1955 [1752]: 70) and noted how it eased the cash constraints within which merchants could transact. The Bank of Scotland adopted the cash account system in 1729. During the note duel of 1728 it had furthermore begun actively to solicit deposit accounts by offering interest upon them. After 1731 it offered such accounts on a regular basis. Checkland comments that 'Scottish banking was thus attracting deposits by the payment of interest long before this happened in England' (1975: 68). This innovation was a natural outgrowth of the competition for reserves between the two banks.

Competition had a dramatic effect on the profits of the Old Bank. It is reported (Wenley 1882: 124, 127) that from 1696 to 1728 its proprietors had received dividends ranging from 0 to 30 per cent (no dividends were declared during two years) and averaging 15.5 per cent. From 1729 to 1743 the dividends ranged from 3.75 to 6.25 per cent and averaged just 5 per cent.

A number of non-issuing private banking houses appeared in Edinburgh in the 1730s and 1740s. These were small partnerships dealing primarily in bills of exchange and commercial loans, many holding cash credit accounts at the chartered banks. The typical private banker was a merchant whose dealings in bills of exchange had grown gradually from a sideline into his primary business. The private bankers played a limited role in the industry, but are notable for demonstrating the freedom of entry that prevailed.

Rivalry between the two chartered banks[4] continued into the 1740s. To counteract the Royal Bank's popularity with Glasgow merchants, the Bank of Scotland in 1749 granted a large cash advance to a partnership in Glasgow for the purpose of forming the Glasgow Ship Bank. The partners promised to promote circulation of Bank of Scotland notes in Glasgow, just as private bankers promoted their circulation in Edinburgh. In competitive fashion, the Royal Bank sponsored the formation of the Glasgow Arms Bank in 1750. To the surprise of the two Edinburgh banks, the Ship Bank and the

Arms Bank both soon began issuing their own notes. At this the chartered banks ceased feuding with one another. The Bank of Scotland's historian tells how their directors met together in 1752 to consider means of dealing with the problem of 'private persons erecting themselves into Banking Companies without any public authority, particularly the two Banking Companies lately set up at Glasgow' (Malcolm [n.d.]: 59–64). They decided to withdraw their credits from the Glasgow banks and to stop credit to any Edinburgh or Glasgow customer circulating Glasgow notes. By 1756 the Glasgow banks were ready to come to terms with the Edinburgh banks, and in fact proposed a geographical division of the Scottish market between the pairs of banks. No agreement on terms could be reached. Once again the inherent instability of cartels had preserved competition in Scottish banking. The chartered banks then allegedly turned jointly to the tactic of note duelling, but their Glasgow rivals survived the assault by a series of evasive manoeuvres.

An agent of the public banks eventually brought suit against the Arms Bank for non-payment of notes. After three years of proceedings an out-of-court settlement was reached. One historian (Graham 1911: 57–8) has correctly commented that the Glasgow banks would never have had to resort to ruses had they kept sufficient specie reserves against their notes. The sufficient quantity of reserves, however, was something that bankers could learn only through trial and error.

The Banking Company of Aberdeen, a joint-stock venture established in 1747, was less fortunate in maintaining its foothold in the industry. The bank issued a great quantity of notes and was evidently unprepared to cope with the reflux of notes upon it. Drained of specie by the notes returned from Edinburgh, it retired in 1753. A petition for summary diligence by a noteholder was refused on the grounds that this remedy was enforceable on bills but not on promissory notes such as bank notes. The Act chartering the Bank of Scotland had provided for summary diligence on its notes, but this provision did not extend to other banks. The question of summary diligence against bank notes was finally settled in 1765, when the option clause was outlawed and summary diligence made enforceable. Until then the notes of the banks circulated despite the notes' unclear legal standing.

The most important entrant during these years was the British Linen Company, a corporation chartered in 1746 to promote the linen trade as wholesalers. The company began providing banking services to its clients much in the manner of the Edinburgh private bankers.

The company's historian reports that in 1747 its directors started issuing interest-bearing promissory notes with which to pay its 'agents, weavers, manufacturers, and other customers' (Malcolm 1950: 26). In 1750 it began issuing non-interest-bearing bank notes, payable on demand. In the 1760s the company began to withdraw from the linen trade and to devote itself entirely to banking. Expanding vigorously, it enjoyed Scotland's – and the world's – first success with branch banking. The branches began on a small scale as agents appointed in various cities to discount bills and circulate the bank's notes. By 1793 the British Linen Company had twelve branches in operation, with six added shortly thereafter. As a result of its extensive branching the bank had the industry's greatest bank note circulation in 1845. The evolution of the British Linen Company into a banking firm (eventually renamed the British Linen Bank) illustrates once more the freedom of entry into banking that prevailed in Scotland.

A number of small private bankers entered the industry in the late 1750s, followed by several provincial banking companies in the early 1860s. Many of these new banks, apparently in response to the denominational disequilibrium created by a loss of coin through an external drain occurring at the time, issued notes for fractions of £1. The banks typically included the option clause in their larger notes but did not include it in notes smaller than 10 shillings. The Royal Bank and the British Linen Company adopted the option clause for the first time in 1762, though not for their 20 or 10 shilling notes. The directors of the Dundee Bank went the option clause one better by promising to redeeem their larger notes, on demand or with interest after six months, in specie or in the notes of either the Royal Bank or the Bank of Scotland, at the directors' option. This 'double optional clause' appears to have been an aberration rather than part of any wider movement toward pyramiding of reserves. The issue of pyramiding is further discussed later in this chapter.

As numerous small traders began issuing optional notes for sums of 5 shillings and 1 shilling and other private traders minted copper coins for still smaller change, there arose some public agitation against the option clause and the small notes. One later commentator, viewing the circulation of the small notes as a natural response to the scarcity of specie, characterized their opponents as 'country gentlemen, led on most probably by some who visited Edinburgh occasionally, and there picked up theories on religion, politics, and commerce, of a very unpractical character', whose speeches and resolutions contained 'the same exaggerated assertions, fallacious inferences, and ridiculous fears that have pervaded the more modern discussions on the circulating medium' (Boase 1867: 2). Some industry historians (e.g., Kerr 1884: 67–74), apparently taking the provincial resolutions more at face value, have described a 'small note mania' taking hold. Public dissatisfaction may also have stemmed from the difficulty, occasioned by the ongoing external drain, in getting the banks to provide short-dated bills on London or specie for their notes (Logan 1839: 43–4). Recall that the legal remedy of summary diligence had been denied to noteholders. The inconvenience led noteholders in 1763 to memorialize the British Parliament on the subject. In 1764 the government in London intervened, after receiving a memorial from the Glasgow banks and after hearing from a joint committee of the Bank of Scotland and the Royal Bank. Effective from 1765, notes bearing the option clause and notes of denomination smaller than one pound were prohibited in Scotland. All notes were to be either explicitly redeemable in gold on demand, or explicitly post-dated. The right of note issue remained universal, despite the chartered banks' rent-seeking attempt to have the right legally restricted to themselves (Checkland 1975: 120–1). The Act of 1765 left Scotland with free banking in most respects, though it raised an entry barrier against very small-scale banks of issue. Shortly after passage, five of the small-partnership note issuers in the city of Perth amalgamated into a single bank.

Entry continued apace during the late 1760s. The total number of Scottish banks (both issuing and non-issuing) having risen from five in 1740 to fourteen in 1750, to twenty-three in 1760, and to twenty-seven in 1765, reached thirty-two in 1769. The year 1769 saw the establishment of Douglas, Heron & Co. in the town of Ayr. The Ayr Bank, as it was known, showed little sign of having learned the lesson of the Bank of Scotland's suspensions and the Banking Company at Aberdeen's retirement. In three years the bank's reckless management extended a great quantity of bad credit via its note issues and achieved a spectacular insolvency. The discipline of the market soon asserted itself. The bank came to grief in 1772 with losses estimated at some two-thirds of a million pounds (see Hamilton 1956). The failure of the Ayr Bank brought down thirteen small private bankers in Edinburgh,[5] thinning the number of private banks from nineteen to six. A provincial banking company in Perth also ended sometime in 1772, leaving the industry with sixteen institutions in 1773 (Checkland 1975: 132–5).

In order to tell the story of the Ayr Bank crash, it is necessary first to discuss the formation of the Scottish note-exchange system. Selgin and White (1987) provide a theoretical account of why such a system would evolve. Charles W. Munn (1975; 1981a: 21–9) has recounted the particular facts surrounding the origin of the Scottish note exchange. The Bank of Scotland and the Royal Bank of Scotland agreed to accept and regularly exchange one another's notes as part of the accommodation they reached in 1751. Provincial banks, as they entered the industry in the 1750s and 1760s, did not initially accept one another's notes as a general practice. In 1768 the Aberdeen and Perth United Banking Companies initiated a policy of mutual acceptance and exchange. This arrangement was in the profit-seeking interest of both firms, for as Munn (1975: 48) points out, it promoted the demand to hold the notes of both banks by merchants doing business between the two cities. The Perth United made a similar arrangement with the Dundee Banking Company.

The Ayr Bank arranged from the outset for mutual acceptance and regular exchange of notes with a number of the provincial banks. The exchange was conducted weekly by the Edinburgh agents of the participating banks. The British Linen Company soon entered the exchange. In 1771 the Bank of Scotland and the Royal Bank agreed to join in accepting and exchanging provincial notes, recognizing that they could thereby promote the demand to hold their own notes. Some provincial bankers were apparently reluctant at first to enter the exchange with the chartered banks, but soon recognized that exchanging regularly was more convenient than confronting irregular demands for redemption of notes collected by the Edinburgh banks. Following a brief hiatus in the wake of the Ayr Bank crash, the note-exchange system revived to encompass all the Scottish issuing banks from 1774 on (Checkland 1975: 140–1). Membership in the exchange became recognized as a valuable brand-name capital asset. One historian records:

> So completely did opinion change, that instead of the senior banks needing to coerce their juniors towards the practice, it became an object of emulation amongst the latter to share in the rank and respectability enjoyed by members of the note exchange.
>
> (Graham 1911: 59)

In accordance with our theory, each member of the industry benefited from the note exchange as its notes gained in negotiability. This quality improvement meant that the Scottish public's margin of preference between specie and notes shifted in favour of notes. Bank notes thereby displaced specie in circulation to a large extent. The Scottish note-exchange system long antedated the well-known Suffolk system of New England (see Trivoli 1979), whose origin and impact can be explained in a similar way.

The episode of the Ayr Bank failure did not impugn but, in fact, confirmed the effectiveness of the Scottish note-exchange system in preventing overissue by a single bank. Settlement between two clearing-house members, for the difference in the sums of notes exchanged, was made in bills negotiable in London, or in specie.[6] As the clearing-house rapidly returned the Ayr Bank's notes to it, the bank piled up ever greater liabilities in the form of bills on London. The bank was in effect borrowing from the other banks to re-lend to the public. This was not a profitable strategy, as Adam Smith noted in 1776, especially when so many of its loans went sour. The bank soon found it difficult to roll over, let alone retire, its obligations. Public confidence in the bank broke when its London correspondent failed and its bills were refused by other brokers. At liquidation the bank's liabilities consisted of £300,000 in deposits, £220,000 in notes, and £600,000 in outstanding drafts on London.

The crash of the Ayr Bank, spectacular as it was for its day, did not imperil the Scottish banking system as a whole. Other banks of issue were not dependent on the Ayr Bank's survival for their own. They did not hold large quantities of its notes, thanks to the operation of the clearing-house. Sir William Forbes, a leading private banker, recorded that a 'smart demand for money' confronted the Edinburgh banks for less than a day. Even this brief run 'was a new and unexpected circumstance, for nothing of the kind had occurred' following the failure of one private bank in 1764 or another in 1769 (Forbes 1860: 43). Only those private banking houses involved with the Ayr Bank's circulation of bills were brought down. The 3 chartered banks, 4 strong private banks in Edinburgh, 3 banks in Glasgow, and 3 provincial banks escaped trouble, having prudently avoided holding the liabilities of the Ayr Bank. The Merchant Bank of Glasgow found it necessary to suspend payments for three months, and a private bank in Edinburgh to close for a month, but both resumed business. The repercussions of the Ayr failure on the industry were short-lived (Checkland 1975: 133). Private banking revived in the next few years, with new entrants in Edinburgh and in provincial towns. The Bank of Scotland took the opportunity finally to establish successful branches of its own in five cities.

Any possible erosion of general confidence in bank notes from the Ayr failure was halted by joint action of the Bank of Scotland and the Royal Bank. On the day before the Ayr Bank went into liquidation the two banks advertised that they would accept the notes of the defunct bank. The potential benefits of this action to the two banks are clear: it would bolster public confidence, attract depositors, and help put their own notes into wider circulation. The potential cost was surprisingly low because of one of the most remarkable features of Scottish free banking: the unlimited liability of a bank's shareholders. Despite their magnitude the Ayr Bank's losses were borne entirely by its 241 shareholders. The claims of its creditors, including noteholders, were paid in full.

New provincial banks continued to spring up all about Scotland in the decades following 1772. Many had extensive networks of bill-discounting agents to promote note circulation.

According to the typology of S.G. Checkland's authoritative chronicle of the industry (1975: 320–1), the Scottish banking trade at the start of 1810 was divided among 3 chartered ('public') banks, centred in Edinburgh with branches in a few large towns: 9 private (non-issuing) bankers, 8 of them in Edinburgh and 1 in Glasgow; and 22 provincial banking companies, 3 of them in Glasgow, 12 in secondary burghs, and 7 in lesser burghs. Checkland reserves the term joint-stock bank for enterprises to be founded later, and Charles W. Munn (1981) follows this usage in his history of the provincial banking companies. Previous industry historians had indicated that at least two provincial banks at this time (Wenley 1882: 135), or the majority of them (Fleming 1877: 98), were founded on joint-stock principles. The law made no distinction among provincial, joint-stock and private banks, as the rule of unlimited liability made all non-chartered banks effectively partnerships. The important distinction came along financial lines: the private banks and provincial banking companies were based on their partners' contributions, with shares generally not freely transferable, whereas joint-stock banks raised capital by issuing a limited number of transferable shares. There were important functional differences among the chartered banks, the private banks of Edinburgh and the provincial banks. The chartered banks served as bankers to many of the private banks, whereas the latter specialized in serving certain sorts of borrowers not served by the former. The private bankers also served as Edinburgh agents of the provincial banking companies. The private bankers in Edinburgh did not issue notes, whereas provincial banks typically were banks of issue. The arrangements between the Edinburgh private and chartered banks were so close that private bankers often exercised considerable control as directors of the Royal Bank and the Bank of Scotland. Their vertical division of labour arose from the comparative advantage held by the smaller private bankers in dealing with commercial borrowers whereas economies of scale operated in the business of issuing.

The three 'public' banks were distinctly larger and more prominent in the industry than any of the other banks at the start of 1810. That was about to change.

Schumpeter has remarked that 'the problem usually being visualized is how capitalism administers existing structures, whereas the relevant problem is how it creates and destroys them (1942: 84)'. The 'perennial gale of creative destruction' soon transformed the structure of Scottish banking. The entry of the Commercial Bank of Scotland in 1810, founded on the joint stock of over 650 shareholders, spelled the end of the small private bankers and ushered in an era of extensive branch banking (on this transformation see Munn 1982). A contemporary observer quoted in the bank's history claimed that the perceived aloofness of the chartered banks from the working public gave rise to 'a demand for a bank founded on more liberal principles; . . . hence the origin of the Commercial, professing to be the bank of the citizens' (Anderson 1910: 3–5). The Commercial Bank announced publicly that no private bankers would sit on its board of directors.

By 1819 the Commercial Bank had opened 14 branches, as compared with the British Linen Company's 17, the Bank of Scotland's 14, and the Royal Bank's single branch office in Glasgow. The structure of the industry as of 1826 is shown in Table 9.1. In 1830 the score stood at 30 branches for the Commercial Bank, 28 for British Linen, 18 for the National Bank of Scotland (established in 1825 with over 1,200 shareholders), 17 for the Bank of Scotland, and still only 1 for the Royal Bank. Smaller banks also branched out. The following decade saw the 7 leading banks alone add another 110 branches, bringing the national total to more than 300 branch banking offices in 1840. On the eve of 1845 there were 19 banks of issue in Scotland with 363 branches, providing one bank office for every 6,600 persons in Scotland, as compared with 1 for 9,405 in England, and one for 16,000 in the United States (Macfarlan 1845: 12).

The Scottish free banking system had thus evolved by 1844 the following features to which free banking advocates in England and elsewhere pointed. There were many competing banks; most of them were well capitalized by a large number of shareholders; none was disproportionately large; all but a few were extensively branched. Each bank issued notes for £1 and above; most banks' notes passed easily throughout the greater part of the country. All the banks of issue participated in an effective note-exchange system. All offered a narrow spread between deposit and discount (loan) rates of interest.

In contrast to their 'big three' dominance in 1810, the public banks now ranked first, fourth, and seventh in size of circulation (see Table

Table 9.1 Scottish banks, 1826

Name of bank, date established	Head office	Number of partners	Number of branch Offices
Chartered banks			
1 Bank of Scotland, 1695	Edinburgh	–	16
2 Royal Bank of Scotland, 1727	Edinburgh	–	1
3 British Linen Co., 1746	Edinburgh	–	27
Provincial banks, joint-stock banks, and private banks of issue			
4 Sir William Forbes & Co., *c.* 1730	Edinburgh	7	0
5 Ramsay, Bonars, & Co., *c.* 1738	Edinburgh	8	0
6 Glasgow Ship Bank, 1749	Glasgow	3	0
7 Thistle Bank, 1761	Glasgow	6	0
8 Dundee Banking Co., 1763	Dundee	61	0
9 Perth Banking Co., 1766	Perth	147	5
10 Banking Co. of Aberdeen, 1767	Aberdeen	80	6
11 Hunters & Co., 1773	Ayr	8	3
12 Commercial Bank of Aberdeen, 1778	Aberdeen	15	0
13 Paisley Banking Co., 1783	Paisley	6	4
14 Greenock Banking Co., 1785	Greenock	14	3
15 Paisley Union Bank, 1788	Paisley	4	3
16 Leith Banking Co., 1792	Leith	15	4
17 Dundee New Bank, 1802	Dundee	6	1
18 Renfrewshire Banking Co., 1802	Greenock	6	5
19 Dundee Union Bank, 1809	Dundee	85	4
20 Glasgow Bank, 1809	Glasgow	19	1
21 Commercial Banking Co. of Scotland, 1810	Edinburgh	521	31
22 Perth Union Bank, 1810	Perth	69	0
23 Montrose Bank, 1814	Montrose	97	2
24 Exchange & Deposit Bank, 1818	Aberdeen	1	4
25 Shetland Banking Co., 1821	Lerwick	4	0
26 Aberdeen Town & County Bank, 1825	Aberdeen	446	4
27 Arbroath Banking Co., 1825	Arbroath	112	2
28 Dundee Commercial Bank, 1825	Dundee	202	0
29 National Bank of Scotland, 1825	Edinburgh	1,238	8
Nonissuing private banks			
30 Thomas Kinnear & Co., 1731	Edinburgh	–	–
31 James & Robert Watson, *c.* 1763	Glasgow	–	–
32 Donald Smith & Co., 1773	Edinburgh	–	–
33 Alexander Allan & Co., *c.* 1776	Edinburgh	–	–
34 Robert Allan & Son, 1776	Edinburgh	–	–
35 Inglis, Borthwick & Co., 1805	Edinburgh	–	–

Sources: Graham (1911: 192); Kerr (1884, appendix D); Checkland (1975b: 320–1)

Table 9.2 Scottish banks of issue, 1845

Name of bank, date established	Head office	No. of shareholders	No. of branches	Paid-up capital £	Note-issue[a] £
Bank of Scotland, 1695	Edinburgh	654	33	1,000,000	300,485
Royal Bank of Scotland, 1727	Edinburgh	854	6	2,000,000	183,000
British Linen Co., 1746	Edinburgh	206	43	500,000	438,024
Dundee Banking Co., 1763	Dundee	57	1	60,000	33,451
Perth Banking Co., 1766	Perth	185	3	100,000	38,656
Banking Co. of Aberdeen, 1767	Aberdeen	370	15	240,000	88,467
Commercial Bank of Scotland, 1810	Edinburgh	550	52	600,000	374,880
National Bank of Scotland, 1825	Edinburgh	1,482	34	1,000,000	297,024
Aberdeen Town & County Bank, 1825	Aberdeen	489	10	150,000	70,133
Union Bank of Scotland, 1830	Glasgow	598	30	1,000,000	327,223
Ayrshire Banking Co., 1830	Ayr	109	12	50,000	53,656
Western Bank of Scotland, 1832	Glasgow	703	39	1,000,000	284,282
Central Bank of Scotland, 1834	Perth	405	7	65,000	42,933
North of Scotland Banking Co., 1836	Aberdeen	1,605	27	300,000	154,319
Clydesdale Banking Co., 1838	Glasgow	947	11	500,000	104,028
Eastern Bank of Scotland, 1838	Dundee	552	4	600,000	33,636
Caledonian Banking Co., 1838	Inverness	938	10	75,000	53,434
Edinburgh & Glasgow Bank, 1838	Edinburgh	1,546	20	1,000,000	136,657
City of Glasgow Bank, 1838	Glasgow	906	6	1,000,000	72,921
Totals		13,156	363	11,240,000	3,087,209

Source: Wenley (1882: 144); Checkland (1975: 372–3).

Note: [a] As authorized by the Act of 1845, equal to the bank's average outstanding note-issue for the year ending 1 May 1845.

9.2). Five of the joint-stock banks had paid-up capitals as large as the Bank of Scotland's £1 million, and eight had capitals as large or larger than the British Linen Company's £500,000. The Commercial Bank had more branches than any of the three public banks, and the National Bank more branches than two of the three. The National Bank, the North of Scotland Banking Company and the Edinburgh and Glasgow Bank each had more shareholders than any of the public banks. Randomly arranging the rows of Table 9.2 and removing the dates of establishment, there would be no way to guess which three banks were the senior members of the industry.

Competition among the public banks and large joint-stock banks was clearly vigorous in note issue, deposit-taking, lending and discounting, inland exchange, and other aspects of banking. Profit margins were squeezed.[7] Competitive bidding for loans and deposits kept the interest differential between them down to 1 per cent (Checkland 1975: 384–8). As Munn notes, 'the competitive nature of the business' meant that 'all earning assets had to be managed with fine attention to detail. There was no room for error or even slackness if dividends were to be maintained' (1982: 118). Attempts were made in the 1830s and 1840s to limit interest rates and activity charges through cartel agreements, but such agreements proved unsustainable in the face of strong competitive pressures (Checkland 1975: 449–50; Munn 1982: 122).

The rise of branch banking on a nation-wide scale in the half-century prior to 1826 was preceded by the network of agents employed by the major banks for the discounting of bills in distant towns. Fully fledged branch offices became profitable only as deposit accounts became a major part of the banking business, while the growth of deposits awaited the growth of real per capita income. Broadly based banks tended increasingly to displace one-office banks because secularly falling costs of communication between areas allowed branched networks profitably to take advantage of economies of scale in fund gathering and asset management, particularly opportunities for risk spreading among various localities. The failure of a local industry whose bills the bank held or an annual variation in the local demand for coin would not imperil the local branch of a national bank so much as it would a purely local bank.

The rise of nationally branched banks went hand in hand with the demise of the small local institutions. Edinburgh's last non-issuing private bankers were gone by 1835. Provincial banks unable to meet the new competition either failed or sold out. The Glasgow Union Banking Company, founded in 1830 with a partnership of 488 shareholders, soon grew to be a major national bank by acquisition of small local banks (Rait 1939).

The Union Bank also pioneered the competitive practice of regularly publicizing its asset and liability status, in 1836 becoming the first British bank to publish an annual balance sheet. Previously the Bank of Scotland had published its accounts to demonstrate its solvency during the suspension of 1704 and 1728.

The rise of nationally branched joint-stock banks and the decline of local banks in Scotland by 1844 indicates that there emerged substantial economies of scale in producing bank-note services, that is, the public confidence, easy redeemability (through branching and reserve management), and other qualities necessary to keep bank notes in circulation in a competitive environment. But these economies were always limited.[8] Thomas Kinnear, an Edinburgh private banker who also served as director of the Bank of Scotland, testified (British Sessional Papers BSP 1826: 132) that the Bank of Scotland had been forced to abandon some of its branch offices due to competition from local banks. No one bank could serve the entire market so cheaply as to exclude others. Scottish experience offers no reason to suppose that there exist 'natural monopoly' characteristics in the production of convertible currency.

Freedom of entry into the banking trade in Scotland was closed off by Peel's Act of 1844 and the subsequent Scottish Bank Act of 1845 (see White 1984b: 76–80). The years prior to 1845 had seen the entrances of some 109 distinct banking firms. Of those, 36 had failed or been wound up, 12 had disappeared for reasons unrecorded, 11 had retired voluntarily or ended without apparent failure, and 30 had merged into other banks (Checkland, 1975: tables 2, 3, 9, 11). Twenty banks remained in business in 1845, 19 of them banks of issue (see Table 9.2). 9 of these 19 had entered since 1830. The Clydesdale Bank, established in 1838, is notable for being one of three Scottish banks issuing notes even today (the others are the Bank of Scotland and the Royal Bank, the industry's first two entrants). Since 1845 the number of native Scottish banks has declined steadily, primarily through merger, to today's three banks.

THE CONTRAST BETWEEN SCOTTISH AND ENGLISH BANKING

J. Shield Nicholson noted that the Scottish system from 1716 to 1845 was 'more than any existing system, the result of continuous development', and owed 'less than any to the direct interference of the legislature'. (1893: 502). James Wilson, first editor of *The Economist*, commented that 'we have only to look to Scotland to see what has been the effect of a long career of perfect freedom and competition upon the character and credit of the banking establishments of that country (1847: 30)'.

Its freedom from legislative intervention sharply distinguishes Scottish banking prior to 1844 from banking in England and Wales.[9] After the lapse of the Bank of Scotland's legal monopoly in 1716, no Scottish bank enjoyed the legal privileges bestowed on the Bank of England. Correspondingly the Scottish provincial and joint-stock banks suffered under none of the peculiar series of makeshift restrictions placed on English country banks (apart from a small-note ban).

The original charter of the Bank of England in 1694 did not grant it exclusive privilege in note issue or in other aspects of banking. In 1697 Parliament resolved that no other bank would be chartered while the Bank of England remained, but left the field open to private bankers. Shortly thereafter, as a quid pro quo for the bank's taking up more Exchequer bills (the bank actually originated in a war loan to the government), an Act of 1708 barred any English private joint-stock bank of greater than six partners from issuing bank notes or any other obligations with maturities shorter than six months during the continuance of the Bank of England.

The business of supplying bank notes in the English countryside was thereby left to a host of poorly capitalized, locally based banks. Bank of England notes hardly circulated outside London in 1708, and even 120 years later were not commonly encountered outside the city. The Bank of England faced diseconomies of scale in providing bank notes with desired qualities. Local country notes circulated more freely because their authenticity was more easily ascertained, and their acceptance by nearby bankers for redemption or deposit was more likely. Bank of England notes bore unfamiliar signatures, could be redeemed for specie only in London, and were not widely accepted by country bankers. In addition – and here the bank seems to have overlooked a profit opportunity – its notes were issued only in denominations too large for common use, the smallest being £20 until a £10 note was introduced in 1759 and a £5 note in 1793.

Smaller notes were issued by the country bankers who, incidentally, often failed. It became popular in England to attribute the instability of these banks to their issues of small notes rather than their undercapitalization. Parliament in 1775 prohibited English banks from issuing notes smaller than £1. Two years later notes smaller than

£5 were banned. Token coins issued by local manufacturers, differing from bank notes only in form, soon arose to meet the demand for money of small denominations. The £1 notes of Scottish banks, already circulating in northern England, gained greater currency in the northern counties.

Bank of England notes did not gain widespread circulation until the bank finally began opening branches after being prompted by the government to do so in 1826. Their circulation was furthered in 1833 by their becoming a form of legal reserve for the country banks. Country banks had previously been obliged to redeem their own notes in gold or silver coin; now they could redeem them either in coin or in Bank of England notes. J. R. McCulloch remarked that 'Bank of England notes are now legal tender everywhere except at the bank and her branches (1837: 170)'. The notes of the bank became a form of high-powered or base money, giving the bank substantial short-run influence over the English money stock.

In Scotland neither native bank notes nor Bank of England notes were legal tender. Yet the notes of the major Scottish banks circulated freely throughout the country. One-pound notes performed the great bulk of the transactions. An anonymous English writer commented:

> Whoever has been to Scotland knows that, notwithstanding the appearances which denote real wealth, no coin but that of copper is common; gold and silver are scarcely visible; it is even difficult sometimes to get silver in change of a twenty shillings Bank Note. Purchases and payments of all kinds are commonly made in paper.
> (Anonymous 1802: 108)

Unlike Bank of England notes, the notes of a major Scottish bank came in conveniently small denominations (though notes smaller than £1 had been outlawed by the Act of 1765). Unlike English country bank notes, their value was secure and their acceptance by other banks commonplace. In the early days, immediately following the Aberdeen, Glasgow and Ayr Bank episodes, the Edinburgh banks refused for a while to accept provincial notes, although they freely accepted one another's notes. Even so, private brokers in the city would change the provincial notes at a discount of 1/2 pence per 20 shillings (0.6 per cent). General acceptance, as we have noted, was the norm after 1774. An individual bank thought overextended by the industry would occasionally be disciplined by the threatened refusal of its notes.

It is sometimes suggested that free banking is inherently attended by a counterfeiting problem of major dimensions. Counterfeiting was not a significant problem in the Scottish experience. Counterfeiting was a problem for the Bank of England, however, especially during the period of the suspension of payments. The likelihood of undetected counterfeiting varies directly with the length of time a note circulates before returning to the issuing bank – where it passes under a teller's discriminating gaze – for deposit or payment. Coppieters (1955: 64–5) points out that Scottish notes had a very brief average period of circulation, as other issuing banks would not hold them as till money, but would return them through the clearing-house. The same could not be said for Bank of England notes.

Because of competition, moreover, we should expect each Scottish bank to pursue a policy towards forgeries of its notes designed to bolster public confidence in its notes (to the point where the marginal revenue of increased circulation equalled its marginal cost of confidence bolstering). Thomas Kinnear testified (British Sessional Papers 1826: 126) that the Bank of Scotland generally honoured forgeries of its notes tendered over the counter by innocent parties. The bank did not honour forgeries accepted by other banks and returned through the note exchange, since presumably that policy would have been more costly. By raising the costs to the bank of discovering who had forged the notes, and hence of discouraging forgeries, it would have invited a greater supply of forgeries. The accepting banks could not be expected to keep an eye out for forgeries of Bank of Scotland notes unless the burden fell upon them.

The six-partner rule of the Act of 1708 prevented England from experiencing the rise of strong nationally based joint-stock banks like those whose branches superseded local and private banks in Scotland. As Sir Henry Parnell explained:

> What has been the cause of the failures of Country Banks in England? The facility with which every cobbler and cheesemonger has been able to open a Bank, in consequence of the limitation of the numerous opulent Banks. What has been the cause of so few failures in Scotland? The freedom of the Banking Trade, and the establishment of opulent Banks.
>
> (Parnell 1833: 73)

Good banks could drive out bad, given the chance. In 1826, a recent banking panic having made the inferiority of the English system plain, Parliament granted a limited concession to public agitation on behalf of Scottish principles of joint-stock banking. An Act of 1826 removed the old Act's restriction on the number of partners permitted to establish a note-issuing bank, but only for banks to be housed more than 65 miles from London. Joint-stock banks could do business in London only if they did not issue notes. The new Act also encouraged the Bank of England to open branches outside London. At least one banking historian (Macleod 1866: 335–7) has argued forcefully that the 65-mile restriction continued to deny England the best feature of the Scottish system, the freedom to develop a broad banking network based in the country's financial centre. The freedom to branch into *Britain's* financial centre – London – was, however, equally denied to the Scottish banks.

In the event of failure of a Scottish bank, a call would go out to its shareholders – who were publicly listed – for some percentage of the nominal value of their shares. The most severe call on record seems to have followed the failure of the Fife Bank in 1829. The holder of each £50 share was assessed at £5,500. All liabilities were paid in full. By one account (Wenley 1882: 142), all failed banks having more than nine partners were able to pay their liabilities to the public in full. The loss to the Scottish banking public from all failures to date was estimated in 1841 at only £32,000. Public losses during the previous year in London alone were estimated at twice that amount (Aytoun 1844: 678). This experience enhanced the great confidence the Scottish public put in bank notes and contributed importantly to the cyclical stability of Scottish banks.

Limited liability was not available to the non-chartered banks[10] until 1862. Compulsory unlimited liability can be viewed as a potential barrier to entry, because it may have restricted new banking firms to a suboptimal sharing of bankruptcy risk between shareholders and debt-holders (Carr and Mathewson 1988: 776–7; Cowen and Kroszner 1989: 225–7). It is possible, however, that the restriction was not binding. The unchartered Scottish banks chose to retain unlimited liability even after limited liability became available to them through the Companies Act of 1862. In Checkland's view the Scottish banks 'preferr[ed] that the obligation should continue to rest on shareholders; they felt that such a step [adopting limited liability] would reduce public confidence in them, and so harm their business' (1975: 480). Not until 1882, after the 1878 failure of the City of Glasgow Bank helped to change shareholders' perceptions of the risks they faced, and after the 1879 passage of a revised Companies Act, did the remaining seven non-chartered Scottish banks agree to limit their shareholders' liability. (For more on this issue see White 1990a: 42–4.)

As an investment to bolster public confidence in its obligations, it was not unusual in the eighteenth century for a local bank to lodge with the town clerk a personal bond guaranteeing payment of its notes. One of the points of contention in the case against the Glasgow Arms Bank was that it had violated its bond by inserting the option clause into its notes. Enforcement of liability was facilitated by Scottish bankruptcy law, which was stricter than English law. In England only the personal estate of an insolvent debtor could be attached. A Scottish creditor was legally entitled to the debtor's real and heritable estate as well. The amount of real and heritable estate an individual possessed could be easily determined by consulting public records. This enabled each partner of a local banking venture to gauge his personal exposure to loss and aided a bank in verifying the collateral property pledged against loans and cash credits. It also enabled members of the public, if they wished, to ascertain the ultimate assets of a local banking partnership. The great security provided to creditors under Scots law helped immunize Scottish banks against any danger of a panic-induced run.

English country banks were never able to create adequate public confidence in their notes. The limitation of English banks to a partnership of six hamstrung their confidence-creating efforts. Joint-stock banking with unrestricted capitalization and freedom of issue was never allowed to evolve. Its trial was limited to eleven years and prejudiced by its exclusion from London. The fact that Scottish notes crossed the border to form the common circulation of the northern counties of England – there is no evidence of English notes travelling north – stands as clear evidence of the superior reliability of the Scottish banks. In 1826 the citizens of Cumberland and Westmorland counties in northern England petitioned Parliament against the proposed restriction of their Scottish note circulation. Their petition, setting forth the facts of their situation, supports the argument that high-quality bank notes will out compete low-quality notes in gaining public circulation. The petition noted that the freedom of Scotland from the six-partner rule

> gave a degree of strength to the issuers of notes, and of confidence to the receivers of them, which several banks established in our counties have not been able to command. The natural consequence has been, that Scotch notes have formed the greater part of our circulating medium.
>
> (quoted by Graham 1911: 366–7)

The petitioners added that they had, with one exception, never suffered any losses from accepting Scottish notes for the last fifty years, 'while in the same period the failures of banks in the north of

England have been unfortunately numerous, and have occasioned the most ruinous losses to many who were little able to sustain them'.

Because of the legal limitation on their capitalization and their consequently restricted ability to spread risks through portfolio diversification and office branching, the English country banks were artificially prone to failure. Experience with country bank failure in turn made the banks less trustworthy and hence more susceptible to sudden panic-induced demands for redemption of notes.

The Scottish banks were both stable and competitive. The English country banks lacked the first of these attributes; the Bank of England lacked the second. The Bank of England did not open branches until the Act of 1826 specifically encouraged it to do so. Adhering to the policies of the London office, the branch offices offered no interest-bearing current accounts, unlike the Scottish banks, and even no interest-bearing six-month time deposit accounts, unlike many country banks. The branches did not allow overdraft privileges, although these (on the model of the Scottish cash credit system) had become popular with merchants. The branches of the Bank of England refused to accept country notes as a matter of course.

Though the country banks operated regular note exchanges in a number of localities, they were excluded from operating on a nation-wide basis by their legal exclusion from London and by the Bank of England's refusal to enter into arrangements with the country banks for mutual acceptance and exchange of notes. Competition had long since led the Scottish banks to accept one another's notes. The sole competitive impact of the Bank of England branches seems to have come in their driving down local rates of discount on bills.

Free banking was beneficial to the Scottish public not only for its improvement of the payments mechanism. The unrestricted note issue of Scottish banks also aided their intermediation. The contrast between Scottish and English deposit practices – only the Scottish banks paid interest on deposits as small as £10 and paid interest on current accounts without charging a fee for withdrawals – may be attributed to the effectiveness of competition in the supply of bank notes in Scotland. The cash account system, original to Scotland, was similarly the product of competitive note issue. Perhaps the most distinctive feature of the Scottish system was the extensive branching of the national joint-stock banks. Freedom of note issue, by allowing each bank to hold its own paper rather than precious metals as till money for redemption of deposits, made it economically feasible for banks to establish numerous and dispersed branch offices. Competition in maintaining a national circulation gave them the incentive to branch. The broad basis for the Scottish banks, especially after 1810, was a major source of their stability in the 1775–1845 period.

In light of the evolution of the English banking system, as told in Bagehot's celebrated *Lombard Street*, it is noteworthy that Scotland prior to 1844 did not develop an inverted-pyramid structure of specie reserves. It rather maintained a system of 'each tub on its own bottom'. Each bank held onto its own specie reserves.[11] The English 'one-reserve system', whereby the Bank of England alone held substantial specie, was, as Bagehot explains, the product neither of conscious design nor of natural market evolution (1912 [1873]: 100). It was instead 'the gradual consequence of many singular events, and of an accumulation of legal privileges on a single bank'. There is no reason to suppose any tendency toward centralization of reserves in the absence of government intervention.[12] Bagehot comments at length that 'the natural system – that which would have sprung up if Government had let banking alone – is that of many banks of equal or not altogether unequal size', and cites Scotland as an example of a system 'where banking has been left free' and where there is 'no single bank with any sort of predominance'. In such a system no bank 'gets so much before the others that the others voluntarily place their reserves in its keeping' (1912 [1873]: 66–8).[13]

CYCLICAL STABILITY OF SCOTTISH BANKS, 1793–1837

The Scottish free banking system proved far hardier during periods of commercial distress than did its English counterpart. As a result, Scottish industry as a whole seems to have suffered less severe cyclical variation than English industry. Even critics of the idea of allowing free banking in London, like J. R. McCulloch, acknowledged 'the comparative exemption of this part of the empire [Scotland] from the revulsions that have made so much havoc in England' (1826: 281). Non-bank-related differences between Scotland and England may be cited in explaining the relative mildness of Scottish cycles – McCulloch invoked the greater role of agriculture in the Scottish economy, for example – but these are of secondary importance. Scotland largely caught up with England in industrialization during the free banking period but retained its advantage in macroeconomic stability. Cameron (1967: 97) has plausibly argued that the more rapid growth of the Scottish economy itself owed much to competition in banking.

Scottish and English experiences may be contrasted for the crises of 1793, 1797, 1825–6 and 1837.[14] The weaknesses of the English country banks led to their frequent failure even in good times. This record in turn enhanced their cyclical instability, for it undermined public confidence in them. Klein has rightly remarked that 'the major way in which monetary confidence is produced is successful past performance' (1978: 6). The slightest suspicion could touch off a run on the country banks. These smallish banks could not turn to one another for financial support in such a circumstance; neither did they appear an attractive investment opportunity to the Bank of England. The Scottish banks, by way of contrast, stood ready to lend one another liquid funds in the event of a short-term disturbance. During the Ayr Bank episode in 1772, for example, the Bank of Scotland and the Royal Bank advanced cash to the three Glasgow banks.

Threat of war from France apparently prompted a great demand for cash in Great Britain in early 1793. The crisis was severe in England. MacPherson's *Annals of Commerce* reports: 'Many houses of the most extensive dealings, and most established credit, failed; and their fall involved vast numbers of their correspondents and connections in all parts of the country' (1805: 266). The numbers involved are disputed. MacPherson reports the failure of more than 100 of the banks in England and Wales (their total variously estimated at 280 and above 400). Macleod (1866: vol. 1, 383; vol. 2, 103) avers that of some 400 country banks, 300 were 'much shaken' and 100 failed. Gilbart (1837: 109), however, reports only twenty-two bankruptcies. The demand for cash was felt in Scotland as well. Two of the Glasgow banks (the Arms Banks and the Merchant Banking Co.) succumbed in March, but both met their liabilities in full. Hamilton notes that 'other banks weathered the storm by paying out freely and by helping each other' (1963: 334). The house of Sir William Forbes, James Hunter & Co., alone extended more than a quarter of a million pounds to other houses. Most of the distress experienced by Scottish businesses was attributed at the time to the tightness of the London discount market.

An even greater trade crisis occurred in 1797. An ongoing outflow of gold prompted the Bank of England to restrict its discounts in 1795. This action checked the external drain temporarily, but an internal drain (public redemption of bank notes following a rise in the domestic demand to hold gold, attributable to reduced confidence in bank obligations) became serious in the following year. An alarm caused in February 1797 by threat of French invasion accelerated the drain and finally led the Bank of England, with the permission of the Privy Council, to suspend payment on its notes. The suspension was approved by Parliament and was not to be lifted until 1821. Scottish banks confronted only a minor internal drain, as noted by Henry Thornton in his account of the events of 1797:

> The fear of an invasion took place, and it led to the sudden failure of some country banks in the north of England. Other parts felt the influence of the alarm, those in Scotland, in a great measure, excepted, where, through long use, the confidence of the people, even in paper money of a guinea value, is so great (a circumstance to which the peculiar respectability of the Scotch banks has contributed), that the distress for gold was little felt in that part of the island. A great demand on the Bank of England was thus created . . . on the account of people in the country.
>
> (Thornton 1802: 112–13)

Upon receiving news of the suspension, the managers of the four leading banks in Edinburgh at this time – the Bank of Scotland, the Royal Bank, the British Linen Company, and Forbes, Hunter & Co. – met and decided to follow the Bank of England's example. Had they made specie available while the Bank of England refused, they feared English demand would rapidly have drained them of their reserves. The suspension of convertibility by Scottish banks was illegal under the Act of 1765, but curiously enough no one seems to have challenged them seriously in court.[15] There is evidence (Checkland 1975: 222) that in practice the banks continued quietly to redeem some notes for favoured customers. The suspension brought on a severe disequilibrium in the denominational structure of Scottish currency. The banks would officially no longer give change, and the public hoarded gold and silver coins. The public resorted to making change by tearing £1 notes into halves and quarters, and token coins (though illegal under the Act of 1765) began to be issued by merchants, until the issue of fractional notes by existing banks was temporarily authorized by Parliament.

The period of the suspension provided no let-up in English country bank failures. Thomas Joplin observed that 300 bankruptcies of English banks had occurred in the thirty years prior to 1821, 'an average of failures . . . in all probability far exceeding that of any regular business' (1826: 5). He noted that no Scottish joint-stock bank had failed in over forty years. McCulloch reported that 'no fewer than ninety-two commissions of bankruptcy were issued against English country banks' during the period 1814–16: 'and one in every seven and a half of the total of these establishments existing in 1813 . . . was entirely destroyed' (1826: 272). An annual record of country bank licensures and bankruptcies for the period 1809–30 is provided by the history of Gilbart (1837: 110). This record is reproduced as columns 1 and 2 of Table 9.3. The differing bankruptcy statistics of Pressnell (1956) are also shown. From Gilbart's figures a failure rate has been computed (column 3) and compared with the failure rate for Scottish banks (column 5). The table shows that over this period the average annual failure rate was more than twice as high for English banks as for Scottish banks.[16]

The crash of 1825–6, attributable to Bank of England policy, brought down a number of England's most reputable country banks and London banking houses as well as scores of smaller banks. A single month in 1825 saw seventy-three banks stop payment, only ten of which eventually resumed business. One member of Parliament took note that 700 or 800 country banks – virtually the entire industry – had asked the Bank of England for assistance during the general panic. The Bank of England itself, in the words of Bagehot (1873: 15), 'was within an ace of stopping payment' due to depleted specie reserves. Gilbart records eighty commissions of bankruptcy issued against English country bankers for the years 1825–6. Macleod puts the number at seventy-six, but adds that 'from the different ways of making compositions, etc, the number of failures should probably be estimated at four times the number of commissions of bankruptcy' (1866: vol. 2, 103). Repercussions of the distress reached Scotland in late 1825, but unsettled only four small members of the banking trade. One retired, apparently still solvent, in 1825; another was taken over by the Commercial Bank of Scotland in 1825 with no inconvenience to depositors or noteholders; a third failed in 1826 but paid its liabilities in full; and the Fife Banking Co. stopped payment in 1825 but did not wind up until 1829 (Checkland 1975: 314–15).

English joint-stock banks, newly legalized by the Act of 1826, sprang up in great numbers in the English countryside after further liberalization of entry in 1833. Over 200 fresh banks were established in the years 1835 and 1836, a period of Bank of England expansion. Their inexperience in maintaining adequate reserves became evident in the panic of 1837, precipitated by the Bank of England being compelled to reverse course and contract. 'In the heavy losses and banking failures which ensued,' one historian notes in passing, 'Scotland had little share' (Graham 1911: 202). Robert Bell commented that 'while England, during the past year, has suffered in almost every branch of her national industry, Scotland has passed comparatively uninjured through the late monetary crisis' (1838: 8).

Table 9.3 English and Scottish bank failures, 1809–30

Year	Licensed English note issuers [a] (1)	English bankruptcies [b] (Gilbart) (2)	English bankruptcies [b] (Presnell) (2)	English bankruptcies per thousand (3)	Scottish banks year end (4)	Scottish bankruptcies per thousand (5)
1809	702	4	5	5.7	37	0
1810	782	20	13	25.6	38	26.3
1811	789	4	11	5.1	37	0
1812	825	17	11	20.6	37	0
1813	922	8	6	8.7	36	27.8
1814	940	27	20	28.7	37	0
1815	916	25	33	27.3	37	0
1816	831	37	16	44.5	36	27.8
1817	752	3	1	4.0	36	0
1818	765	3	8	3.9	37	0
1819	787	13	9	16.5	37	0
1820	769	4	6	5.2	37	0
1821	781	10	12	12.8	36	0
1822	776	9	5	11.6	35	28.6
1823	779	9	11	11.6	35	0
1824	788	10	3	12.8	35	0

Year	Licensed English note issuers [a] (1)	English bankruptcies [b] (Gilbart) (2)	(Presnell)	English bankruptcies per thousand (3)	Scottish banks year end (4)	Scottish bankruptcies per thousand (5)
1825	797	37	60	46.4	36	27.8
1826	809	43	–	53.1	35	28.6
1827	668	8	–	11.9	35	0
1828	672	3	–	4.5	35	0
1829	677	3	–	4.4	34	29.4
1830	671	14	–	20.9	36	0
Total	–	311	–	–	–	–
Average year	781.7	14.1	–	18.1	36.1	7.8

Notes:

[a]Beginning 1808 a licensing duty was imposed on note-issuing English banks. The number of licensed note issuers represents roughly, but probably overstates, the number of country banks, because banks having more than one note-issuing office were required to take out a separate license for each office up to the fourth. On the other hand, non-issuing banks were not licensed. If the figures in column (1) overstate the number of country banks, then the figures for bankruptcies per thousand in column (3) are biased downward. An earlier version of this table in White (1984, p. 48) adjusted the Scottish figures similarly by counting a bank's first three branches as separate banks, but because Scottish banks were more commonly branched, this adjustment probably biased the Scottish bankruptcy rate figures downward more severely. Columns (4) and (5) are not adjusted in this way, so that the computation is now most likely biased *against* showing lower rates in Scotland. The Scottish bankruptcy rates now shown are consequently higher than those appearing in the earlier version of this table. Column (5) has also been revised to square the years in which Scottish bank failures are recorded with the accounts of Munn (1981b) and Checkland (1975); I thank Larry J. Sechrest for drawing my attention to previous discrepancies.

[b]Although Gilbart (1837) and Pressnell (1956) offer differing figures on the number of English bank failures in each year 1809–25, their totals for those years are the same.

Sources: Gilbart (1837: 110); Pressnell (1956: 538); Checkland (1975: 177–9, 320–21); Munn (1981b: 69, 86–7).

ACKNOWLEDGEMENT

I thank Cambridge University Press for permission to reprint this essay, with revisions, from White (1984b: ch. 2).

NOTES

1 The original version of this chapter overstated the case when it said that Scottish banking had 'virtually no' political regulation and 'complete' freedom of entry. An Act of 1765, mentioned below, banned banknotes that gave the issuer an option to delay redemption, and also banned notes smaller than one pound. Contractual limitation of bank-owners' liability was not freely allowed. All of these were regulatory barriers to entry, though I do not believe they significantly impeded competition in practice. See White (1990a; 1990b).

2 This section draws its historical facts primarily from the works of Checkland (1975), Munn (1981), Graham (1911), Kerr (1884), Boase (1867), Munro (1928), and Wenley (1882). Other earlier accounts are Fleming (1877) and Somers (1873).

3 This event incidentally inspired Scotsman John Law to the belief that a bank run could correspondingly be forestalled at any time by an announcement of an imminent devaluation of coin. That belief was put to the test in Law's ill-fated Mississippi Scheme.

4 Strictly speaking, the Bank of Scotland was not created by royal charter, but by act of the Scottish Parliament. It is none the less expedient to refer to the Bank of Scotland and the Royal Bank of Scotland (and the British Linen Company, after 1746) as 'the chartered banks'.

5 I am indebted to Larry Sechrest for pointing out that my previous figure of eight was in conflict with Checkland (1975: 132).

6 The original version of this chapter said that settlement was also made in Exchequer bills, but I have been unable to discover the basis for that statement.

7 This contradicts Cowen and Kroszner (1989: 226), who hypothesize that the charters of the public banks had the effect of 'reducing competitive pressures (hence relaxing the zero-profit condition)' throughout the free banking period. My response here draws on White (1990a; 1990b).

8 In stating my conclusion this way, I am admittedly downplaying the fact that the Scottish banks, like other banks typically, produced a number of outputs jointly with bank note services.

9 This theme has been emphasized by Cameron (1967: ch. 3). For a contrary view see Checkland (1968). For rejoinders see Cameron (1982) and White (1990a: 38–42). Of course, Scotland did not enjoy literally *perfect* freedom. See n. 1 above.

10 More precisely, only the Bank of Scotland, the Royal Bank of Scotland and the British Linen Company enjoyed limited liability during the free banking era. The Commercial Bank and the National Bank were granted charters in 1831, but these charters expressly retained unlimited liability. On the question of the liability of joint-stock companies in Scotland, see

Campbell (1967); on the liability of the banks in particular, see Logan (1839: 1).

11 Munn (1981: 141) provides statistics on the ratios of specie to demand liabilities held by six provincial Scottish banking companies during various decades. In the second half of the eighteenth century their ratios, averaged for each bank by decades, stood between 10 and 20 per cent in six out of ten cases reported, and over 20 per cent in one case. In the first half of the nineteenth century the ratios were substantially lower, ranging from 0.5 to 3.2 per cent. The drop may be attributed to lower costs of obtaining specie on short notice and possibly to lower risk of substantial specie outflows.

The claim that Scottish banks held much of their reserves in the form of Bank of England liabilities, and thus characteristically 'pyramided credit on top of the Bank of England' (Rothband 1988: 231; see also Sechrest 1988: 247), is in error. See White (1990a: 49–53).

12 This point is made by Vera Smith (1990 [1936]: 170).

13 In order that the 'natural system' may prevail it is important that the central government not play favourites in placing its deposits among the banks. This was an issue that concerned the Jacksonian free banking advocates in the United States (e.g., Leggett 1984: 119–26) and led to their insistence on an 'independent Treasury'. The argument that a favoured bank of the central government must play a special role in the banking system and tends to become a central bank has recently been raised as an objection to Hayek's (1978) proposal for 'denationalization of money' by Congdon (1981). This argument may be regarded not as pointing to an insurmountable obstacle to free banking, however, but merely as re-emphasizing the importance of government neutrality toward banks in placing its deposits.

14 The evidence that follows is suggestive. It is certainly not a substitute for a detailed comparative study of Scottish and English business cycles.

15 It is not immediately clear why the Scottish banks (and likewise the English country banks) did not remain tied to specie and let their currency float against the Bank of England note. One answer focusing on the banks' self-interest points to the fact that, London being Britain's financial centre, suspensions by the London banks made the Scottish banks unable to get extra gold from their correspondent banks or from sale of securities in the London market. In other words, their secondary reserves were immobilized. Another answer, focusing on the self-interest of Scottish bank customers, suggests that they preferred a note convertible into what had become London's basic cash due to the importance of trade with London. In other words, Britain as a whole was the natural currency area.

Irish banks, by the way, were directed to suspend by the British government, a directive ratified by the Irish parliament. Northern Ireland, where bank notes did not circulate, continued on the gold coin standard. On this see Fetter (1955: 12–16).

16 The limitation of the table to the years 1809–30 is due to the limitation of Gilbart's figures to those years.

10 Free banking in Switzerland after the liberal revolutions in the nineteenth century

Ernst Juerg Weber

THE LIBERAL REGIME: 1830–81

The development of the Swiss monetary system is closely linked to the political evolution of Switzerland from a loose association of independent states to a federal republic.[1] After liberal revolutions in the 1830s and 40s, several Swiss cantons deregulated their financial systems, chartering new banks and allowing the free issue of paper money. Private bankers with ties to the aristocracy had dominated earlier Swiss commercial banking, but by the mid-1840s the liberals had gained control of the industrialized cantons in the rolling plains between the Alps and the Jura mountains. A rift then developed between the industrialized cantons and the Alpine cantons on the question of federation. The conflict was aggravated by the fact that the population of the industrialized cantons was Protestant, whereas that of the Alpine cantons was Catholic. After a brief civil war in 1848, the victorious liberals transformed Switzerland into a federal republic. The new federal government removed the cantonal barriers to the free movement of goods, capital and people which had impeded earlier industrialization. It also reformed the Swiss currency system and replaced the large number of cantonal and local currencies with a new unified currency – the Swiss franc.

The cantons retained jurisdiction over the issue of paper money until the enactment of the Federal Banking Law in 1881. The steady increase in the number of banks that issued bank notes suggests that in most cantons it was easy to get a charter to issue notes. The first Swiss bank that issued notes was the Depositokasse der Stadt Bern, which was set up by the City of Berne in 1826. It was followed by the Kantonalbank von Bern in 1834, and the Bank in Zürich and Bank in St Gallen in 1837–8. The number of issuers continued to rise until it reached thirty-six in 1880. There was one note-issuing bank per 80,000

Table 10.1 The Swiss issuers of paper money, 1829–1906

Banks	(A)	(B)	Bank notes[a] 1840	1850	1860	1870	1880	1890	1900
I Commercial banks									
1 Bank in Zürich	1837–1906	1837–94	873	1,651	2,154	1,753	4,964	19,873	–
2 Bank in St. Gallen	1837–1907	1838–1907	598	1,967	1,580	1,364	3,986	8,984	17,860
3 Bank in Basel	1844–1907	1845–1907	–	1,179	809	1,277	7,874	19,687	23,825
4 Banque du Commerce de Genève	1846–1907	1846–1907	–	2,025	1,798	3,172	16,214	19,915	23,903
5 Banque de Genève	1848	1848–99	–	328	927	1,526	4,657	4,820	–
6 Banque Cantonale Neuchâteloise[b]	1855–83	1855–83	–	–	1,372	1,982	5,935	–	–
7 Banque Générale Suisse	1853–69	1857–69	–	–	58	–	–	–	–
8 Eidgenössische Bank	1864	1864–82	–	–	–	933	4,883	–	–
9 Banque Commercial Neuchâteloise	1883–1907	1883–1907	–	–	–	–	–	3,352	7,969
II Cantonal banks									
10 Kantonalbank von Bern	1834	1834–1910	217	200	579	1,685	7,644	9,692	19,463
11 Banque Cantonale Vaudoise	1864	1847–1910	–	350	3,666	3,385	5,054	9,874	11,384
12 Aargauische Bank	1855	1856–1910	–	–	250	315	2,610	3,961	5,888
13 Banque Cantonale du Valais	1858–70	1858–70	–	–	399	–	–	–	–
14 Solothurnische Kantonalbank[c]	1857	1858–1910	–	–	138	388	2,020	3,984	4,954
15 Basellandschaftliche Kantonalbank	1864	1867–1910	–	–	–	28	713	1,499	1,989
16 St. Gallische Kantonalbank	1868	1868–1910	–	–	–	1,418	5,948	9,982	13,981

Table 10.1 The Swiss issuers of paper money, 1829–1906 (continued)

Banks	(A)	(B)	Bank notes[a]						
			1840	1850	1860	1870	1880	1890	1900
17 Zürcher Kantonalbank	1870	1870–1910	–	–	–	1,897	14,042	23,653	29,328
18 Thurgauische Kantonalbank	1871	1871–1910	–	–	–	–	1,289	1,483	4,974
19 Graubündner Kantonalbank	1870	1873–1910	–	–	–	–	1,988	2,976	3,923
20 Caisse d'amortissements de la dette publique Fribourg[d]	1868–93	1874–93	–	–	–	–	746	1,468	–
21 Luzerner Kantonalbank	1850	1877–1910	–	–	–	–	984	1,985	5,694
22 Appenzell A.-Rh. Kantonalbank	1877	1877–1910	–	–	–	–	1,978	2,976	2,979
23 Ersparniskasse des Kantons Uri	1837	1878–1910	–	–	–	–	261	498	1,450
24 Nidwaldner Kantonalbank	1879	1879–1910	–	–	–	–	175	497	995
25 Banque Cantonale Neuchâteloise	1883	1883–1910	–	–	–	–	–	2,962	7,981
26 Schaffhauser Kantonalbank	1883	1883–1910	–	–	–	–	–	1,495	2,462
27 Glarner Kantonalbank	1884	1884–1910	–	–	–	–	–	1,489	2,481
28 Obwaldner Kantonalbank	1887	1887–1910	–	–	–	–	–	493	983
29 Kantonalbank Schwyz	1890	1890–1910	–	–	–	–	–	500	2,974
30 Zuger Kantonalbank	1892	1893–1910	–	–	–	–	–	–	2,967
31 Banque de l'Etat de Fribourg	1893	1893–1910	–	–	–	–	–	–	4,948
32 Basler Kantonalbank	1899	1900–10	–	–	–	–	–	–	–
33 Appenzell I.-Rh. Kantonalbank	1900	1900–10	–	–	–	–	–	–	–

Table 10.1 The Swiss issuers of paper money, 1829–1906 (continued)

Banks	(A)	(B)	Bank notes[a]						
			1840	1850	1860	1870	1880	1890	1900
III Local Banks									
34 Depositokasse der Stadt Berne[e]	1826	1826–69	170	87	9	–	–	–	–
35 Banque Cantonale Fribourgeoise	1850–1910	1851–1910	–	–	330	378	1,677	996	1,246
36 Thurgauische Hypothekenbank	1852–1914	1852–1908	–	–	470	322	735	963	983
37 Bank in Glarus	1852–1912	1852–82	–	–	492	657	1,275	–	–
38 Bank in Luzern	1857–1912	1857–1907	–	–	125	216	1,969	3,987	4,977
39 Banque Populaire de la Gruyère	1853	1857–92	–	–	–	65	168	173	–
40 Banca Cantonale Ticinese	1861–1914	1861–1908	–	–	–	168	2,119	1,952	1,894
41 Bank für Graubünden	1862	1863–82	–	–	–	108	693	–	–
42 Bank in Schaffhausen	1862	1863–1908	–	–	–	136	667	1,989	3,424
43 Toggenburger Bank	1863–1912	1864–1907	–	–	–	350	987	990	978
44 Banque Populaire de la Broye	1864	1865–82	–	–	–	18	18	–	–
45 Caisse Hypothécaire du Canton de Fribourg	1854	1865–82	–	–	–	115	22	–	–
46 Crédit Agricole et Industriel de la Broye	1866	1867–1910	–			70	216	799	994
47 Leihkasse Glarus[f]	1863–84	1870–84				92	292	–	–
48 Banca della Svizzera Italiana	1873	1874–1907				–	1,395	1,996	1,991
49 Crédit Gruyérien	1873	1874–92				–	163	170	–
50 Credito Ticinese	1890–1914	1891–1907				–	–	–	2,231
51 Banca Populare di Lugano	1888	1898–1910				–	–	–	1,992

(A) Years of operation. The final year is only shown if the banks closed before World War I. (B) Years in which bank notes were issued. (a) 1000 francs. End of year. (b) Succeeded by the Banque Commerciale Neuchâteloise and the (new) Banque Cantonale Neuchâteloise. (c) Before 1886 Solothurnische Bank. (d) Succeeded by the Banque de L'État de Fribourg. (e) The circulation of bank notes amounted to Fr. 88,000 in 1830. (f) Succeeded by the Glarner Kantonalbank.

Source: ...131y (1915, volume II, tables 1 and 2, diagram 1) people and at least one bank in twenty of the twenty-five cantons by then. Table 10.1 lists Swiss note-issuing banks between 1826 and 1906. There were three types of banks: incorporated commercial banks, cantonal banks run by cantonal governments, and local savings banks with private and municipal ownership. The table shows when the banks were in operation and when they supplied notes (columns 2 and 3), as well as the circulation of notes at the end of each decade (columns 4–10). The table does not include the aristocratic private bankers who abandoned the bank-note business (but not banking) in the 1840s.

In the liberal period the issue of paper money was free from government interference. Unlike modern central banks, the cantonal banks did not monopolize the circulation of paper money in their home cantons. And since there were no cantonal legal tender laws and the Federal Constitution of 1848 had removed all cantonal exchange controls, there was free currency substitution even in those cantons where the cantonal bank was the sole issuer of notes. Private banks were usually obliged to submit their articles of association to the cantonal government. These articles often included reserve and capital requirements and in some cases direct restrictions on the issue of notes. Yet these provisions did not constrain the banks' issuing power as most allowed for large margins and the authorities were usually ready to relax them when they interfered with the development of a bank. The banks included the restrictions in their articles in order to reassure the public. In particular, banks with nominally less restrictive articles did not grow faster than those with more stringent ones.[2] And in the early 1870s Swiss banks had no difficulty in expanding the circulation of bank notes more than threefold in response to a dramatic increase in the real demand for paper money. This important event will be discussed in due course.

Free entry implied that the number of note-issuing banks was determined by the net return from issuing notes. New banks took up the issue of bank notes until the return was equal to that from other business activities. It should be emphasized that the majority of Swiss banks did not supply notes, including several commercial banks that were formed in the second half of the nineteenth century and a large number of savings banks that had been set up in the first half of the century.[3] These banks stayed out of the note business, not because entry was restricted but because the return would have been too low. This view is confirmed by the fact that there were several banks that provided for the issue of bank notes in their articles of association without actually issuing notes.[4]

The large number of Swiss note-issuing banks disproves the popular notion that the issue of paper money constitutes a natural monopoly.[5] All banks experienced rising costs which limited the amount of bank notes that each bank could profitably keep in circulation. The largest banks operated in the industrial and commercial centres and in the fertile agricultural regions in the western part of Switzerland where the real demand for bank notes was high. But none of these banks dominated the Swiss monetary system. The note circulation of the large commercial banks actually stagnated from 1850 to 1870, and most of the increase in the total circulation in this period was accounted for by the issues of new local banks (See Table 10.1). In 1880 the Banque du Commerce de Genève was the largest issuer of bank notes, supplying 15 per cent of the Swiss circulation of paper money. The Zürcher Kantonalbank followed with 13 per cent, and the Bank in Basel and the Kantonalbank von Bern tied at 7 per cent.

The banks financed their assets by issuing bank notes and bonds and accepting demand and time deposits. Cost minimization required that each source of funds was employed until the costs of raising a franc through every source were equal. The banks paid interest on the bonds and time deposits and provided clearing services on the chequing accounts. The issue of bank notes was a costly source of funds because each bank faced a real demand for bank notes that depended on the usefulness of those notes in commercial transactions. Even the commercial banks in the industrial centres found it difficult to keep bank notes in circulation for a significant period of time. In 1855 the notes of the Bank in Basel on average returned to the bank after 36 days (Table 10.2). In 1865 they stayed in circulation for only 10.5 days, which is not much more than the time it now takes for a personal cheque to clear. In 1875, reflecting an increase in the real demand for paper money, the 100-franc notes stayed in circulation for 70 days, the 500-franc notes for 37 days and the 1,000-franc notes for 18 days. The large bank notes were less popular than the small-notes because people preferred to use cheques and bills of exchange as media of exchange in large commercial transactions.

The banks incurred costs for printing bank notes, for teller services and for storing specie reserves. But the most significant costs arose from clearing notes, which was a major concern of the banks because bank notes are only suitable as media of exchange if they are traded at par. Discounts that vary with market conditions reduce the real demand for bank notes by imposing information costs on the users of notes.[6] Therefore, the banks concluded a large number of clearing agreements in which they agreed to accept each others'

Table 10.2 The duration of the circulation of the bank notes of the Bank in Basel, 1851–1905 (days)

Year	Face Values (francs)			
	50	100	500	1,000
1851		154	162	
1855		36[a]		
1860		22[a]		
1865		10.5[a]		
1870		31	10	
1875		70	37	18
1880	126	99	34	23
1885	203	128	41	24
1890	215	183	52	34
1895	304	210	65	38
1900	272	173	71	60
1905	355	300	121	153

Source: Mangold (1909)

Note: [a] Fr. 100 and Fr. 500

notes either at par or at a predetermined discount. These clearing agreements could be very costly because the banks had to cover the transport of gold and silver when inter-regional trade flows did not match. As a consequence, the banks continuously renegotiated the agreements. In fact, the clearing agreements provided a sensitive

Table 10.3 The share of bank notes in the balance sheets of Swiss note-issuing banks, 1826–1906 (%)

Year	Commercial Banks[a]	Cantonal Banks	Local Banks[a]	All Banks
1831– 40	19.2[b]	4.4[c]	10.8	11.1
1841– 50	25.2	3.5	5.6	16.9
1851– 60	20.9	9.4	4.4	12.9
1861– 70	13.8	6.8	3.5	7.3
1871– 80	31.7	10.2	8.3	13.6
1881– 90	41.9	11.8	8.6	16.1
1891–1900	47.4	12.1	8.5	15.7
1901– 6	50.9	9.6	7.2	12.3

Source: Jöhr (1915: Volume II, table 4)

Note: [a] The Banque Générale Suisse and the Eidgenössische Bank are included among the local banks.
[b] 1838–40.
[c] 1835–40.

Table 10.4 The Swiss bank-note circulation, 1825–1906[a]

1826–1850		1851–1880		1881–1906	
		1851	7,667	1881	99,401
		1852	8,335	1882	98,235
		1853	10,920	1883	102,228
		1854	10,816	1884	114,801
		1855	11,291	1885	123,431
1826	35	1856	12,262	1886	127,064
1827	71	1857	13,900	1887	134,835
1828	90	1858	14,177	1888	139,637
1829	50	1859	13,752	1889	145,461
1830	58	1860	13,826	1890	152,444
1831	84	1861	12,697	1891	163,487
1832	40	1862	14,939	1892	163,344
1833	23	1863	16,004	1893	167,369
1834	87	1864	16,831	1894	171,285
1835	181	1865	17,818	1895	179,221
1836	458	1866	18,276	1896	190,155
1837	335	1867	16,537	1897	199,415
1838	1,171	1868	17,466	1898	207,665
1839	1,991	1869	18,465	1899	214,685
1840	2,050	1870	18,982	1900	216,673
1841	2,472	1871	24,822	1901	214,456
1842	2,720	1872	31,613	1902	222,963
1843	2,711	1873	47,804	1903	221,811
1844	2,564	1874	65,376	1904	228,431
1845	2,929	1875	77,290	1905	233,466
1846	3,737	1876	80,594	1906	234,897
1847	3,937	1877	83,135		
1848	5,575	1878	82,580		
1849	6,556	1879	83,664		
1850	7,582	1880	92,851		

Source: Jöhr (1915: 496).
Note: [a] 1,000 francs. Annual averages of monthly figures.

tool for the management of the bank-note circulation (and specie reserves) because they directly affected the usefulness of bank notes as media of exchange.

As bank notes were a costly source of funds, their share in the balance sheets of banks was low, fluctuating between 7.3 per cent in the 1860s and 16.9 per cent in the 1840s (Table 10.3). Moreover, the share of notes was much lower for cantonal banks and local banks than for commercial banks. This is not surprising in the case of local banks which operated in the less developed regions of Switzerland where the real demand for bank notes was low. But in most cantons the issue of bank notes by the cantonal bank was privileged in one way or another. The notes of the cantonal banks were usually guaranteed by the cantonal government, and they could be used at par for tax payments and other transactions with cantonal authorities. In addition, in the 1870s private banks in some cantons were subject to regulations and taxes that did not apply to cantonal banks. Yet despite these advantages, the cantonal banks were not able to drive out the private banks as issuers of paper money. The poor performance of the cantonal banks suggests that in a competitive monetary system government banks do not have a comparative advantage in issuing paper money.

THE FEDERAL REGIME: 1881–1906

In the 1860s and 1870s the political tide turned against the liberals. The popular dissatisfaction with the *laissez-faire* policy of the liberals, which had led to the rapid restructuring and industrialization of the Swiss economy, gave rise to the so-called democratic movement. After constitutional reforms, several cantons in the north-eastern part of Switzerland became active in economic and social regulation. The democratic movement did not spread to the western cantons, where the radical wing of the liberals had already anticipated parts of the democratic platform, in particular the demand for cantonal banks. (The radicals had established the Kantonalbank von Bern, the Banque Cantonal Vaudoise and the Banque de Genève immediately after the revolutions in the 1830s and 1840s.)

The democratic cantons set up cantonal banks and regulated the private issue of bank notes. By the end of the century there were twenty-one cantonal banks. Several cantons imposed a tax of 1 per cent per annum on the circulation of private notes. This was a substantial rate, considering that the banks could raise funds through current accounts that were usually interest free. Despite these regulations, the degree of competition remained high in the Swiss monetary system in the 1870s – and it was actually increased by the newly established cantonal banks. Zürich was the only canton where the private issue of bank notes was seriously affected. The cantonal banking law of 1869 imposed substantial costs on the Bank in Zürich, accounting for the subsequent rise in the circulation of notes of the Zürcher Kantonalbank relative to that of the Bank in Zürich. In 1880 the circulation of the cantonal bank amounted to 14 million francs, whereas that of the Bank in Zürich was only 5 million (see Table 10.1). In 1876 the voters passed a referendum that would have made the cantonal bank the sole issuer of paper money in the canton of Zürich. The Bank in Zürich, however, successfully appealed to the federal government.

In 1874 the federal constitution was revised along democratic lines after a more radical draft had been narrowly defeated in a referendum two years earlier. The revised constitution authorized the federal government to regulate the issue of paper money and provided the basis for the Federal Banking Law of 1881. Although a large number of banks continued to issue bank notes until the Swiss National Bank took over between 1907 and 1910, the free issue of paper money had ended in Switzerland by 1881. The following are the most important provisions of the Federal Banking Law. (i) The issue of paper money was restricted to incorporated banks and cantonal banks, and private individuals were excluded. This was no longer of much importance because the private bankers, who had issued notes under the aristocrats, had already voluntarily abandoned the bank-note business. (ii) The banks were required to hold at least 40 per cent of their bank note circulation as specie reserves. In addition, those banks whose notes were not guaranteed by a canton had either to hold the remaining 60 per cent in the form of approved domestic and foreign government securities or, under very restrictive conditions, as commercial bills. This regulation strongly favoured the cantonal banks. (iii) The capital had to amount to at least one third of the bank-note circulation. (iv) Each bank was required to accept the bank notes of the other banks at par as long as those banks redeemed their bank notes on demand. (v) The tax that the cantons could levy on the circulation of bank notes was reduced to a maximum of 0.6 per cent. In addition, there were federal and cantonal fees of 0.2 per cent. (vi) The federal government provided the banks with standardized bank notes with face values from 50 to 1,000 francs. Earlier, notes with smaller face values were common. (vii) The banks were required to submit weekly and monthly statements to the federal government and they were regularly examined by the Eidgenössische Noteninspektorat.

Despite the fact that the banking law of 1881 put the private banks at a disadvantage, the cantonal banks could only raise their share in the total circulation of bank notes from 43 per cent in 1880 to 47 per cent in 1890 and that mainly because the Eidgenössische Bank (the name is best translated as the Confederate Bank of Switzerland) and five small banks ceased to issue notes (see Table 10. 1). Then, in an 1891 referendum, voters authorized the federal government to establish a central bank. As it became clear that the issue of paper money would soon be nationalized, the Bank in Zürich and the Banque de Genève phased out the bank-note business. Belatedly and not very successfully, the Bank in Zürich tried to join the group of commercial banks that did not issue bank notes; in 1905 it merged with the Schweizerische Kreditanstalt. These further exits raised the share of cantonal banks in the total circulation of notes to 60 per cent by 1900.

THE PURCHASING POWER OF THE BANK NOTES

Competition forced the Swiss banks to issue their bank notes as unconditional promises to redeem to the bearer on demand in specie currencies. Before the enactment of the Federal Banking Law of 1881 the banks could easily have provided for suspensions of payments in their articles of association. This would have lowered the costs of issuing bank notes by reducing the need for specie reserves. Yet the banks did not provide for suspensions of payments because each faced a real demand for bank notes that was very sensitive to changes in the purchasing power of those notes. Indeed, in a competitive monetary system the issuers of bank notes cannot keep depreciating notes in circulation because people can easily substitute notes. Therefore, the marginal revenue of inflating is negative and each issuer is a 'price level taker'.

The Swiss banks denominated their bank notes in the specie units in use in commercial transactions in order to reduce the information costs to the users of their notes. Before the currency reform all but one bank used foreign currency units which had driven out the debased cantonal and local currencies in commercial transactions.[7] The Depositokasse der Stadt Bern, which denominated its bank notes in the so-called old Swiss franc, was not able to keep a significant amount of notes in circulation. The old franc was a silver unit of account that had been adopted by nineteen cantons for transactions with the embryonic federal administration in 1819.[8] The users of those notes incurred information costs because, as there were no coins denominated in old francs, they faced the risk to be redeemed in the momentarily least valuable silver currency. Similarly, the circulation of bank notes of the Bank in Zürich fell when that bank rendered the purchasing power of its bank notes uncertain by making them either redeemable in French gold francs or in silver brabanterthaler in the period from 1841 to 1847.

In 1850 the federal government replaced the cantonal and local currencies with the Swiss franc. Switzerland was on the silver standard from 1850 to 1860 and on a bimetallic standard afterwards. The silver and gold parities of the Swiss franc equalled those of the French franc.[9] The currency reform of 1850 coincided with a worldwide rise in the price of silver relative to gold, and *French* gold coins drove out the new Swiss silver coins. This was in violation of Swiss legal tender laws and several creditors took legal action (see Banque Nationale Suisse 1925: 4). Nevertheless, by the mid-1850s there had been a complete reversal in the unit of account. In particular, Swiss banks used French gold coins at par, implying that domestic silver coins were traded at a premium. The breakdown of the Swiss legal tender laws is a unique occurrence. People accepted the overvalued French gold coins at par because the domestic silver coins were inconvenient in commercial transactions. The face value of the only full-valued silver coin – the écu – was five francs, whereas gold coins reached 100 francs.[10] In 1860 the federal government sanctioned the *de facto* use of foreign gold coins by making the gold coins of France and Sardinia legal tender.

The Swiss banks were free to choose the currency denomination of their bank notes until the enactment of the Federal Banking Law in 1881 or, in some cantons, of the democratic banking laws. The banks voluntarily adopted the new Swiss franc when it became used in commercial transactions in the early 1850s, and they deliberately switched from the domestic silver franc to the French gold franc when the latter drove out the former in the mid-1850s. In 1852 the Bank in Zürich and the Bank in St Gallen issued notes both in Swiss francs and in the foreign currency units that they had used before the currency reform. But the demand for old bank notes turned out to be small and the two banks abandoned them after several months. The public preferred new bank notes because the exchange rate fluctuations between the franc and the formerly used foreign currencies imposed information costs on the users of old notes. This sheds light on the nature of money. The inability of the banks to keep their old notes in circulation after the introduction of the franc shows that bank notes were primarily demanded for transactions purposes. There was no asset demand for old notes because people who wished to hold foreign exchange invested in interest-yielding bills of exchange that arose from international trade.

In 1865 Belgium, France, Italy and Switzerland founded the Latin Monetary Union, and three years later they were joined by Greece. The members of the union shared a common monetary base that consisted of the full-valued coins of the participating countries. The Bank of France provided for the free coinage of gold and silver in Switzerland. The Swiss government did not mint gold coins until the 1880s and it only supplied a limited amount of écus. Unlike the supply of paper money,

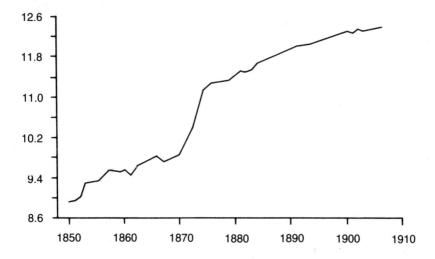

Figure 10.1 Swiss bank notes, 1850–1906 (natural log)
Source: See Table 10.4

the supply of *full-valued* coins involves economies of scale that give rise to a natural monopoly. Therefore, small countries cannot compete with large countries in the production of full-valued coins.[11] The Latin Monetary Union suffered from the shortcomings of bimetallism. In the early 1870s the fall in the price of silver relative to gold led to the massive coinage of écus, which drove out the gold coins. Between 1874 and 1878 the free coinage of silver was phased out, giving rise to a substantial overvaluation of the écu. Afterwards, the union was *de facto* on an écu standard. The Swiss banks continued to redeem their bank notes in the momentarily circulating coins until the Federal Banking Law required them to use legal tender.

THE CIRCULATION OF BANK NOTES

The Swiss circulation of bank notes rose from 7.6 million francs in 1850 to 234.9 million in 1906 (Figure 10.1). This increase represents a rise in the real demand for paper money as Switzerland was on a succession of specie standards with no significant increase in the price level. The available price figures confirm that the inflation

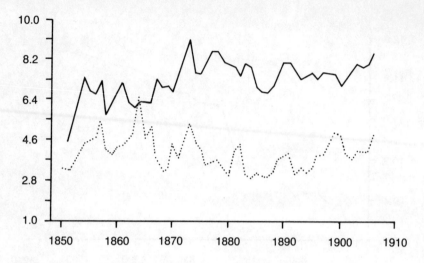

Figure 10.2 Swiss prices and interest rates, 1850–1906
Source: Prices: Brugger (1978: 251); interest rates: Jöhr (1915: 508)

rate was small in the long-run. Despite large price changes in the short-term, the average price of agricultural products remained almost unchanged in the second half of the nineteenth century (Figure 10.2). In addition, the interest rate on commercial bills fluctuated between 3 and 6.5 per cent. The circulation of paper money expanded in three stages with moderate monetary growth until the 1860s, rapid expansion in the early 1870s, and again moderate growth afterwards. Excluding the early 1870s, the annual rate of growth in the circulation of paper money amounted to 4.4 per cent from 1850 to 1870 and to 3.7 per cent from 1875 to 1906. These figures provide estimates for the trend in real output, if it is assumed that changes in real output induced proportional changes in the real demand for paper money.

Economic growth cannot by itself explain the surge in the circulation of paper money in the early 1870s. From 1870 to 1875 it jumped from 19.0 million to 77.3 million francs. This amounts to an expansion by a full 307 per cent at an annual rate of 32.4 per cent. It should be noted that an increase in the real demand for paper money accounts for most of the increase in the circulation of paper money. From the 1860s to the 1870s food prices rose by only 22.6 per cent (Figure 10.1). Three factors explain the dramatic increase in the real demand for paper money in the early 1870s:

1 In July 1870 France declared war on Prussia. During the war the convertibility of the bank notes of the Bank of France was suspended and France resorted to exchange controls. This gave rise to a peculiar situation in the Latin Monetary Union. Swiss bank notes continued to be redeemable in French gold francs, whereas French bank notes were no longer redeemable. As seen, there were no Swiss gold coins and the silver and gold parities of the Swiss franc equalled those of the French franc. In the following months Swiss (and Belgian) bank notes drove out the depreciating French bank notes (certainly outside France and to some extent also in France) as the public preferred bank notes with stable purchasing power. In particular, the banks in the French-speaking part of Switzerland benefited from the additional demand for Swiss bank notes. The bank note circulation of the Banque du Commerce de Genève by far exceeded that of the other banks at the end of 1870 (see Table 10.1). The experience of the Bank of France shows that even a large government bank cannot keep depreciating bank notes in circulation if it has to compete with other banks. The Swiss banks would have captured a substantial market share in the French districts at the Swiss border had there been no exchange controls. This incident also shows that in a competitive monetary system the majority of banks will maintain the purchasing power of their bank notes if a large bank breaks ranks by depreciating its notes. The war-induced increase in the demand for Swiss bank notes contributed to the increase in the circulation of paper money in 1870–1.

2 The public substituted bank notes for silver money on a large scale. In the 1850s and 1860s the price of silver in terms of gold was above the ratio implied by the gold and silver parities of the franc, and hence gold coins served as media of exchange. The real demand for bank notes was small because they did not provide a decisive advantage over gold coins in commercial transactions. Gold coins involved low information costs because they did not carry a default risk, and they were almost as convenient to handle as bank notes as their size was small and their face values overlapped with those of the popular small-notes. The extremely short duration of the circulation of bank notes of the Bank in Basel (see Table 10.2) and the small share of notes in the balance sheets of all banks (see Table 10.3) confirm that the real demand for bank notes was low when gold coins were used as media of exchange in the 1860s. In 1872 the price of silver fell and the silver écu replaced the gold coins as media of exchange. But the écu, whose face value was only

five francs, was not suitable for commercial transactions, and people substituted bank notes for écus until there arose a silver-reserve standard. The substitution of bank notes for écus accounts for most of the increase in the real demand for paper money in the early 1870s. It also explains why the increase in the circulation of paper money was permanent as the gold coins never returned.[12]

3 Real output expanded strongly and raised the real demand for bank notes. The early 1870s are known as the *Gründerjahre* (foundation years) in the German-speaking countries. The economic boom ended with the financial crash in Vienna in 1873 but the Swiss economy prospered for another two years. Monetary factors partly accounted for the expansion of the Swiss economy. The substitution of bank notes for silver money had provided the banks with a large amount of base money. Despite an import boom that must have given rise to a current account deficit, the specie reserves of the banks increased from 10.3 million francs in 1872 to 20.5 in 1874 (Jöhr 1915: vol. II, table 3). There exists no generally accepted estimate of the rise in Swiss real output. Still, it can be inferred that from the beginning of 1870 to the end of 1874 the expansion in real output raised the real demand for paper money by 47 per cent, if it is assumed that the demand for bank notes was as sensitive to changes in real output as the demand for bank deposits (Jöhr 1915: II, table 3). Although this is a substantial figure, it is only a small portion of the total increase in the demand for paper money in the early 1870s.

BANK DIFFICULTIES

The competitive issue of paper money provided a secure monetary system with only one bank failure. The Banque Cantonale du Valais failed as a result of the persistent cantonal budget deficits, thus foreshadowing the inflationary bias of modern central banks. The bank had granted substantial loans to the cantonal government which it had financed through borrowings from banks outside the canton. In addition, it also suffered loan losses. The bank collapsed when the cantonal legislative council refused an application for an issue of bonds for the refinancing of the bank's borrowings in 1870. Given the pressure of the cantonal government, this bank would almost certainly have overissued paper money had it been able to do so. But like the other banks, it was not able to keep large amounts of bank notes in circulation at a profit (see Table 10.1). It could not monetize the cantonal budget deficits because the real demand for bank notes was small in the rural canton of Valais. Moreover, it would not have been able to keep depreciating bank notes in circulation in the competitive Swiss monetary system. The failure of the cantonal bank led to a political scandal and the resignation of several executive councillors in the canton of Valais. The cantonal government eventually redeemed all bank notes at par.

Two banks aspired to a leading role in the Swiss financial system but both ran into difficulties. In 1853 the radical politician and financier James Fazy, who had already founded the Banque de Genève, established the Banque Générale Suisse. The bank, which was structured after the French *crédit mobilier*, operated as a finance company participating in railways, industrial companies and real estate. The capital was very large, exceeding the aggregate capital of all other Swiss banks that issued notes. The scope of the bank was international with a board of directors that included personalities from Geneva, Paris and London. The bank suffered heavy losses on its investments, and it experienced a run after the branch office in Paris had to defer payments over a weekend in April 1859. Within one day it had had to redeem two-thirds of its bank-note circulation of close to one million francs in value. Afterwards, there were prolonged take-over fights until the bank went into liquidation in 1870.

The founders of the Eidgenössische Bank intended to set up a private central bank. Accordingly, this bank was located in the capital of Switzerland (Berne), it was headed by a former member of the federal executive council, Jakob Stämpfli, and it issued bank notes with the Swiss emblem and German and French text. The bank, which was strongly opposed by the commercial banks, established an elaborate network of branches throughout Switzerland and it concluded a large number of clearing agreements with domestic and foreign banks. But it was only moderately successful, accounting for 7 per cent of the Swiss circulation of bank notes in 1869, after five years of operation. Then, it was hit by a massive fraud at the branch office in Zürich and had to be restructured. The difficulties of the Banque Générale Suisse and the Eidgenössische Bank confirm that the optimal size of banks was small in the competitive Swiss monetary system.

SUMMARY

The world-wide deregulation of financial markets has generated a renewed interest in monetary systems in which media of exchange are supplied competitively. Many models of competitive monetary systems have recently been developed, but empirical research is still in its infancy because in the twentieth century central banks have almost universally either directly or indirectly controlled the supply of currency. Thus it is necessary to reach back in time, before the formation of central banks, for the study of deregulated monetary systems.

The main finding of this chapter is that competition provided a stable monetary system in Switzerland in which the purchasing power of bank notes equalled that of specie and only one bank failed. The Swiss banks did not overissue bank notes because there was no demand for depreciating notes in the competitive Swiss monetary system. Each bank faced a real demand for bank notes that depended on the usefulness of those notes in commercial transactions. And the marginal revenue of inflating was negative for each bank because depreciating notes impose information costs on their users, and people could easily substitute notes. In contrast, modern central banks can inflate at a profit because (i) they have the exclusive right to issue currency and (ii) currency substitution is limited by legal tender laws and – if necessary – by exchange controls. The Swiss monetary system was also stable in the sense that rising costs prevented a central-bank-like monopoly by a single issuer.

ACKNOWLEDGEMENTS

I am indebted to Kenneth Clements, Kevin Dowd, Jürg Niehans, Larry Sjaastad and Pamela Statham for helpful comments. This chapter is based on a paper that originally appeared in *Kyklos*, 41 (3): 459–78.

NOTES

1 Important sources on the Swiss monetary system in the nineteenth century are: Banque Nationale Suisse (1921), Blaum (1908), Bleuler (1913), Debes (1909), Gygax (1907, 1901), Jöhr (1915), Kalkmann (1900), Mangold (1909), Völlmy (1967) and Weisskopf (1948). Bibliographies are provided by Ritzmann (1973) and Schweizerische Nationalbank (1957).

2 Jöhr (1915: 84–8) surveys the restrictions on the issue of bank notes in the articles of association of banks.

3 The most important commercial bank that did not issue paper money was the Schweizerische Kreditanstalt, which was founded in 1856. Other large banks that did not issue notes included the Schweizerische Bankverein, the Basler Handelsbank, Leu & Cie., the Bank in Winterthur and the

Schweizerische Volksbank. Ritzmann (1973: 305–73) records 234 banks in 1850 and 538 in 1880. Most of these banks were minute savings associations.

4 These banks included the Bank in Winterthur, the Bank in Zofingen, the Berner Handelsbank, the Hypothekarbank in Winterthur and the Solothurnische Volksbank (Jöhr 1915: 72–3).

5 King (1983) draws the same conclusion in his study of the private issue of paper money in New York in the nineteenth century.

6 For an analysis of the demand for money that stresses information costs see Brunner (1989) and Brunner and Meltzer (1971).

7 Weber (1988) deals with the issue of paper money in Switzerland before the currency reform.

8 One old Swiss franc equalled 6.665 grams of silver.

9 4.5 grams of silver and 0.2903226 grams of gold (15.5 grams of silver per gram of gold).

10 Before the rise in the price of silver, people would naturally have accepted the then undervalued gold coins but nobody would have offered them at par in a transaction.

11 Similarly, the Swiss cantons minted only small amounts of full-valued coins before the currency reform.

12 The gold coins that were minted by the federal government in the 1880s and 1890s were either hoarded or melted down (by the watch industry?).

11 US banking in the 'free banking' period

Kevin Dowd

The two decades preceding the American Civil War . . . witnessed something approaching a natural experiment. During those years the Federal government withdrew from the regulation of banking, a policy that was the final outcome of Andrew Jackson's war with the Second Bank of the United States. A wide range of experiments concerning entry into commercial banking were tried, from 'free' banking to 'socialized' banking. Moreover, other kinds of legislation affecting banking varied from state to state as well. While the regions of the United States differed in terms of economic structure, a common language, a common legal tradition, and, to some extent, a common culture permeated all regions. Thus the period provides excellent conditions for observing the effects of financial legislation on . . . financial intermediation.

(Rockoff 1975b: 160)

INTRODUCTION

Banking has always occupied a unique place in American history. When the republic was founded, entry to other industries was normally free, but banking was made an exception. Those who wished to set up a bank had to obtain explicit authorization in the form of a charter, and the constitution assigned the power to grant charters to the state legislatures to use as they saw fit. A typical charter would give the shareholders some limit on their liability and place restrictions on the ratio of notes to capital. Following on from English practice, the law interpreted a 'bank' as an institution that issued notes, and this narrow interpretation implied that while the issue of notes was quite restricted, the issue of deposits for a long time was not. (The restrictions on notes were important, none the less, in that notes were still a considerable part of the circulating medium.[1]) The controlled entry to the industry implied that charters normally involved a degree of monopoly privilege. They were therefore valuable, and state legislatures were often inclined to sell them for financial favours (e.g., cheap loans) rather than give them away. In addition, charters often restricted the bank to operate only in one county and one office – a restriction that would have propped up the value of charters, and, therefore, what they could be sold for, by restricting competition at the local level. Not surprisingly, perhaps, the state chartering process was often highly politicized and frequently controversial. The chartering of federal banks was even more so, and although the federal government did grant banking charters, the constitutionality of its power to do so was always controversial.[2] Whether the charter of the (second) Bank of the United States (BUS) should have its charter extended on its expiry in 1836 became a key issue in national politics, and the 'war' against the Bank was the dominant theme in Andrew Jackson's presidency. Jackson eventually succeeded and vetoed the bill to re-charter the Bank. The Bank's charter then expired and the federal government effectively withdrew from the banking industry to leave the field almost entirely to the individual states.[3]

'FREE BANKING' IN NEW YORK

New York had a particularly controversial charter system. The legislature had long been accustomed to grant charters 'as patronage to political favorites' (Holdsworth 1971 [1911]: 31), and the corruption surrounding the chartering process was widely regarded as scandalous. As early as 1825, a report to the State Senate recommended opening entry to the banking industry by repealing the laws against non-chartered banks. If noteholder safety was a major concern, the report suggested that the law could require that non-chartered banks deposit approved bonds with the state authorities, and these bonds could then be used to repay noteholders of any banks that failed. These two features – free entry and a bond-deposit condition – were to become the distinguishing characteristics of the 'free banking' laws,[4] and numerous petitions were subsequently presented to the legislature for the passage of a 'free banking' act. The charter system meanwhile had become 'so shameless and corrupt that it could be endured no longer',[5] and a 'free banking' act finally became law in April 1838.[6]

The New York law allowed free entry to the industry subject to a number of conditions.[7] Banks had to have at least $100,000 in capital, they were to observe a 12.5 per cent specie reserve requirement against notes, and their notes had to be redeemable on demand. Their notes were also to be secured by deposits of eligible assets with the state comptroller, and these assets included US bonds and the bonds of New York and other 'approved' states, and certain mortgages. Shareholders of 'free banks' were also allowed limited liability, and noteholders had first lien on the assets that were deposited to secure the note issue. The act was revised in 1840 when the reserve requirement was eliminated and US bonds and the bonds of other states were removed from the list of eligible bonds – a move, incidentally, that Knox (1969 [1903]: 418) says was expressly intended to promote the demand for New York bonds. A revised state constitution in 1846 also altered the 'free banking' law and made shareholders personally liable for notes up to the amount of their capital subscription ('double liability').

A large number of 'free banks' was set up immediately after the passage of the act – Hammond (1957: 596) suggests that 50 were set up very soon after, and 120 within two years. The early years of New York 'free banking' coincided with the financial difficulties of the late 1830s and early 1840s, however, and a number of banks failed when a group of southern and western states defaulted on their debts and inflicted large losses on them (see Root 1895: 20).[8] (As an illustration, Rolnick and Weber (1985: 8) note that the 17 banks that closed in the period from January 1841 to April 1842 held no less than 95 per cent of their asset portfolio in the form of bonds issued by defaulting states.) After this initial growth spurt, the New York banking system settled down to two decades of fairly steady expansion. From 1841 to 1861,

> the banking sector's volume of outstanding circulating notes doubled. . . . Even more dramatically, deposits at New York banks increased by more than six times as New York City became the financial center of the US economy. . . . There was also substantial growth in the total number of banking institutions, which more than doubled between 1838 and 1863, rising from 133 to 301.
>
> (King 1983: 143)

The impression of rapid growth is also borne out by Rockoff's observation that per capita bank money in New York grew at an annual rate of 4.41 per cent in the period from 1845 to 1860 (Rockoff 1975b: 162–3). (Rockoff notes, too, that this growth rate compares to national average of 2.56 per cent over the same period.) The losses that noteholders suffered in the first few 'free banking' years were also substantially reduced in the later period. To quote King again

In the twenty year period from October 1842 through September 1862. . . . [the] average annual percentage loss was about 0.04 percent, described by a contemporary observer as being far less than the loss arising from wear, tear, and shaving of specie coins. The largest percentage loss – about one third of one percent – occurs during a period of general financial distress and sharp economic decline.

(King 1983: 148)

The success of 'free banking' in New York was widely acknowledged. Rockoff (1975a: 11) describes New York 'free banking' as 'brilliantly successful', and even Knox (who is often quite hostile to 'free banking') acknowledged that 'New York in 1863 had an excellent banking system; the banks under it were sound and solvent and issued a satisfactory and safe currency' (1903: 392).

'FREE BANKING' LAWS ELSEWHERE

The New York 'free banking' law was widely imitated, and eighteen states eventually passed versions of it by 1860. The list of eligible assets that could be used to secure the note issue almost always included the bonds of the state that passed the law, and it usually also included US bonds. The bonds of other states were often included as well, and other assets such as mortgages were sometimes allowed. These laws also required that banks redeem their notes on demand at face value, on pain of dissolution – chartered banks were normally under the same obligation too – and they had a minimum (and sometimes a maximum[9]) capital requirement. As with earlier charters, 'free banking' laws sometimes included restrictions against investments in real property (Rockoff 1975b: 162), restrictions on branch-banking, and (usually) restrictions on the maximum ratio of the note issue to bank capital. In addition, banks were often subject to usury laws[10] and a variety of restrictions on the minimum denominations of their notes.[11] And while early laws normally limited shareholders' liability to the amount of their initial investment, there was a tendency to extend their liability as time went on, and most states had 'double' liability for the shareholders of 'free' (and chartered) banks by 1860 (Klebaner 1974: 11). As we saw, already in New York, there was also a gradual tendency to strengthen noteholder protection, and most states eventually gave noteholders preferred status as creditors and first lien on the assets deposited with the state authorities. Early restrictions on the note–capital ratio were also supplemented as time went by with explicit reserve requirements, and twelve states had reserve requirements of one sort or another by 1860.[12]

Apart from New York, 'free banking' laws were passed in Michigan (1837), Georgia (1838), Alabama (1849), New Jersey (1850), Illinois, Massachussetts, Ohio and Vermont (1850), Connecticut, Indiana, Tennessee and Wisconsin (1852), Florida and Louisiana (1853), Michigan again (1857), Iowa and Minnesota (1858) and Pennsylvania (1860). The spread of 'free banking' appears to be due to a variety of factors. One is New York's clear success with it. One suspects, too, that it was not just the success of New York in achieving a stable and growing banking system that accounts for its imitation, but also the realization by state legislatures that it offered a good way to raise revenue by promoting the demand for state debt. The usefulness of 'free banking' in this regard is illustrated by the fact that the New York 'free banking' system held no less than 57 per cent of New York's state debt in 1860 (Rockoff 1975a: table 4). In a number of southern states the adoption of 'free banking' also appears to have been facilitated by the fact that the earlier controversies over banking that had been so pronounced in the 1830s and 1840s had to some extent burned themselves out by the 1850s. As the protagonists fought themselves to a standstill, they gradually converged to more liberal policies as a matter of pragmatism rather than principle (see, for example, Schweikart 1987: 47). There was also considerable dissatisfaction in many states with state banking systems which either prohibited banking entirely or else implied a large degree of political control through a state bank or a politicized charter system. Dissatisfaction with the results of prohibition thus led to its replacement with 'free banking' in Iowa and Wisconsin, and dissatisfaction with the politicized process by which bank capital was allocated was a major factor behind the adoption of 'free banking' in Ohio and Tennessee. Rockoff observes that the 'sentiment for free banking was especially strong in the West' (1975a: 50) because of these sorts of difficulties, and these restrictions were felt particularly acutely in areas of new settlement where there was scope for rapid economic development (1975b: 163–4). There appears to have been a general perception that 'free banking' would promote economic and financial development, and that more restrictive systems would hold it back, and these beliefs appear to be borne out by a comparison of different states' experiences, especially in the 1850s.

We turn now to take a closer look at the various experiences of 'free banking'.

'Free banking' in Michigan (1837)

Michigan was the first state actually to pass a 'free banking' law. As in New York, there was considerable dissatisfaction with the existing 'monopoly' in banking, and a 'free banking' law was passed in March 1837 modelled on a bill that was still before the New York legislature. Hammond (1948: 6) reports that 40 banks were set up very quickly after the passage of the new law and all were in liquidation within a year, while Knox (1903: 735) reports that 42 banks were in liquidation and only 6 banks – 2 chartered banks and 4 'free banks' – still remained in operation by the end of 1839. The 'free banking' act itself was suspended in 1838, and it was subsequently repealed in 1839 and declared unconstitutional in 1844. What had happened?

The most important factor behind the failures appears to be a suspension law that resulted from a special legislative session in June 1837 – three months after the 'free banking' law – that authorized all banks in the state to stop specie payments. This law effectively removed the discipline against overissue – if banks' notes are convertible, then a bank is limited in its ability to issue notes by the legal requirement that it redeem them on demand for specie. The suspension law removed that requirement and thereby eliminated any effective check on the note issue. As Rockoff put it,

> a unique situation was set up in which a group of men could issue bank notes with practically no risk to themselves. Few free banks had been started up to this time, but now the rush to start began in earnest, and in fact, nearly all the Michigan wildcats lived their brief lives during the period of general suspension.
>
> (Rockoff 1975a: 95)

Far from telling us much about 'free banking' as such – recall that 'free banking' laws required that banks maintain convertibility – the Michigan experience thus appears to tell us more about the dangers of suspension laws.[13] Yet the Michigan experience, ironically, had a profound impact on later generations' perceptions of 'free banking', and 1837 Michigan was remembered when the successes of 'free banking' in New York and other states were all but forgotten. Many of the colourful stories about 'wild-cat' banking that were later regarded as the natural outcome of 'free banking' stem from episodes in late 1830s Michigan. With convertibility suspended, banks had no need to keep reserves other than to satisfy the bank commissioners, and the famous episodes of barrels of nails covered with coins and of specie being moved around the country to fool the commissioners were perhaps only to be expected.

Illinois

In 1835 the state of Illinois set up a state bank ostensibly modelled after Indiana's,[14] but the bank defaulted (as, indeed, did the state itself) in 1842, and the state constitution was subsequently amended in 1847 to ban state involvement in banking and to submit all banking legislation to referendum. A 'free banking' act modelled on New York's was then approved in 1851 (see, for example, Hammond 1948: 5, 13–14) and 141 'free banks' were subsequently formed (Economopoulos 1988, table 1). The Illinois 'free banking' system 'escaped practically unscathed' from the crises of 1854 and 1857 (Rockoff 1975a: 113), and Economopoulos reports that it 'worked reasonably well prior to 1861' (1988: 254). He notes, too, that it outperformed three out of Rolnick and Weber's four states during this period (1988: 113). However a potential problem was highlighted in a bank commissioners' report of 1857 which revealed that over two-thirds of Illinois banknotes were secured by bonds from the state of Missouri, and the Illinois banking system was therefore vulnerable to a fall in the price of Missouri state debt (Economopoulos 1988: 253). Relatively little was done to reduce the banking system's vulnerability to the prices of Missouri bonds, and a large number of bank failures followed when Missouri bond prices plummeted at the start of the Civil War. The prices of Missouri 6s fell from over 80 per cent of par in mid-1860 to under 40 per cent of par a year later (Rolnick and Weber 1984: figure 2). Only two banks had failed prior to 1861, with losses of only 8 cents on the dollar, but eighty-nine failed in 1861 and noteholders took average losses of 33 cents per dollar (Economopoulos 1988: 254). 'Free banking' in Illinois thus had a successful run until it was undermined by the fiscal instability associated with the outbreak of the Civil War.

Wisconsin

Wisconsin had a 'free banking' experience similar to Illinois. The territorial legislature was initially very hostile to banking and did what it could to prevent it,[15] and the prohibition on banking was continued under the constitution of the new state until it was reversed and a 'free banking' law passed in 1852 (Hammond 1948: 8). One hundred and forty 'free banks' were set up, and thirty-seven eventually failed (Rolnick and Weber 1983: table 2). Wisconsin's 'free banking' appears to have been relatively successful throughout the 1850s and there were no failures until 1860–1 (Rolnick and Weber 1984: 280). The balance-sheet data provided by Rolnick and Weber (1985: table 3) indicate that those Wisconsin 'free banks' that failed had secured 48.8 per cent of their note issues with the Missouri 6s that subsequently lost over half their market values in 1860–1 and inflicted such damage on the 'free banks' of Illinois, and an additional third or more of their note issue was secured by the bonds of other southern states that also fell very heavily in price. The failed 'free banks' of Wisconsin were thus the victim of the same fiscal instability as their Illinois counterparts.

Ohio

Ohio had a charter system until its banking system was overhauled in 1845 and a dual system established in which a state bank was established to operate beside 'independent' ones (Holdsworth 1971 [1911]: 33). Branches of the state bank were obliged to contribute to a safety fund, and independent banks were subject to a bond-deposit provision but there was no automatic free entry (Rockoff 1975a: 121–2). These reforms helped develop the banking system, but there was still a feeling in 1850 that the state did not have enough banks or enough bank capital (Rockoff 1975a: 56), and this feeling led to the passage of a 'free banking' law in 1851. The 'free banking' law was apparently successful – one Ohio historian noted that 'The banks organized under the general banking laws of 1845 and 1851 were attended by a high degree of success, and furnished a currency well adapted to the business wants of the people' (Huntington 1964: 479) – and while there were some failures, noteholder losses were trivial at most (Rockoff 1975a: 16).

Indiana

Indiana set up what was nominally a state branch bank but really a system of private chartered banks in 1834 (see Calomiris 1989: 15).[16] Yet despite the fact that many modern historians have regarded this system as very successful, the legislature none the less chose in 1852 to pass a 'free banking' law modelled on that of New York. Ninety-four banks were established in three years and the circulation increased from $3.5 million to $9.5 million (Hammond 1948: 12), and 104 'free banks' were established altogether (Rolnick and Weber 1982: table 2). Some 86 per cent of these banks closed, but only 31 per cent actually closed without paying their creditors at par (i.e., failed). Most of these failures occurred in 1854–5 (Rolnick and Weber 1983: table 5) and can be traced to the large falls in the prices of Indiana state bonds which occurred just before the failures, and which would have inflicted capital losses on the holders of Indiana bonds (see, for example, Rolnick and Weber 1984: figure 1). These failures notwithstanding, Indiana's 'free banking' appears to have been reasonably successful – Rockoff (1975a) quotes the state auditor's assessment in 1856, 'The experiment of free banking in Indiana, disastrous as it has been in some particulars, has demonstrated most conclusively the safety and wisdom of the system' (p. 22) – and there were eighteen 'free banks' still operating on the eve of the Civil War (p. 98).

Minnesota

Minnesota had an unusual experience with 'free banking'. A 'free banking' law was passed in July 1858, and sixteen 'free banks' subsequently opened (Rolnick and Weber 1982: table 2). Seven of these then failed in the period from June to September 1859, and two more in the period from June 1860 to June 1861 (Rolnick and Weber 1986: 884). The cluster of failures in 1859 and the low redemption rates of these failed institutions – Rolnick and Weber (1988: 57) report an average redemption rate of only 21.25 cents on the dollar – had led many earlier writers to the conclusion that 'free banking' in Minnesota had been a failure, but Rolnick and Weber (1988) have put forward an interpretation of the Minnesota experience that suggests it was more successful than had hitherto been realized. The Minnesota law was amended in August 1858 to allow US or Minnesota bonds valued at par to be used as eligible assets, and the 'free banking' laws were passed at almost the same time as the 'five million dollar' loan bill which provided for an issue of Minnesota state debt – the Minnesota 7s – secured *de facto* by the assets of the railroad companies whom the bill was designed to assist (Rolnick and Weber 1988: 54–7). What was effectively private debt was thus classified as state debt, and was therefore eligible security for a note issue. Five banks were then set up which secured their note issues with Minnesota 7s, and they all failed the next summer when the railroad boom ended and the railroad companies themselves failed (Rolnick and Weber 1988: 57). (The reasons for the failures of the other Minnesota banks are not clear.)

While earlier writers interpreted these banks as 'wildcats', Rolnick and Weber suggest they should be interpreted as mutual funds whose liabilities were priced to reflect the riskiness of their assets. They emphasize that the notes of these mutual fund banks were not sold and did not trade at par (1988: 57) – and the implication is that earlier estimates of noteholder losses are inappropriate since they were based on the assumption that the notes had been sold at par. Rolnick and Weber suggest these institutions performed a useful intermediation service – enabling ordinary people to invest in the railroads on the one hand, and providing the railroads with finance on the other – and they present compelling evidence that the public were well-informed and knew the risks involved (1988: 67). The railroad banks were set up by St Paul brokers who appointed nominal owners out-of-state to protect themselves from extended liability, and the first-lien provisions of the laws were circumvented by the banks making loans to the brokers secured only by promises to repay bank notes (1988: 59). To prevent arbitrage at their expense by the public, the railroad banks refused to redeem at par the notes they sold at a discount, and they announced this policy clearly in advance (1988: 59). Noteholders had no incentive to force the issue since they could only recover the risky assets securing the notes, minus the costs of litigation, and no-one apparently tried to protest their notes. This interpretation is supported by various pieces of evidence – the timing of the railroad bank failures shortly after the failures of the railroads themselves, the discussions of the risks involved in the press, the absence of any outcry when the state government announced that it would repay the notes of failed banks at about 20 cents on the dollar, some circumstantial evidence that railroad bank notes were discounted on the market, and the fact that most other 'free banks' continued well past the summer of 1859 (Rolnick and Weber 1988: 64–70).

OTHER 'FREE BANKING' EXPERIENCES

'Free banking' experiences elsewhere can be summarized more briefly. 'Free banking' laws were passed in Alabama, Florida, Georgia, Iowa, Massachussets, Pennsylvania and Vermont, but few (and, in the case of Iowa, no) 'free banks' were ever formed under them.[17] One reason in most of these cases – Florida is an exception, Iowa a possible exception, and the Pennsylvania law was only passed in 1860 – was that charters were already easy to obtain before the Act was passed (e.g., in the New England states) or else the passage of the Act was accompanied by a more liberal chartering policy (e.g., in Alabama). An additional reason seems to be that the constraints implied by the bond-deposit requirements of the 'free banking' law sometimes bound so tightly that 'free banks' were not set up because they would not have been able to compete effectively. A case in point is Massachussetts where the 'free banking' law was passed in 1851, but no 'free banks' were set up until 1859 despite the very considerable growth of the Massachussetts banking industry from a capital of just over $4 million in 1850 to nearly $19 million in 1857 (Knox 1903: 364; Rockoff 1975a: 125). The Massachussetts law restricted eligible assets to US (federal), New England and New York bonds which all sold at substantial premiums in the 1850s and yet were valued at par when used as collateral for a 'free bank' note issue. Banking entrepreneurs presumably preferred to apply for a conventional charter so they could avoid the tax on a 'free bank' implied by the difference between the high market price of eligible bonds and their par valuation by the authorities.[18]

'Free banking' laws appear to have had more impact on other states. In New Jersey, a 'free banking' law was passed in 1850 and five 'free banks' were set up by August 1852 (Rockoff 1975a: 11, 102). The original act authorized issues of bank notes against US bonds or the bonds of selected states, but Virginia bonds were added to the list in 1852 at about the same time as Virginia was running a large fiscal deficit. Much of this debt was absorbed by the New Jersey 'free banks', and a number of them then failed in 1853 when the price of Virginia debt fell and undermined their net values (Rockoff 1975a: 102–4). Dissatisfaction with the restrictiveness of the financial system in Louisiana led to the passage of a 'free banking' law in 1853 (see, for example, Schweikart 1987). Six banks were chartered under the 'free banking' law in the 1850s and there was some growth, albeit slow, in the banking industry that decade, growth being restricted, perhaps, by the 'stiff' reserve requirements that Louisiana banks had to observe (Green 1972: 201; Rockoff 1975b: 163). The Louisiana banking system was strong and solid, and in common with a number of other southern banking systems was able to avoid any suspensions in the crisis of 1857 (Pecquet 1990: 3).[19] Ongoing controversy in Tennessee about the siting of the branches of the state bank apparently led to the abolition of the state bank and the passage of a 'free banking' law in 1853. The number of banks then rose rapidly and the industry boomed (Rockoff 1975a: 11; Schweikart 1987: 276–7). As Schweikart recently observed, 'Contrary to the oft-cited assumptions of some modern historians . . . free banking in the southern states of Louisiana and Tennessee . . . produced fairly sound institutions and increased competition' (1987: 170).

We now leave the different states' experiences of 'free banking' and turn to some of the broader issues raised by *ante bellum* banking.

'WILDCAT BANKING'

'Wildcat banking' is a subject on which traditional histories of *ante bellum* banking have placed considerable emphasis. The notion of a 'wildcat' bank is misleadingly easy to grasp – it suggests an institution that is unsound and irresponsibly run, and that probably sets out deliberately to 'rip off' the public – but it defies attempts to pin it down precisely despite its superficial intuitive appeal. The difficulty is illustrated by Rockoff's definition – and note that earlier writers usually sidestepped the problem by avoiding definitions altogether – of a wildcat as a 'bank that issued notes in a much greater volume than it could continuously redeem, and that came into being as a result of a liberal entry provision in a free banking law' (1975a: 5). It is not at all clear what this definition effectively amounts to. Most banks operate on a fractional reserve, so it is questionable whether they 'could' redeem their notes continuously anyway. But one would presumably be reluctant to say that all fractional reserve note-issuing banks in this period were 'wildcats' – to do so would concede that the notion was more or less useless – and yet it is not clear what alternative construction one can make of this clause that drives the appropriate wedge between 'wildcat' banking on the one hand and 'good' fractional-reserve banking on the other. And the fact that Rockoff then ties the notion of a 'wildcat' to an institution that operates under a 'free banking' law in no way clarifies the issue – it relates 'free' and 'wildcat' banking in terms of definition, but does not tell us what 'wildcat' banking actually *was*. The term 'wildcat' is ultimately a colourful label, but it does not capture any well-defined theoretical construct. If 'wildcat' banking exists at all, it exists, like beauty, only in the eye of the beholder.

Many observers have nonetheless looked at *ante bellum* banking and thought they saw 'wildcats' – whatever they might be – and they have insisted, furthermore, that 'wildcat' banking was an important, indeed, critical, element in the *ante bellum* banking experience. These claims seem to boil down to the hypothesis that an important proportion of banks in this period were unsound in some sense, but such a hypothesis would seem to be both implausible a priori and empirically refuted. It is implausible because it fails to explain why people would choose to patronize such institutions in the first place. If the public preferred 'responsible', solid banks, then how could 'wildcat' banks attract any business when they were presumably out-competed? The wildcat hypothesis also seems to presuppose that the banker can simply issue notes and then disappear with the proceeds. He would lose the bonds deposited with the state authorities, of course, but the hypothesis maintains that it would be worth his while if the value of those bonds fell below the value of the liabilities outstanding (see, for example, Rockoff 1974, 1975a.) One difficulty here is that such behaviour is effectively fraud, and various laws already existed to prevent it. At a more basic level, if noteholders were afraid of being ripped off, then they would have insisted on adequate security from the banker – that he has 'respectable' people on his board of directors whom they believe are unlikely to sanction 'misbehaviour', that he acquires a stake in the local community (e.g. by making loans to it), and so on – and the threat of losing this security undermines his incentive to disappear with his proceeds (see also Rolnick and Weber 1984: 272). And, to take the argument full circle, it is precisely this security that gives the 'good' banker the competitive edge over the 'wildcatter'.

The wildcat hypothesis also appears to be rejected empirically. As Rolnick and Weber (1982: 14) point out, the bank note *Reporters* which warned of counterfeit and dishonoured notes would surely have said something had it been common for bankers to abscond with whatever assets they could take. They also present empirical evidence which indicated that two of the empirical predictions of the wildcat hypothesis – that wildcat banks should stay in business only a short time, and that noteholders should suffer losses when they failed – were only satisfied for 7 per cent of failed banks in their sample of failed banks from Indiana, Minnesota, New York and Wisconsin (1982: table 2). One should note, too, that the conditions that Rolnick and Weber test are only necessary conditions, and (in the absence of a well-defined notion of a wildcat bank) cannot be treated as sufficient ones. Their evidence indicates, therefore, that 7 per cent is only an upper bound on the proportion of bank failures that might be explained by wild-cat banking. Their claim that 'wildcatting' was relatively unimportant is also supported by the empirical work of Economopoulos on Illinois. He identified three characteristics of a 'wildcat' – that it should last less than a year, that it should be set up when there was a 'wildcat' profit to be made on the note issue, and that it should be set up in an inaccessible location – and finds that only one 'free bank' out of 141 satisfied all three conditions, and only eight even satisfied two (Economopoulos 1988: 261).

In short, the notion of wildcat banking is entertaining but ultimately provides little understanding of *ante bellum* banking. Hammond (1948: 24) was not far off the mark when he wrote that 'wildcat' banking is falsely taken as 'typical, being in accord with picturesque notions of frontier life [but that] fancy and theory have gone hand in hand to exaggerate the 'wildcat' banks' importance'. And Rockoff himself wrote

> To a remarkable extent the reigning view [about wildcats] is derived from purely anecdotal evidence . . . the traditional interpretation has been influenced by a small number of stories about wild-cat banks. It is not surprising that these stories are repeated frequently, for wild-cat banking is a romantic diversion from the usual dull recitation of statistics that makes up the backbone of most banking histories . . . little quantitative evidence has been presented that wild-cat banking was sufficiently frequent and harmful to constitute a basis for condemning free banking, and . . . few theoretical arguments have been advanced to show that wild-cat banking could not have been prevented without abandoning free banking.
>
> (Rockoff 1975a: ii)

THE CAUSES OF THE 'FREE BANK' FAILURES

Much ink has been spilt over the causes of the 'free bank' failures. Earlier writers often ascribed the failures to 'wildcatting', but as we have just seen, the wildcat hypothesis is unsatisfactory as a theoretical explanation, and recent empirical work indicates that it is consistent with only a small proportion of the failures anyway. We therefore have to look elsewhere, and two other factors suggest themselves. One of them was the occasional tendency of state governments to intervene to suppress the convertibility of bank money. As the Michigan experience of 1837 illustrated, this intervention could eliminate the check on banks' issues and open the way for a major over-expansion, and while the Michigan suspension law was perhaps the most notorious example, many other states also adopted suspension laws during the panics of the late 1830s and 1857. Such laws illustrated what Smith (1990 [1936]) regards as 'probably the worst feature of the American system' – the 'extreme laxity with which the principles of bankruptcy were applied to insolvent banks'.

A second major cause of the failures was the capital losses inflicted on 'free banks' by falls in the values of the state bonds held in their asset portfolios. A bank's liabilities were basically fixed in value, so its net worth depended on it maintaining the value of its assets, and a sufficiently large fall in the value of these assets could wipe out that net worth. There is considerable evidence to link 'free bank' failures with such capital losses, and these losses, in turn, can be linked to the fiscal instability that certain states experienced at particular times. Some evidence is presented by Rolnick and Weber using data for the states of New York, Indiana, Minnesota and Wisconsin over the years 1852–63 (1982: table 3). They use Indiana bonds as a proxy for the assets held by the 'free banks' in these states, and the prices of these bonds fell 25 per cent in the second half of 1854, 20 per cent from March to October 1857, and about 20 per cent from October 1860 to August 1861 (1982: 16). The bonds therefore fell for a combined period of about two years out of the total sample period, and yet 54 (or 79 per cent) of the 68 known 'free bank' failures in these states during the sample period occurred during these two years (1982: table 3). Rolnick and Weber present comparable results for the same states over the longer period of 1841–61 (1984: table 9) – which, in effect, means the same sample plus New York over the additional period – and found that 76 out of the 96 known failures (i.e., 79 per cent again) occurred during periods of falling bond prices (Rolnick and Weber 1984: 288). Economopoulos provides even stronger evidence from Illinois. He takes the whole population of known 'free bank' failures – 91 in all – and finds that all of them occurred in periods of falling bond prices (1988: 262). The severity of these bond price falls and the amounts of them held by failed 'free banks' also lends support to the view that they contributed in a major way to the failures. Rolnick and Weber's figure 1 (1984) indicates that Indiana 5s fell about 80 per cent in value from January 1841 to April 1842, for example, and we already noted Rolnick and Weber's observation (1985: 8) that the seventeen New York 'free banks' that closed in the first four months of 1842 held no less than 95 per cent of their asset portfolio in the form of the bonds of states which defaulted on their debts. Similarly, there were large falls in the prices of southern bonds with the onset of the Civil War – for example, Lousiana 6s fell 53 per cent, Missouri 6s 57 per cent, North Carolina 6s 56 per cent, and Virginia 6s 59 per cent – and Rolnick and Weber's 'free banks' that failed in 1860–1 secured about 84 per cent of their note issues with southern bonds that fell severely in price (Rolnick and Weber 1984: 288; 1986: 887). The history of the period also makes it clear that these bond price falls were related to fiscal factors. The fall in the prices of Indiana state bonds in the early 1840s were related to fears that Indiana would default on its debt (Rolnick and Weber 1986: 884), and the falls in the prices of southern bonds in 1860–1 were related to fears of southern repudiation with the outbreak of the Civil War. In the final analysis, the losses that put so many of the 'free banks' out of business were ultimately caused by fiscal and, at an even more basic level, by political factors.

BANKING STABILITY DURING THE *ANTE BELLUM* PERIOD

A number of issues have been raised regarding the stability of American banking during this period. A key concern has been that banking problems may have been contagious – that the difficulties of one bank or one group of banks should adversely affect public confidence in other banks. If noteholders or depositors are imperfectly informed, so the argument goes, then

> they might have – rightly or wrongly – interpreted the redemptions and failures at some banks as evidence that their own bank was also in trouble. In this way a local shock . . . could have caused . . . a large number of bank failures and closings that were not warranted by the local shock.
>
> (Rolnick and Weber 1985: 5)

Rolnick and Weber looked for contagion using their data set for New York, Indiana, Minnesota and Wisconsin, but they found very little evidence of it. Bank failures tended to be clustered, and they found that clustered failures in one state – in New York in 1841–2, in Indiana in 1854, in Minnesota in 1859, and in Wisconsin in 1860–1 – were associated with shocks that were specific to particular groups of banks (in fact, as already noted, these banks failed because they held large amounts of particular state bonds whose prices fell dramatically). In fact, they found that there was little tendency for these banking problems to spread to other states (1985: 5–8; 1986: 885–7). Rolnick and Weber also looked for evidence of intrastate contagion, and found little evidence of that either (1986: 887, n. 7).[20]

The *ante bellum* period also saw some experience with private banking 'clubs' that both helped member-banks and 'regulated' them. These clubs can be viewed as attempts to reap economies external to the individual banking firm, but internal to the industry, in a context where the most direct means of exploiting these economies – amalgamation – was subject to legal restrictions. Perhaps the most famous example is the Suffolk system in New England. (For more on the Suffolk system, see Trivoli 1979, Mullineaux 1987 and Selgin and White 1988.) In 1819 the Suffolk Bank of Boston attempted to counter the Boston circulation of out-of-town ('country') banks by buying up-country bank notes at their currently discounted prices in Boston and then presenting them to their issuers for redemption. The Suffolk system gradually developed into a multilateral clearing system, membership of which involved certain obligations – members had to maintain permanent deposits at the Suffolk, and to 'behave themselves' – but also gave member-banks a public signal of 'good standing' and access to credit facilities provided by the Suffolk. Most banks judged the benefits of membership to be worth the costs, and the Suffolk system gradually spread over much of New England (see, for example, Sumner 1896: 417). It 'created lasting benefits for the New England economy' (Trivoli: 1979: 5) and was successful in various specific ways: it initially reduced discounts on the notes of member-banks, and ultimately eliminated them, and thus helped to 'unify' the currency provided by different note-issuers; it provided a cheap and effective clearing system, and ensured the rapid return of notes and cheques to their issuers; it economized on monitoring costs (instead of the public having to monitor each bank themselves, much of the monitoring was delegated to the Suffolk and the public had merely to monitor the Suffolk and take note of any expulsions from the Suffolk system); and it provided emergency loans to member-banks, and was well-placed to do so because it was already monitoring them. The weaknesses of the system were that the Suffolk combined the sometimes conflicting roles of club owner, club manager and club member, and the product provided by the Suffolk was more 'hierarchical' than many member banks wanted. The Suffolk's 'dictatorial' attitude provoked frequent complaints, and after earlier attempts had failed, a group of banks at last succeeded in 1855 in obtaining a charter for a rival bank – the Bank for Mutual Redemption (BMR) – which was to take-over the Suffolk's note-exchange function and offer a less hierarchical product. (It was to impose less irksome conditions on members but provide no overdraft or vetting facilities as the Suffolk did.) The BMR finally opened in 1858 and a brief struggle ensued which ended with the withdrawal of the Suffolk from the note-exchange business. The Suffolk system was replaced by that provided by the BMR, and the new system lasted until it was destroyed by the note restrictions of the National Banking System in the 1860s.

A related institution was the clearing-house association (see Timberlake 1984: 3–4). Like the Suffolk system, these institutions initially arose to economize on redemption costs. Banks would tend to take in each other's notes in the course of business, and they soon realized that it would be more convenient for bank representatives to meet together at a central clearing-house than it would be to arrange a series of bilateral note exchanges. One bank would typically be assigned to administer the clearing process, and member banks would keep balances with it with which they could settle their accounts. Later on, the administration of the clearing process would be transferred to a clearing-house institution established for the purpose, and the clearing-house would economize on specie by issuing certificates of its own which would be used in the clearing process in place of coins. The most important clearing-house association was the one in New York which was founded in 1853, and the role of the New York association soon expanded significantly during the crisis of 1857. While the banks' initial reaction to the crisis was to want to curtail their loans, the New York association arranged a co-ordinated response by which they allowed their reserve ratios to fall while the association began to issue loan certificates which were to be used to supplement specie and which were secured against clearing-house assets. These certificates helped to alleviate the specie shortage and enabled lending to continue, and they were retired after the crisis had subsided. The role of the clearing-house expanded further when it arranged for the issue of more loan certificates and a co-ordinated bank policy in the run-up to the Civil War (Timberlake 1984: 4–5). Unlike the system provided by the BMR, the clearing-house associations survived the National Banking legislation and continued to evolve until the crisis of 1907.

This period also saw the establishment of the first systems of state-sponsored liability insurance. Like the Suffolk–BMR systems and the clearing-house associations, these schemes are perhaps best viewed as substitute means by which banks could reap the economies of scale which legal restrictions implied they were not allowed to exploit by the more direct means of amalgamation. In this regard it is significant that southern banks faced relatively few amalgamation restrictions, and were generally comparatively large, reasonably well-diversified, and noticeably more stable than many of their northern counterparts. Northern banks were frequently hemmed in by amalgamation restrictions (e.g., restrictions on branching), and their greater instability was almost certainly due, in part at least, to their restricted ability to diversify risks. This instability gave rise to political pressure to protect the small banks, and some state governments responded by instituting liability insurance schemes to protect them – New York in 1829, Vermont in 1831, Indiana in 1834, Michigan in 1836, Ohio in 1845 and Iowa in 1858 (see Calomiris 1989). The schemes fall into one of two main classes, though the particulars vary somewhat in each case. There were the New

York 'safety fund' and the Vermont and Michigan systems loosely modelled on it, which Calomiris (1989: 12) characterizes as 'complete failures' and which ultimately defaulted. Insurance premiums were fixed and there was little or no attempt to relate them to banks' risk-taking, there was little incentive for banks to monitor each other and no effective supervision (i.e., the systems created moral hazard and failed to control it) and the systems tended to attract bad-risk institutions (i.e., had a bad adverse selection problem). The other systems were 'mutual guarantee' schemes modelled after the one introduced by Indiana which Calomiris (1989: 16) assesses as 'extraordinarily successful'. These schemes were actuarially much sounder, they provided more effective supervision and a stronger incentive for banks to monitor each other, and they were mostly managed by the banks themselves. All three were successful and lasted until the suppression of state note issues by the National Banking System.[21]

DE FACTO **FREE BANKING**

One feature of *ante bellum* banking experience that has often been touched upon but seldom addressed in any depth is the extent to which many states experienced free or competitive banking *de facto* (as opposed to banking under a 'free banking' law). While no state ever had pure *laissez-faire* in banking, many states had banking regimes which imposed relatively lax restrictions and which therefore gave a reasonable approximation to banking *laissez-faire*. Massachussetts provides a good example. Massachussetts operated a charter system, but charters were apparently granted relatively routinely after 1820 (Sylla 1985: 108) and the banking industry was widely regarded as competitive and successful (e.g., E. White 1990: 27). Pennsylvania also operated a charter system with a reasonably liberal chartering policy, and the Pennsylvania banking industry appears to have been at least moderately competitive and successful.[22] New York had something close to free banking after the passage of its 'free banking' law in 1838, and the success of New York banking has already been noted. Alabama also enjoyed something like free banking after the passage of its 'free banking' law in 1849 – few 'free banks' were actually chartered, but the legislature simultaneously adopted a more liberal chartering policy – and the more liberal regime of the 1850s saw the Alabama financial sector recover from its earlier decline (Schweikart 1987). Banks were theoretically prohibited in Florida from 1845 until the passage of the 'free banking' law in 1853, but unchartered banks apparently operated there with considerable success. Schweikart (1987: 170) could say that these 'private bank agencies had preempted the revised banking law and operated so effectively that no reason to welcome new banks existed', and he went on to note that 'Florida had experienced free banking for a decade before it became official' (1987: 174).[23] The south also provides other interesting examples of approximate free banking. South Carolina had chartered banks which were allowed to branch state-wide, and the South Carolina banks were sound as well as competitive. As Knox observed,

> The laws regulating banks in South Carolina gave satisfaction throughout the country, affording as they did a sound currency and ample accommodation to the people. A Bank of Charleston note was current from Maine to Texas, and even circulated in England and the Continent of Europe.
>
> (Knox 1903: 567–8)

Virginia is another example. Virginia had a system of chartered branch-banks, and as in South Carolina, the banking system was both stable and competitive. Schweikart (1987: 126) observes that there were no failures, and consequently no noteholder losses, and he concludes that on the eve of war, Virginia 'could look back upon a decade marked by generally wise legislation and adequate, if not notable, growth in its banking system' (1987: 275).[24] Altogether, at least seventeen states could reasonably be said to have had approximate free banking – there were probably more, but it is hard to assess the competitiveness of the banking regimes in a number of other states (see Table 11.2, n. 1) – and it is surely highly significant that all appear to have been at least moderately successful and there are no obvious 'failures'.

GENERAL ASSESSMENT

The most obvious (and overwhelming) feature of US banking experience over this period is its sheer diversity. Some idea of the extent of this diversity can be gauged from the Appendix which lists the main features of each state's legislative regime and the most noticeable aspects of its banking experience (as far as I could assess them). Legislative regimes ranged from the total prohibition of banking at one extreme to something close to free banking towards the other, with state monopoly banks and various forms of state charter and 'free banking' systems at points in between. Some of the main

Table 11.1 States with 'free banking' laws[1]

State	Date of Act	Outcome
Alabama	1849	Few 'free banks'
Connecticut	1852	Unknown
Florida	1853	Few 'free banks'
Georgia	1838	Few 'free banks'
Illinois	1851	Successful until 1861
Indiana	1852	Moderately successful
Iowa	1858	No 'free banks' established
Louisiana	1853	Moderately successful
Massachusetts	1851	Few 'free banks'
Michigan	1837	Apparent disaster
Michigan	1857	Unknown
Minnesota	1858	Quite successful
New Jersey	1850	Some failures
New York	1838	Very successful
Ohio	1851	Successful
Pennsylvania	1860	Few 'free banks'
Tennessee	1852	Successful
Vermont	1851	Few 'free banks'
Wisconsin	1852	Successful until 1860

Note: [1] In addition, Kentucky, Missouri and Virginia adopted bond-deposit laws but not 'free banking' laws as such (in 1850, 1858 and 1851 respectively).

features of these experiences are summarized in tables 11, 1–4. Table 11.1 lists the states that adopted 'free banking' laws and gives an assessment of the outcome in each case. As the table indicates, eighteen states adopted 'free banking' at some point, and Michigan did twice. The first three 'free banking' laws were passed in Michigan, New York and Georgia in 1837–8, the fourth in Alabama in 1849, and the remainder in the period from 1850 to 1860. In seven cases – Alabama, Florida, Georgia, Iowa, Massachussets, Pennsylvania and Vermont – few 'free banks' if any were ever set up. In two other cases – Connecticut and Michigan in 1857 – I could find no real indication of the outcome. Of the remaining ten, 'free banking' was very successful in New York, and at least moderately successful in Illinois, Indiana, Louisiana, Minnesota (apparently, if one adopts the Rolnick and Weber (1988) mutual fund interpretation of the railroad banks), Ohio, Tennessee and Wisconsin. A considerable number of failures occurred in Illinois and Wisconsin around the outbreak of the Civil War, and in New Jersey in 1853, but these failures can be traced to the losses banks suffered on their asset portfolio and be plausibly attributed to government policy, and the apparent disaster of Michigan in 1837 can be largely attributed to the state-induced suspension that quickly followed it. As far as one can tell, therefore, 'free banking' appears to have a reasonably good record, and most of the problems it encountered can be put down to government policies of one sort or another.[25, 26]

Table 11.2 States with (reasonably) competitive banking regimes[1]

State	Dates	Outcome
Alabama	1849 on	Financial recovery
Florida	1843 on?	Moderately successful
Georgia	1850s?	Successful
Illinois	1851 on	Successful until 1861
Indiana	1852 on	Moderately successful
Louisiana	1853 on?	Moderately successful
Maryland	Throughout	Successful
Massachusetts	Throughout	Successful
Minnesota	1858 on	Quite successful
New York	1838 on	Very successful
North Carolina	1850s, and maybe earlier	Very successful
Ohio	1845 on	Successful
Pennsylvania	Throughout	Successful
South Carolina	Throughout?	Very successful
Tennessee	1852 on?	Successful
Virginia	Throughout?	Successful
Wisconsin	1852 on	Successful until 1860

Note: [1] The table only includes states where one can reasonably maintain the banking system was competitive. The competitiveness of the banking systems of Connecticut, Delaware, Iowa, Kentucky, Maine, Michigan (1857), New Hampshire, New Jersey, Rhode Island and Vermont is hard to assess. Note that Michigan (1837) is omitted as a misleading case in view of the suspension law that followed.

If 'free banking' has a good record, free banking has an even better one. Table 11.2 lists the states that had reasonably competitive banking regimes (i.e., *de facto* free banking, or a reasonable approximation to it), the periods roughly when this occurred, and a brief assessment of the outcome. Seventeen states appear to have had *de facto* free banking over some period. All appear to have been at least reasonably successful, and four (Massachussetts, New York and North and South Carolina) were arguably very successful indeed. Unless one includes the perverse case of Michigan in 1837 – which is of questionable relevance anyway due to the suspension law –

there were no cases in which *de facto* free banking can be said to have demonstrably 'failed'. One should also bear in mind that the table almost certainly *understates* the success of free banking in so far as it excludes a number of cases – New Jersey and a number of New England states, among others – where the competitiveness of the banking system could not easily be assessed, but where one would be very surprised if the banking system was not both reasonably free and relatively successful. What is also striking is the extent to which the cases of 'free banking' and free banking differ. While there are some experiences that can be considered as both 'free' and free – Alabama (perhaps), Florida, Georgia and Ohio (in part), and Illinois, Indiana, Minnesota, New York, Tennessee and Wisconsin – many belong to one category but not the other. Connecticut, Michigan, New Jersey and Vermont all had 'free banking' laws, but I have not been able to find any notable evidence that they had free banking. A number of other states (Florida, Louisiana, Maryland, Massachussetts, North and South Carolina, Pennsylvania, and Virginia) had something like free banking over periods for which they had no 'free banking' laws – some of these states in fact never passed 'free banking' laws at all – and these experiences include some of the most successful cases of *de facto* free banking (e.g., the cases of Massachussetts and the Carolinas). There is thus a considerable discrepancy between the experiences of 'free banking' and free banking, and we must be careful not to confuse the two.

Tables 11.3 and 11.4 examine other aspects of *ante bellum* banking. Table 11.3 lists three cases where states had monopoly state banks – Illinois until 1842, Iowa for a brief period in 1858, and Missouri until 1857. Two of these experiments – Illinois and Missouri – clearly failed and the Iowa case is (perhaps not surprisingly) hard to assess. State monopoly banks thus had a poor record, and there are no cases where any (*de facto*) monopoly banks succeeded. Table 11.4 looks at the experiences of those states that prohibited banking entirely – banks were banned over various periods in Arkansas, California, Florida, Iowa, Oregon, Texas and Wisconsin. The effects of the bans in California, Oregon and Wisconsin are not clear, but the prohibitions failed to achieve any sensible purpose in any of the four cases where the outcome is easily ascertainable. In Arkansas the prohibition retarded the state's financial development, in Iowa and Texas it led people to use out-of-state notes, and in Florida it led people to resort to private bankers instead. Sumner (1896: 416) notes that 'states which had no banks . . . generally had a worse currency than those which had banks', and they presumably

Table 11.3 States with monopoly state banks[1]

State	Period	Outcome
Illinois	Until 1842	Failure
Iowa	1858	?
Missouri	Until 1857	Failure

Note: [1] Table excludes Indiana, which had a state monopoly bank in name only, and Michigan which chartered a bank that 'imitated almost exactly' the Indiana bank (Sumner 1896: 330) but was already in liquidation by the end of the next year.

Table 11.4 States which prohibited banking

State	Period of Prohibition	Outcome
Arkansas	1846 on[1]	Failure
California	1849 on	?
Florida	1845–53	Failure[2]
Iowa	Until 1858	Failure
Oregon	1857 on	?
Texas	1845 on	Failure
Wisconsin	Until 1852	?

Notes: [1] New charters were prohibited in 1846, but the last already existing bank only disappeared in the 1850s.
[2] The Florida ban only failed in the sense that it failed to achieve its objectives. Private bankers actually provided Florida with a reasonably good banking system (see Table 11.2).

made other banking services (e.g., loans and savings facilities) more expensive to obtain. Prohibition thus failed along with monopoly banking.

In a nutshell, *ante bellum* banking experience strongly suggests that liberal financial regimes were broadly successful and that state intervention by and large failed. There was also a tendency to imitate successful systems, and New York-style 'free banking' was widely copied, especially in the 1850s. By the eve of the Civil War more than half the states in the union had adopted 'free banking' in one form or another, and a number of others had liberal financial regimes even though they never passed 'free banking' laws. There was a significant improvement in banking in most states over this period – illustrated, for instance, by the growth in per capita bank money from $7.64 in 1840 to $14.21 in 1860 (Rockoff 1975b: 165) –

and, as Smith wrote,

> The improvement that took place in American banking in the twenty years preceding the Civil War was especially noticeable in the eastern region. The banking system was by no means perfect at this period, but except for the international crisis of 1857 . . . the situation was far steadier than before. It is very probable that this improvement was not attributable to any considerable extent to State regulations relating to bond deposit guarantees for notes. In fact, the State authorities seem to have become, after a time, rather lax in the enforcement of the law. . . . Much the greater weight is to be attached to the more rigid enforcement of specie payments between banks by frequent exchange of notes due in great part to the spread of the Suffolk system and to the institution of the New York clearing-house.
>
> (Smith 1990 [1936]: 45–6)

The Civil War then broke out and the federal government intervened once again to pass the National Banking legislation of 1863–5 by which the bond deposit provision was adopted at the federal level and the state note issues were effectively taxed out of existence. These measures were prompted by fiscal considerations and not by any well-established dissatisfaction with the existing state systems. They were also initially intended as emergency (and therefore, transitory) measures to help finance the federal government's wartime expenditures, but the wartime regime was left substantially intact after the war ended and it survived with relatively little alteration until the Federal Reserve Act was passed in 1913. And so it happened that

> The fiscal exigencies of the Civil War checked the process of evolution and fastened upon the country the incubus of a cumbersome and unscientific banking system. But for this check it is highly probable that some such organization as the free banking system of New York . . . would have spread throughout the entire country . . .
>
> (Holdsworth 1971 [1911]: 23)

NOTES

1 As an illustration, the ratio of note to deposits was 27 per cent in New York city in 1849 (Klebaner 1974: 26).
2 The argument made by opponents of federal chartering was that the federal government did not have any powers not expressly granted to it, and the chartering power was among these. For more on this issue, see Dowd (1990b) and Timberlake (1990).
3 The expiration of the charter of the BUS in 1836 saw the federal role cut down to imposing restrictions on banks that had federal deposits, and even these restrictions were removed by the adoption of the Independent Treasury System in January 1847 (Rolnick and Weber 1983: 1082; see also Scheiber 1963: 212, and Timberlake 1978).
4 Note that the adjective 'free' used in this context 'referred solely to freedom of entry' – the term 'automatic' would be more accurate, however, since entry was 'free' only subject to certain conditions – 'The free banking laws ended the requirement that banks obtain their charters through special legislative acts' (Rockoff 1975b: 161).
5 These were the words of New York comptroller Millard Fillmore looking back later in 1848 (quoted in Klebaner 1974: 9).
6 Knox (1903: 413–15) and E. White (1990) have detailed discussions of the origins of the New York 'free banking' law. See also Holdsworth (1971 [1911]: 31).
7 Details of the New York legislation are given in Rockoff (1975a: table 12), King (1983: 142–8), Knox (1903: 414–15), and E. White (1990: 9 and 22).
8 Arkansas, Florida, Indiana and Mississippi defaulted in 1841, and Illinois, Lousiana, Maryland, Michigan and Pennsylvania in 1842 (Rolnick and Weber 1985: 6; see also Schweikart 1987).
9 Examples are Vermont and Pennsylvania whose 'free banking' laws limited the capital of a 'free bank' to no more than $200,000 and $1 million respectively (Knox 1903: 357, 459).
10 For more on usury laws, see Rockoff (1975b: 169–72). These laws varied considerably, both in the interest ceilings they imposed and in the penalties imposed for violating those limits. His discussion suggests that they probably had some impact at some times, but were often ineffective.
11 Eugene White (1990) has a good account of the history and effects of denominational restrictions. Notes under $1 were banned in Ohio in 1819, in Florida in 1828, and in Georgia in 1830, and the federal Treasury and a number of states attempted to discourage the use of notes less than $5 in the 1830s. There were also some attempts to impose even higher minimum denominations (e.g., Missouri banned notes under $20 in 1836). Denominational restrictions were sometimes highly controversial, and opposition to them led to the repeal of the New York ban on notes under $5 in 1837. They were often ineffective, and led to a flood of 'foreign' (i.e., out-of-state notes) (see also Klebaner 1974: 19). Where they were effective, on the other hand, they tended to put banknotes out of reach of the ordinary man.

12 Reserve requirements were generally applied to chartered and not just to 'free' banks. Virginia was the first state to introduce one (1837), and other states soon followed suit. (New York's was repealed in response to opposition from the bankers.) While early reserve requirements stipulated reserves against the note issue, Louisiana was the first state to introduce a reserve requirement against deposits as well as notes (in 1842; see Klebaner 1974: 43).

13 The argument that it was the suspension law rather than the 'free banking' law that was the principal factor behind the failure is also supported by the observation that only two of the chartered banks remained in operation by the end of 1839 (Knox 1903: 735). It is questionable however whether all the 'free bank' failures can be blamed on the suspension law alone. Rockoff (1975a: 94) states that many banks 'were simply frauds which operated in violation of the free banking law'. He also suggests (1975a: 18) that 'only a small portion of the notes entered circulation at par' which suggests that the mutual fund model of Rolnick and Weber (1988) might be appropriate, as with Minnesota, or that losses might have been exaggerated.

14 Banking histories often regard the Illinois bank as modelled on the Indiana one (e.g., Hammond 1948), but this interpretation of the Illinois bank is misleading – see n. 16.

15 See n. 8 to the Appendix.

16 While many previous writers have admired Indiana's state monopoly bank – Holdsworth (1971 [1911]: 32) comments that it 'stands out as the most striking exception to the rule of failure among state-owned banks' – the Indiana bank was a state monopoly in name only. As Calomiris (1989) points out, the Indiana branches were 'separately owned and operated' (p. 15), and the language of state monopoly was required because the 'state constitution only provided for the chartering of a state bank and its branches' (p. 29, n. 21). The state monopoly in Indiana only appeared to work because it only appeared to be a state monopoly, and the state banks of Illinois and Missouri failed because they were apparently real state monopolies.

17 'Free banking' laws were also passed in Connecticut and Michigan in 1857, but their effects are difficult to determine.

18 This claim presupposes that the bond collateral restrictions of the 'free banking' legislation were binding, but it seems reasonable to suppose that they were. As White (1986: 893) puts it, it appears that 'collateral restrictions forced banks to hold unbalanced asset portfolios overloaded with state bonds. Such portfolios exposed the banks unduly to the risk of declining state bond prices'. He notes further that 'It seems unlikely that banks would deliberately so overload themselves absent regulatory distortions of their asset-holding choices'. While this hypothesis needs more investigation, the fact that banking entrepreneurs were sometimes so slow to set up 'free banks' (e.g., in Massachussetts) would appear to provide it with some support. Further work might focus on whether 'free banks' held more than the required amounts of state bonds in their portfolios. If they did not, as White (1986: 893, n. 3) points out, then there is *prima facie* evidence that the restrictions were binding; if they did, on the other hand, then the restrictions clearly were not. Assuming that the

hypothesis is valid, then one can properly attribute the 'free bank' failures not only to the fiscal instability that produced the bond price falls, but also to the bond-deposit requirements as well. It was the latter that exposed the banks to capital losses, and the former that inflicted the losses on them.

One objection also needs to be considered. King (1983: 147) disputes the claim that the bond-deposit requirements were responsible for the failures and argues that 'there are natural means for any bank to undo any pure portfolio restriction. Banks should simply have as owners or creditors individuals who would otherwise hold amounts of government debt'. However this irrelevant result does not apply when there are limitations on agents' liability (see Dowd 1989: 149–50, n. 31). (It would be interesting to test the issue, nonetheless, since King's argument makes the empirical prediction that bond-deposit requirements should have no impact on the prices of state bonds. I would expect that such a test would find this prediction to be rejected.)

19 Pecquet also notes that 'This solid banking system depended upon a unique state constitution which forbade the legislature or governor to authorize or aid specie suspension in any way' (1990: 3) – an assessment which would seem to reinforce the earlier comments about the potential damage done by suspension laws.

20 The claim that there was little or no contagion has however been challenged recently by Hasan and Dwyer (1988) who present some circumstantial evidence and the results of logit analysis. In their model the probability of failure depends on the value of bonds relative to capital, the remoteness of the bank's location, and a dummy variable which takes the value one if another bank failed in that county, and zero otherwise, and they interpret the positive sign and statistical significance of the dummy variable as evidence of contagion. This interpretation of their results is open to the objection, however, that while the dummy *might* pick up contagion, it will also pick up *any other* factor that the first two variables proxy inadequately, but which is also linked to the failure of a neighbouring bank – conditions in the local economy come to mind – and these alternative explanations need to be ruled out before one can claim to have established the presence of contagion.

21 The stability of the banking industry of the period is also borne out by other indicators. Particularly important is its capital adequacy. Salsman (1990: 95) notes that 'the banking system restored its capital adequacy in the first decade of free banking from 40.5 percent in 1836 to 55.1 percent in 1842, the greatest capital adequacy level and the swiftest rise in the entire history of banking'. He also notes that there was 'no appreciable deterioration of banking capital adequacy' in the remaining 'free banking' period. Sechrest (1990: 102) also notes that capital adequacy was very high, and he notes too that capital ratios became more stable towards the end of the 'free banking' era. Indicators of banking liquidity reinforce the impression of the industry's stability. Salsman's cash–deposit ratio shows a steady climb from over 42 per cent in 1836 to 54.2 per cent in 1844, and it varies thereafter between 36.2 per cent and 41.5 per cent (Salsman 1990: table 17). Sechrest's reserve ratio, on the other hand, has a value of just over 20 per cent for 1834–49, and almost 18 per cent for the period

1850–62 (1990: 100–2). Sechrest also points out that commercial paper rates were lower and less variable in the period 1850–62 which saw the large-scale switch to 'free banking' than they had been in the earlier period 1834–49 (1990: 110).

22 There is however some controversy over how competitive the Pennsylvania banking system actually was. Evidence in favour is suggested by casual observation and a comment by the state auditor-general in 1863 that the reason so few 'free banks' were formed was the ease with which special charters could be obtained which, incidentally, also imposed less onerous conditions than the 'free banking' law (Knox 1903: 460). However Rockoff (1975a, 53) suggests that Philadelphia banks enjoyed a rather high profit rate which he attributes to restrictions on entry, and he presents anecdotal evidence that Philadelphia banks were undercapitalized.

23 The experience of Florida underlines the importance of private (i.e., uncharted or unincorporated) banking in the *ante bellum* USA. Schweikart writes that

> Unaccounted currencies, especially small-note issues, played an extremely important role in the antebellum southern economy but have defied attempts at measurement . . . [for example] Georgia chartered 150 'potential currency-issuing organizations' between 1810 and 1866, and more than fifteen hundred varieties of currency of this type circulated in the state . . . Florida, without chartered banks of its own, relied heavily on unaccounted currencies for its circulating medium.
>
> (Schweikart 1987: 80)

Sylla also indicates that they were a widespread and important phenomenon. He notes that though 'Quantitative information . . . is scarce, . . . what there is of it suggests that the private banker was considerably more important than previously thought' (1976: 181), and he presentts some indicative evidence to back that claim up (e.g., how some restraining acts were successful in 'smoking out' private bankers). Also revealing is a comment by James Gurthrie, the Treasury Secretary, who reported to the House in 1856 that the capital of private banks was more than a third of that employed in chartered banks (Sylla 1976: 184). Hammond (1948: 16) and Klebaner (1974: 12) indicate that private banking was important in the West as well, and the latter observes that by 1860, private banks in Ohio, Indiana, Illinois, Michigan and Wisconsin had more deposits than the combined liabilities of chartered banks in those states.

24 Virginia gives a good example of the difference between 'free' and free banking. It had supplemented its chartered banks with a law to allow bond-deposit banking in 1851 – although note that this law omitted the 'free entry' principle (Rockoff 1975b: 163) – but bond-deposit banks were not allowed to branch as easily as chartered ones. Aided by branch-banking, Virginian banks were 'strong and stable', and there were no failures (Schweikart 1987: 126). Thirteen bond-deposit banks opened soon after the 1851 law (E. White 1990: 22), but these banks had great difficulty competing against the chartered banks which expanded their branch networks to compete with them (Schweikart 1987: 274; E. White 1990: 22).

25 Despite the fact that 'free banking' laws were often (apparently) intended to lower entry barriers, it is far from clear that they usually did. If entry barriers fell, we would expect to see the state-level output of banks grow after the passage of 'free banking' laws. Ng (1988) tests for this prediction using data for seven 'free bank' states and finds that it is only demonstrably satisfied for New York. He concludes that 'free banking laws did not generally lower barriers to entry [or] increase competition in the banking industry' (1988: 886), and suggests that the explanation might be the conditions attached to the establishment of 'free banks' and that fact that chartered banking in some states was reasonably competitive already (1988: 887). However, Bodenhorn (1990) presents results that suggest that 'free banking' laws might have been more effective in promoting bank competition than Ng's results indicate.

26 The figures for bank failures and noteholder losses also suggest that these have been exaggerated by earlier historians. Rolnick and Weber (1983: 1084) find that in their four states about half the banks closed before 1863, but less than a third actually failed and did not redeem their notes at par (i.e., 15 per cent failed altogether). They also suggest that New York and Wisconsin banks were not very short-lived, and only 14 per cent failed to last a year (1983: 1086). Kahn (1985: 882) is less sanguine, however, and suggests that banks in 'free banking' states had much shorter life expectancies than banks elsewhere. (The explanation, presumably, has to do with the combination of the bond-deposit requirement and the states' fiscal instability discussed earlier.) Estimates of losses vary somewhat – losses were very low in New York, as already mentioned, but they were sometimes higher elsewhere (see, for example, Kahn 1985: 884–5), and these losses presumably reflect the factors that caused the 'free bank' failures.

Appendix Us banking experience, 1837–63

State	Legislative framework	Comments/results
Alabama	Chartered Banks and State Bank until 1849. 'Free banking' law passed 1849[1] and charters now granted liberally.	Chartering policy restrictive. State Bank a failure. 8 chartered and 2 free banks set up. Financial system recovered by 1860.
Arkansas	Real Estate Bank and State Bank chartered 1836. Constitutional amendment 1846 to prohibit further charters.	Both corrupt and eventually failures. Banking system backward. Some private banking.
California	Banking banned 1849.	—
Connecticut	Chartered banks. 'Free banking' law passed 1852.	—
Delaware	Chartered banks.	—
Florida	Charter system until 1845 when banking theoretically prohibited. 'Free banking' law passed 1853.	Evidence that private banks provided *de facto* free banking from 1843 onwards. Only two 'free banks' set up.
Georgia	Charter system with state bank ('Central Bank'). 'Free banking' law passed 1838.	Central Bank defaulted 1840. Only two 'free banks' set up. Chartering policy (apparently) liberal in 1850s. Considerable banking progress.
Illinois	Monopoly state bank until 1842. Constitution amended 1847 to ban state involvement in banking and to submit banking legislation to referendum. 'Free banking' law passed 1851.	State bank defaulted 1842. 'Free banking' very successful until large-scale failures in 1861.
Massachusetts	Charter System. 'Free banking' law passed 1851.	Charters granted liberally, so *de facto* free banking. Large increase in bank capital and number of banks in 1850s. First 'free bank'

State	Legislative framework	Comments/results
Michigan	Charter system. 'Free banking' law passed March 1837, but suspended in 1838, repealed in April 1839 and declared unconstitutional in 1844. Safety fund established 1836. Bank suspension law June 1837. Constitution amended 1850 to require that banking law be submitted to referendum. New 'free banking' law 1857.	formed 1859, no more than seven 'free banks' formed altogether. 40 banks set up in less than a year after passage of 'free banking' law, but most rapidly went into liquidation. Safety fund a failure.
Minnesota	Charter system until passage of 'free banking' law in 1858.	sixteen 'free banks' set up. Nine 'free banks' – mostly railroad banks – failed following the failure of the the railroad companies in 1859.
Mississippi	Charter system.	Flurry of charters in 1836–7. Banking system declined in 1840s and 1850s. By 1860 there were no unchartered banks left and the circulating medium consisted mostly of Tennessee bank notes.
Missouri	State monopoly bank set up 1837. Constitution amended 1857 to allow more banks to be chartered. Law passed to allow bank-secured banks (but not 'free banks') in 1857.	Only 3 banks set up by 1860. Some amount to private banking. Missouri financially underdeveloped.
New Hampshire	Charter system.	–
Indiana	'Free banking' law was passed 1852.[2] Safety fund system throughout period.	State bank apparently successful. Substantial number of 'free banks' rapidly set up, but most went out of business by 1854. 'Free banking'

State	Legislative framework	Comments/results
Iowa	Banking banned by 1846 constitution. Ban lifted in 1858 when a state (branch) bank was set up.[3] 'Free banking' law passed 1858. Safety fund set up 1858.	apparently quite successful. Safety fund successful.
Kentucky	General banking law to allow bond-secured (but not 'free') banks 1850.	Widespread circulation of out-of-state notes during banking ban. No 'free banks' established. Safety fund apparently successful.
Louisiana	Charter system with branches. Banking reformed in 1842. Constitution amended 1845 to prohibit chartering and re-chartering. Constitution amended again in 1852 to allow chartering. 'Free banking' law passed 1853.	–
		Large fall in bank capital after 1840, and banking capital only starts to recover in 1850s. Banking system in 1850s solid but grew slowly.
Maine	Charter system.	–
Maryland	Charter system. General banking law passed in 1853, but this merely consolidated existing laws and the 'free banking' principle was omitted.	Charters granted liberally, so *de facto* free banking.
New Jersey	Charter system. 'Free banking' law passed in 1850. Virginia state bonds added to list of eligible bonds in 1852.	Absorption of VA debt by 'free banks' and 'free bank' failures in 1853.
New York	Charter system with safety fund. 'Free banking' law passed in 1838.	Flurry of 'free banks' set up shortly after passage of 'free banking' law. *De facto* failure of Safety Fund in 1842. 'Free banking' very successful.

State	Legislative framework	Comments/results
North Carolina	Charter system with state bank and branching. Most activities of state bank wound down by 1860.	Banking system competitive and charters readily granted, especially in 1850s. *De facto* free banking.
Ohio	Charter System. Reform act of 1845 set up state bank and specified that its branches contribute to a safety fund, and allowed 'independent' banks subject to a bond-deposit requirement. 'Free banking' law passed in March 1851. Constitutional amendment effective June 1951 required that banking legislation pass a referendum.	Considerable increase in bank numbers following 1945 law. Thirteen 'free banks' established in 1851–2. Laws of 1845 and 1851 apparently successful. Safety fund successful.
Oregon	Banking banned 1857.	–
Pennsylvania	Charter system. General banking law 1850. 'Free banking' law March 1860. Banks suspended November 1860.	Charters granted liberally, but bank profits quite high. Nine 'Free banks' formed.
Rhode Island	Charter system.	–
South Carolina	Charter system with branching and state bank.	Banking system highly stable and successful.
Tennessee	Charter system with branching. New state bank 1838.[4] 'Free banking' law 1852 and elimination of Bank of Tennessee 1857.	Apparent decline in bank numbers from 1839 to 1853. Rapid growth in banks from 1853, and considerable financial development in state banking system. Withstood crisis of 1857 easily. 'free banking' apparently successful.[5]
Texas	Banking banned by state constitution 1845.	Private banking and circulation of out-of-state notes.[6]
Vermont	Charter system. 'Free banking' law passed 1851. Safety fund system established 1831.	Four 'free banks' set up. Safety fund a failure.

State	Legislative framework	Comments/results
Virginia	Charter system with state bank. Charter banks allowed to branch. General banking law 1837. Law passed to allow bank-deposit banking 1851.[7]	Banking system strong and stable – no failures in 1837 and 1857. Thirteen banks set up under bond-deposit law, but had difficulty competing against the branch-banking advantages of the chartered banks. Considerable banking development throughout period.
Wisconsin	Banks banned by territory of Wisconsin.[8] New state constitution of 1848 banned any legislative authorization of banks unless ratified by referendum. 'Free banking' law passed 1852.[9]	140 'free banks' set up. Large number of failures when southern bond prices fell with onset of Civil War.

1 There is some dispute over the date of this Act: Rockoff (1975a: 127) puts it in 1849, but Schweikart (1987: 269) puts it in 1850.
2 There is also some dispute over the date of this Act: Hammond (1948: 12) and Knox (1903: 698) put it in 1853, but Rockoff (1975a: 98) and Rolnick and Weber (1984: 279) put it in 1852. I have gone along with 1852 since Rolnick and Weber give the precise date the Act was passed.
3 Sumner (1896: 542) states that this bank was chartered in March 1858, but Hammond (1948: 10–11) claims it was chartered in 1857. As in note 2, I have gone along with the author who could give the precise date of the act (Sumner).
4 It is not clear when this bank was chartered. Schweikart (1987: 182) gives 1838, but his table 12 gives a date of 1837.
5 Note, however, that Knox (1903: 655) does not concur in this assessment. He suggests it performed badly and says that wildcats 'were as plentiful as grasshoppers', but he does not spell out the evidence behind that conclusion.
6 However, Schweikart (1987: 8, 259) suggests that there was one chartered bank in operation in the 1850s.
7 The 1851 law allowed banks to be set up under a bond-deposit provision, but Rockoff (1975b: 163) states that entry was not automatic. It therefore ought not to be considered a 'free banking' law in the strict sense.
8 Note however, that the Wisconsin Marine and Fire Insurance Company carried out some banking activities, and succesfully fought off legislators' attempts to stop it.
9 There is also some dispute about the date of this act: Hammond (1948: 8) and Rockoff (1975a: 84) say it was passed in 1852, but Knox (1903: 325) says it was passed in 1855 and Sumner (1896: 451) says it was passed in 1853.

Sources: Calomiris (1989), Hammond (1948), Rockoff (1974, 1975a, b), Rolnick and Weber (1982, 1983, 1984, 1985, 1986, 1988), Knox (1903), Schweikart (1987), Sumner (1896).

Bibliography

PARLIAMENTARY REPORTS

1804 Committee
  Select Committee of the House of Commons on the circulating paper, the specie and the current coin of Ireland; and also on the exchange between that part of the United Kingdom and Great Britain, 1804 H.C. 1826, V.
1826 Committee
  Select Committee of the House of Commons to inquire into the state of the circulation of promissory notes under the value of £5 in Scotland and Ireland . . . 1826, H.C. 1826, III.
1837 Committee
  Select Committee of the House of Commons to inquire into the operation of the acts permitting the establishment of joint stock banks in England and Ireland . . . 1837, H.C. 1837, XIV.
1840 Committee
  Select Committee of the House of Commons to inquire into the effects produced on the circulation of the country by the various banking establishments issuing notes payable on demand 1840, H.C. 1840, IV.
1848 Committee
  Select Committee of the House of Commons on commercial distress 1848, H.C. 1848, iv.
1857 Committee
  Select Committee of the House of Commons to inquire into the bank acts of 1844 . . . and of the bank acts for Scotland and Ireland of 1845 . . . 1857, H.C. 1857, X.

BOOKS AND ARTICLES

Alcazar, C. C. (1957) *Historia de los bancos en Peru, 1860–79*, Lima: [n.p.].
Anderson, J. L. (1910) *The Story of the Commercial Bank of Scotland*, Edinburgh: [n.p.]
Andreades, A. (1966) *History of the Bank of England, 1640 to 1903*, 4th edn, New York: Augustus M. Kelley.
Anonymous (1802) *The Utility of Country Banks Considered*, in J. R. McCulloch (ed.). *A Select Collection of Scarce and Valuable Tracts . . .*

on *Paper Currency and Banking*, New York: Augustus M. Kelley, 1966. (Reprint of 1857 edn.)

——(1927) 'The Dai Fook Dollar of Foochow', *Chinese Economic Journal* (February): 127–41.

——(1932) 'Native Banks in Foochow', *Chinese Economic Journal* 10(5) (May): 440–7.

——(1957) '"Circulation Notes" in Rural China', *Far Eastern Economic Review* (11 April): 466–7.

Anti-Cobweb Club (1925) *Fukien: A Study of a Province in China*, Shanghai: Presbyterian Mission Press.

Arndt, E. H. D. (1928) *Banking and Currency Development in South Africa (1652–1927) with an Appendix on the Rise of Savings Banking in South Africa*, Cape Town: Juta & Co.

Avella, M. (1987) *Pensamiento y Politica Monetaria en Colombia, 1886–1946*, Bogotá: Contraloria General de la República.

Aytoun, W. E. (1844) 'The Scottish Banking System', *Blackwood's Edinburgh Magazine*, 56: 671–86.

Bagchi, A. K. (1987) *The Evolution of the State Bank of India*, 2 vols, Bombay: Oxford University Press.

Bagehot, W. (1912 [1873]) *Lombard Street: A Description of the Money Market*, London: Henry S. King. Reprinted New York: Charles Scribner's Sons.

La banque en Belgique, 1830–1980 (1980), Brussels: Centre d'Etudes Financières.

Banque Nationale Suisse (1925) *Le Système Monétaire de la Suisse*, Geneva: Publications du Bureau de Statistique de la Banque Nationale Suisse.

Barclays Bank (Dominion, Colonial and Overseas) (1938) *A Banking Centenary*, Plymouth, England: privately printed.

Barrow, G.L. (1975a) *The Emergence of the Irish Banking System, 1820–1845*. Dublin: Gill & Macmillan Ltd.

——(1975b) 'The Irish Banking System in 1845', *Quarterly Report*, Central Bank of Ireland.

Baskerville, P. (1987) *The Bank of Upper Canada: A Collection of Documents*, Toronto: Champlain Society.

Baster, A. S. J. (1929) *The Imperial Banks*, London: Routledge & Kegan Paul.

Beckhart, B. H. (1929) 'The Banking System of Canada', in H. P. Willis and B. H. Beckhart, (eds). *Foreign Banking Systems*, New York: Henry Holt & Co.

Bell, R. (1838) *A Letter to James William Gilbart . . . on the Relative Merits of the English and Scotch Banking Systems*, Edinburgh: Bell & Bradfute.

Benavides, M. J. (1972) *Historia de la moneda en Bolivia*, La Paz: Ediciones 'Puerto del Sol'.

Bernanke, B. S. (1983) 'Nonmonetary effects of the financial crisis in the propagation of the Great Depression', *American Economic Review*, 73: 257–6.

Bernholz, P. (1989) 'Currency competition, inflation, Gresham's Law and exchange rate', *Journal of Institutional and Theoretical Economics*, 145: 465–88.

Bett, V. (1957) *Central Banking in Mexico: Monetary Policies and Financial Crises, 1864–1949*, Ann Arbor, Michigan: Bureau of Business Research,

School of Business Administration, University of Michigan, vol. 13 (1).

Black, F. (1970) 'Banking and interest rates in a world without money: the effects of uncontrolled banking', *Journal of Banking Research*, 1: 8–20.

Blainey, G. (1958) *Gold and Paper. A History of the National Bank of Australia*, Melbourne: Georgian House.

Blaum, K. (1908) *Das Geldwesen der Schweiz seit 1798*, Strasbourg: Abhandlungen aus dem Staatswissenschaftliche Seminar.

Bleuler, W. (1913) *Bank in Zurich, 1836–1906*, Zurich: Schweizerische Kreditanstalt.

Bloch, K. (1935) 'On the copper currencies in China', *Nankai Social and Economic Quarterly*, VIII (3) (October): 617–31.

Boase, C. W. (1867) *A Century of Banking in Dundee*, 2nd edn, Edinburgh: R. Grant.

Bodenhorn, H. (1989) 'Two episodes of free banking in Ireland: Scotland's forgotten sister', unpublished paper.

——(1990) 'Entry, rivalry and free banking in antebellum America', mimeo, Rutgers University.

Boehm, E. A. (1971) *Prosperity and Depression in Australia 1887–1897*, Oxford: Clarendon Press.

Bordo, M. D. (1984) 'The Gold Standard: the traditional approach', in M. D. Bordo and A. J. Schwartz (1984), see next entry.

Bordo, M. D. and Schwartz, A. J. (eds) (1984) *A Retrospective on the Classical Gold Standard, 1821–1931*, Chicago: University of Chicago Press.

Bordo, M. D. and Redish, A. (1988) 'Was the establishment of a Canadian central bank in 1935 necessary?', in C. England and T. F. Huertas (eds) *The Financial Services Revolution*, Boston: Kluwer Academic Publishers.

Botero, M. M. (1989) 'El Banco de Antioquia: un modelo de Banco Regional, 1872–1888', *Estudios Sociales*, 5, Medellín: FAES.

Brandt, L. and Sargent, T. J. (1989) 'Interpreting new evidence about China and U.S. silver purchases', *Journal of Monetary Economics*, 23: 31–51.

Brecher, I. (1957) *Monetary and Fiscal Thought and Policy in Canada, 1919–1939*, Toronto: University of Toronto Press.

Breckenridge, R. M. (1894) *The Canadian Banking System, 1817–1890*, Toronto: [Canadian Bankers' Association?]

——(1910) *The History of Banking in Canada*, US National Monetary Commission Publications (61st congress, 2nd session, Senate doc. 332), Washington: Government Printing Office.

British Sessional Papers (BSP) (1826) vol. III, no. 402. *Report from the Select Committee Appointed to inquire into the State of the Circulation of Promissory Notes under the Value of £5 in Scotland and Ireland. . . .* Reprinted New York: Readex Microprint [n. d.].

Brugger, H. (1978) *Die Schweizerische Landwirtschaft*, 1850–1914, Verlag Huber Frauenfeld.

Brunner, K. (1989) 'The disarray in macroeconomics', in *Monetary Economics in the 1980s*, F. Capie and G. E. Wood (eds), London: Macmillan in association with the Centre for Banking and International Finance, The City University, 197–233.

——and Meltzer, A. H. (1971) 'The uses of money in the theory of an exchange economy', *American Economic Review*, 61 (1) (December): 784–805.

Buisson, F. (1805) *Dictionnaire universel du commerce*, Paris: Buisson.

244   The experience of free banking

Butlin, N. G. (1962) *Australian Domestic Product, Investment and Foreign Borrowing, 1861–1938/39*, Cambridge: Cambridge University Press.
Butlin, S. J. (1953) *Foundations of the Australian Monetary System, 1788–1851*, Melbourne: Melbourne University Press.
——(1961) *Australia and New Zealand Bank. The Bank of Australasia and the Union Bank of Australia Limited, 1828–1951*, London: Longman.
——(1986) *The Australian Monetary System 1851 to 1914*. Sydney: Ambassador Press.
Butlin, S. J., Hall A. R. and White, R. C. (1971) *Australian Banking and Monetary Statistics 1817–1945*, Occasional Paper 4A, Sydney: Reserve Bank of Australia.
Cabezas Villa, L. (1941) *La moneda en Bolivia*, Potosí: Escuela Tip. Salesiana – Sucre.
Cagan, P. (1963) 'The first fifty years of the national banking system', in D. Carson (ed.) *Banking and Monetary Studies*, Homewood, Ill.: Richard D. Irwin, ch. 2.
Calogeras, J. P. (1910) *La politique monétaire du Brésil*, Rio de Janeiro: Imprimerie Nationale.
Calomiris, C. W. (1989) 'Deposit Insurance: lessons from the record', in Federal Reserve Bank of Chicago, *Economic Perspectives* (May–June): 10–30.
Cameron, R. (ed.) (1972) *Banking and Economic Development: Some Lessons of History*, New York: Oxford University Press.
——(1982) 'Banking and industrialization in Britain in the nineteenth century', in A. Slaven and D. H. Aldcroft (eds) *Business, Banking and Urban History: Essays in Honour of S. G. Checkland*, Edinburgh: John Donald.
Cameron, R. with Crisp, O. White, H.T. and Tilly, R. (1967) *Banking in the Early Stages of Industrialization: A Study in Comparative Economic History*, New York: Oxford University Press.
Campbell, R. H. (1967) 'The law and the joint-stock company in Scotland', in P. L. Payne (ed.), *Studies in Scottish Business History*, London: Frank Cass.
Canadian Bankers' Association (1971) *A Bibliography of Canadian Banking*, Toronto: Canadian Bankers' Association.
Canales, J. M. (1942) *Organizacion y contabilitad bancarias. Evolucion bancaria en El Salvador, 1880–1935*, San Salvador: Imprenta Funes.
Cantillon, R. (1952 [1735]) *Essai sur la nature du commerce en général*, Paris: Institut National d'Etudes Démographiques.
Capie, F. and Webber, A. (1985) *A Monetary History of the United Kingdom, 1870–1982*, 2 vols, London: George Allen & Unwin.
Carbo, L. A. (1978) *Historia monetaria y cambraria del Ecuador desde epoca colonial*, Quito.
Carr, J. L. and Mathewson, G. F. (1988) 'Unlimited liability as a barrier to entry', *Journal of Political Economy*, 96 (August): 766–84.
Castillo Flores, A. (1974) *Historia de la moneda de Honduras*, Tegucigalpa: Banco Central de Honduras.
Chalmers, R. C. (1893) *A History of Currency in the British Colonies*, London, Eyre & Spottiswood, for HMSO.
Chang, G. H. (1938a) 'A brief survey of Chinese native banks', Central Bank of China *Bulletin*, IV (1) (March): 25–32.

——(1938b) 'The practice of Shanghai native banks', Central Bank of China *Bulletin*, IV (4) (December): 310–19.

Chapman, J. M. and Westerfield, R. B. (1942) *Branch Banking: its Historical and Theoretical Postion in America and Abroad*, New York: Harper & Bros.

Chappell, N. M. (1961) *New Zealand Banker's Hundred: A History of the Bank of New Zealand 1861–1961*, Wellington: Bank of New Zealand.

Checkland, S. G. (1968) 'Banking history and economic development: seven systems', *Scottish Journal of Political Economy*, 15: 144–66.

——(1975) *Scottish Banking: A History, 1695–1973*, Glasgow: Collins.

Ch'en, J. (1980) *State Economic Policies of the Ch'ing Government, 1840–1895*, New York, Garland.

Chiang, H. D. (1966) 'The origins of the Malaysian Currency System (1867–1906)', *Royal Asiatic Society Journal of the Malaysian Branch*, vol. 39.

Chinese Economic Bulletin (various dates).

Chisholm, D. (1979) 'Canadian monetary policy 1914–1934: the enduring glitter of the gold standard', Ph.D. thesis, University of Cambridge.

Chlepner, B. S. (1943) *Belgian Banking and Banking Theory*, Washington: Brookings Institution.

Christ, C. F. (1989) 'On free banking', *Market Process*, vol. 7 (1) (Spring): 5–10.

Clapham, J. (1945) *The Bank of England*, 2 vols, London: Macmillan.

Clay, C. (1869) *Manx Currency*, Douglas, Isle of Man: Manx Society.

Coble, Parkes M., Jr (1980) *The Shanghai Capitalists and the Nationalist Government, 1927–1937*, Cambridge, Mass.: Harvard University Press.

Coghlan, T. A. (1918) *Labour and Industry in Australia*, Oxford: Oxford University Press.

Colmenares, G. (1974) 'Censos y Capellanias: formas de credito en una economia agricola', *Cuadernos Colombianos*, 2.

Conant, C. A. (1911) *The Banking System of Mexico*, US National Monetary Commission (61st congress, 2nd session, Senate doc. no. 493), Washington: Government Printing Office.

——(1927 [1896]) *A History of Modern Banks of Issue*, 2nd edn, 6th edn and rev. edn, New York: G. P. Putnam's Sons (6th edn reprinted New York: Augustus M. Kelley, 1969).

Congdon, T. (1981) 'Is the provision of a sound currency a necessary function of the State?' *National Westminster Quarterly Review* (August): 2–21.

Copland, D. B. (1920) 'Currency inflation and price movements in Australia', *Economic Journal*, 30 (December): 484–509.

Coppieters, E. (1955) *English Bank Note Circulation, 1694–1954*, The Hague: Martinus Nijhoff.

Coq, P. (1850) *Le Sol et la haute banque*, vol. 1, Paris: Librarie Democratique.

Coquelin, C. (1845) 'Commercial associations of France and England', *The Merchants' Magazine* (May–June): 403–20, 499–520 (translated from the French *Revue-des-Deux-Mondes*, with remarks and Notes by Henry Charles Carey).

——(1849) 'The causes of commercial crises', *The Merchants' Magazine* (October): 371–89.

——(1874) *Dictionnaire de l'economie politique*, vol. 1, Paris: Guillaumin.

——(1876) *Le Credit et les banques*, Paris: Guillaumin.

Cork, N. (1894) 'The late Australian banking crisis', *Journal of the Institute of Bankers*, 15(4): 175–261.

Courcelle-Seneuil, J. G. (1867) *La Banque libre*, Paris: Guillaumin.

——(1920) *Les Operations de Banque*, 11th edn, Paris: Felix Alcan.

Courtois, A. (1881) *Histoire des banques en France*, Paris: Guillaumin.

Cothren, R. (1987) 'Asymmetric information and optimal bank reserves', *Journal of Money, Credit, and Banking*, 19 (1) (February): 68–77.

Cowen, T., and Kroszner, R. (1987) 'The development of the new monetary economics', *Journal of Political Economy*, 95: 567–90.

——(1989) 'Scottish banking before 1845: a model for *laissez-faire?*', *Journal of Money, Credit, and Banking*, 21 (May): 221–31.

Crawcour, S. (1961) 'The development of a credit system in seventeenth-century Japan', *Journal of Economic History*, 20 (3) (September): 342–60.

Crazut, R. J. (1970) *El Banco Central de Venezuela: notas sobre la historia y evolucion del instituto 1940–1970*, Caracas: Banco Central de Venezuela.

Cribb, J. (1987) *Money in the Bank: An Illustrated Introduction to the Money Collection of the Hongkong and Shanghai Banking Corporation*, London: Spink & Son.

Crick, W. F. (ed.) (1965) *Commonwealth Banking Systems*, Oxford: Clarendon Press.

Croisé, R. and Link, R. (1988) *La Legislation monetaire du Grand-Duché de Luxembourg de 1815 à nos jours; recueil de textes*, Luxembourg: Editions Lux-Numis Luxembourg.

Crossley, J.and Blandford, J. (1975) *The D.C.O. Story*, London: Barclays Bank International.

Cruz Reyes, V. C. (1981) *La moneda hondurena*, thesis, Universidad Nacional Autonomia de Honduras.

Curtis, C. A. (1926) 'The Canadian banking system, 1910–1925', Ph.D. dissertation, University of Chicago.

——(1931) 'Statistics of banking', *Statistical Contributions to Canadian Economics*, vol. 1, Toronto: Macmillan.

Dauphin-Meunier, A. (1936) *La Banque de France*, Paris: Gallimard.

——(1937) *La Banque à travers les ages*, vol. 2, Paris: Banque.

Debes, R. (1909) *Banque du Commerce de Genève, 1845–1907*, St Gallen.

Denison, M. (1966) *Canada's First Bank: A History of the Bank of Montreal*, 2 vols, Toronto: McClelland & Stewart.

Diamond, D. W. and Dybvig, P. H. (1983) 'Bank runs, deposit insurance, and liquidity', *Journal of Political Economy*, 91 (3) (January): 401–19.

Dierschke, K. and Mueller, F. (eds) (1926) *Die Notenbanken der Welt*, 2 vols, Berlin: Verlag für Bergeldlosen Zahlungsverkehr, R. Gruegens.

Diez, J. I. (1989) 'El Banco Nacional, 1880–1904: El Fracaso de la Moneda Legal', *Lecturas de Economia*, 28, Medellín.

Doolittle, J. (1865) *Social Life of the Chinese*, vol. II, New York: Harper & Bros.

Dowd, K. (1988) 'Option clauses and the stability of a laissez-faire monetary system', *Journal of Financial Services Research*, 1 (December): 319–33.

——(1989) *The State and the Monetary System*, Hemel Hempstead: Philip Allan, and New York: St Martin's Press.

——(1990a) 'Did central banks evolve naturally? A review essay of Charles Goodhart's *The Evolution of Central Banks*', *Scottish Journal of Political Economy*, 37 (1) (February): 96–104.

——(1990b) 'Money and banking: the American experience', paper presented to the Durell Foundation conference 'Money and Banking: The American Experience', Washington, May.

Drake, P. (1984) 'Postracion al Debe, 1929–1933', *Economia Colombiana*, 155 (March): 25.

Drake, P. J. (1967) *Financial Development in Malaya and Singapore*, Canberra: Australian National University Press.

Du Pont de Nemours (1789) *Discours prononcé à l'Assemblée Nationale sur les banques en général et sur la Caisse d'Escompte en particulier*, Paris: Baudouin.

——(1806) *Sur la Banque de France, les causes de la crise qu'elle a eprouvée, les tristes effets qui en sont resultés, et les moyens d'en prevenir le retour; avec théorie des banques*, Paris: Delance.

Duverneuil et de la Tynna (1797–1804) *Almanach du commerce de la ville de Paris*, Paris: Valade.

Echeverri, L. (1989) 'Monetary policies and institutions in Colombia 1870–1922', unpublished manuscript, University of Georgia.

Ecklund, G. N. (1973) 'Banking and finance', in Yam-li Wu, (ed.) *China: A Handbook*, New York: Praeger.

Economopoulos, A. J. (1988) 'Illinois' free banking experience', *Journal of Money, Credit, and Banking*, 20: 249–64.

Essars, P. des (1896) 'A history of banking in the Latin nations', in *A History of Banking in All the Leading Nations*, New York: Journal of Commerce & Commercial Bulletin.

Estrada Ycaza, J. (1976) *Los bancos del siglo XIX*, Guayaquil: Archivo Historico del Guayas, Casa de la Cultura Ecuatoriana/Nucleo del Guayas.

Fama, E. (1980) 'Banking in the theory of finance', *Journal of Monetary Economics*, 6: 39–57.

Fane, G. (1988) 'The development of monetary institutions in Australia from Federation to the Second World War', mimeo, Australian National University.

Fernandez, P. (1982, 1984) *Analisis de la historia bancaria y monetaria del Paraguay*, vols 1, 2, Asuncion: Croms.

Ferraris, C. F. (1911) *The Italian Banks of Issue*, US National Monetary Commission (61st congress, 2nd session, Senate doc. no. 578), Washington: Government Printing Office.

Ferrero, R. A. (1953) *La historia monetaria del Peru en el presente siglo*, Lima: [n.p.].

Fetter, F. W. (1955) *The Irish Pound. 1797–1826: A Reprint of the Report of the Committee of 1804, . . .* Evanston, Ill: Northwestern University Press.

Fleming, J. S. (1877) *Scottish Banking: A Historical Sketch*, 3rd rev. edn, Edinburgh: William Blackwood.

Flux, A. W. (1910) *The Swedish Banking System*, US National Monetary Commission (61st congress, 2nd session, Senate doc. no. 576), Washington: Government Printing Office.

Forbes, W. (1860) *Memoirs of a Banking-House*, 2nd edn, Edinburgh: William & Robert Chambers.

248   The experience of free banking

Fortune, R. (1847) *Three Year's Wandering in China*, London: Murray.

Franco, A. Arinos de Melo (1973) *Historia do Banco do Brasil*, 4 vols, Rio de Janeiro: Banco do Brasil.

Fratianni, M. and Spinelli, F. (1984) 'Italy in the Gold Standard period, 1861–1914', in M. D. Bordo and A. J. Schwartz (eds) (1984), *A Retrospective on the Classical Gold Standard, 1821–1931*, Chicago: University of Chicago Press.

——(1985) 'Currency competition, fiscal policy and the money supply process in Italy from unification to World War I', *Journal of European Economic History*, 14 (3) (September–December): 473–99.

Freris, A. F. (1986) *The Greek Economy in the Twentieth Century*, London: Croom Helm.

Friedman, M. (1960) *A Program for Monetary Stability*, New York: Fordham University Press.

Friedman, M. and Schwartz, A. J. (1963) *A Monetary History of the United States 1867–1960*, Princeton: Princeton University Press.

——(1986) 'Has government any role in money?', *Journal of Monetary Economics*, 17 (1) (January): 37–62.

Frost, J. D. (1982) 'The "nationalization" of the Bank of Nova Scotia, 1880–1910', *Acadiensis*, 12 (1) (Autumn): 3–38.

Galbraith, J. A. (1970) *Canadian Banking*, Toronto: Ryerson Press.

Garcia Ruiz, J. L. (1989) 'En torno a la libertad de emision de billetes en España, 1856–1874', unpublished manuscript, Universidad Complutense de Madrid.

Garnier, J. (1874) *Dictionnaire de l'economie politique*, vol. 2, Paris: Quillaumin.

Gibson, J. D. and Schull, J. (1982) *The Scotiabank Story: A History of the Bank of Nova Scotia, 1832–1982*. Toronto: Macmillan.

Gilbart, W. J. (1834) *The History and Principles of Banking*. London: Longman (3rd edn 1837).

——(1865 [1827]) *A Practical Treatise on Banking*, London: Bell & Daley.

Gollan, R. (1968) *The Commonwealth Bank of Australia: Origins and Early History*, Canberra: Australian National University Press.

Goodhart, C. A. E. (1969) *The New York Money Market and the Financing of Trade, 1900–1913*, Appendix A, 'Canadian banks and the New York money market', Cambridge, Mass.: Harvard University Press.

——(1985) *The Evolution of Central Banks: A Natural Development*, London: Suntory Toyota International Centre for Economics and Related Disciplines.

——(1988) *The Evolution of Central Banks*, Cambridge, Mass.: MIT Press.

Goodwin, C. D. W. (1961) *Canadian Economic Thought*, Durham: Duke University Press.

Gorton, G. (1985a) 'Bank suspension of convertibility', *Journal of Monetary Economics*, 15 (2): 177–93.

——(1985b) 'Banking theory and free banking history: a review essay', *Journal of Monetary Economics*, 16 (2) (September): 267–76.

——(1986) 'Banking panics and business cycles', Unpublished manuscript.

Graham, W. (1911) *The One Pound Note in the History of Banking in Great Britain*, 2nd edn Edinburgh: James Thin.

Green, G. D. (1972) 'Louisiana 1804–1861', in R. Cameron (ed.) *Banking and Economic Development: Some Lessons of History*, New York: Oxford University Press.

Greenfield, R. L. and Yeager, L. B. (1983) 'A laissez-faire approach to monetary stability', *Journal of Money, Credit, and Banking*, 15: 302–15.

Greenfield, R. L. and Rockoff, H. (1990) 'A tale of two dollars: currency competition and the return to gold, 1865–1879', unpublished manuscript, Fairleigh Dickinson University and Rutgers University.

Gunasekera, H. A. de S. (1962) *From Dependent Currency to Central Banking in Ceylon: An Analysis of Monetary Experience 1825–1927*, London: G. Bell & Sons Ltd.

Gygax, P. (1901) *Kritische Betrachtung über das Schweizerische Notenbankwesen mit Beziehung auf den Pariser Wechselkurs*, Zürich: Albert Müller's Verlag.

——(1907) *Die Bank in St Gallen, 1837–1907. Die Geschichte einer schweizerischen Notenbank*, St Gallen.

Hahn, O. (1968) *Die Währungsbanken der Welt*, 2 vols, Stuttgart: C. E. Poeschel Verlag.

Hall, F. G. (1949) *The Bank of Ireland 1783–1946*, Dublin: Hodges, Figgis & Co.

Hall, R. O. (1922) *Chapters and Documents on Chinese National Banking*, Shanghai: Commercial Press.

Hall, R. (1983) 'Optimal fiduciary monetary systems', *Journal of Monetary Economics*, 12: 33–50.

Hamilton. H. (1956) 'The Failure of the Ayr Bank, 1772', *Economic History Review*, 2nd series, 8 (April): 405–17.

——(1963) *An Economic History of Scotland in the Eighteenth Century*, Oxford: Clarendon Press.

Hammond, B. (1948) 'Banking in the early west: monopoly, prohibition, and laissez faire', *Journal of Economic History*, 8: 1–25.

——(1957) *Banks and Politics in America from the Revolution to the Civil War*, Princeton: Princeton University Press.

Hanke, S. H. and Schuler, K. (forthcoming 1992) *Currency Reform and Economic Development*, Princeton: Princeton University Press.

Hardcastle, D. (1843) *Banks and Bankers*, London: Whittaker & Co.

Hargreaves, R. P. (1972) *From Beads to Bank Notes*, Dunedin, New Zealand: John McIndoe Ltd.

Hasan, I. and Dwyer, G. P. (1988) 'Contagion effects and banks closed in the free banking period', in *The Financial Services Industry in the Year 2000: Risk and Efficiency*, proceedings of a Conference on Bank Structure and Competition, Federal Reserve Bank of Chicago, May.

Hayek, F. A. (1960) *The Constitution of Liberty*, London: Routledge & Kegan Paul.

——(1976) *Denationalisation of Money: An Analysis of the Theory and Practice of Concurrent Currencies*, Hobart Paper, London: Institute of Economic Affairs.

——(1978) *Denationalisation of Money: The Argument Refined*, London: Institute of Economic Affairs.

HBC (1923) Canada. Parliament. House of Commons, Select Committee on Banking and Currency, *Hearings*.

Henry, J. A. and Siepmann, H. A. (1963) *The First Hundred Years of the Standard Bank*, London: Oxford University Press.

Hepburn, A. B. (1968 [1903]) *History of Coinage and Currency in the United States and the Perennial Contest for Sound Money*, New York: Greenwood Press.

Higgs, H. (1963) *The Physiocrats*, Hamden, Conn.: Archon Books.

Holdsworth, J. T. (1971) 'Lessons of state banking before the Civil War', reprinted in *Proceedings of the Academy of Political Science*, 30: 23–36, originally printed in vol. 1 of the *Proceedings* (1911): 210–24.

Holladay, J. (1938) *The Canadian Banking System*, Boston: Bankers Publishing Co.

Horn, E. (1866) *La Liberté des banques*, Paris: Guillaumin.

Hübner, O. (1854) *Die Banken*, Leipzig: Verlag von Heinrich Huebner.

Hume, D. (1955 [1752]) 'Of the balance of trade', in E. Rotwein (ed.) *Writings on Economics*, Madison: University of Wisconsin Press.

Huntington, C. C. (1964) *A History of Banking and Currency in Ohio before the Civil War*, Columbus, Ohio: F. J. Heer Printing Co.

Ibañez, J. E. (1990) 'Antecedentes legales de la creacion del Banco de la República', in A. Meisel (ed.) *El Banco de la Republica, Antecedentes, Evolucion y Estructura*, Bogotá, Bogotá: Banco de la República.

Imperial Maritime Customs (China) (1882–1922) *Decennial Reports* (various dates).

Jamieson, A. B. (1957) *Chartered Banking in Canada*, rev. edn, Toronto: Ryerson Press.

Jaramillo, E. (1918) 'Proyecto de ley por la cual se autoriza la fundacion de un banco, para darle elasticidad al medio circulante nacional', *Anales de la Camara de Representantes*, 2 (9 July): 6–7.

Jernigan, T. R. (1904) *China's Business Methods and Policy*, Shanghai: Kelley & Walsh.

Jöhr, A. (1915) *Die Schweizerischen Notenbanken, 1826–1913*, Zurich: Orell Fussli.

Jones, S. Mann (1972) 'Finance in Ninpo: the Ch'ien Chuang, 1750–1880', in W. E. Wilmott (ed.) *Economic Organization in Chinese Society*, Stanford: Stanford University Press, 47–77.

Jonung, L. (1989 [1985]) 'The economics of private money: the experience of private notes in Sweden, 1831–1902', unpublished mimeo, Stockholm School of Economics Research Report 282 (first version August 1985, third version April 1989).

Joplin, T. (1826) *An Essay on the General Principles and Present Practice of Banking in England and Scotland*, 5th edn London: Baldwin, Cradock & Joy.

Joslin, D. (1963) *A Century of Banking in Latin America: To Commemorate the Centenary in 1962 of the Bank of London and South America Limited*, London: Oxford University Press.

Kahn, J. A. (1985) 'Another look at free banking in the United States', *American Economic Review* 75: 881–5.

Kalkmann, P. (1900) *Untersuchungen über das Geldwesen der Schweiz und die Ursache des hohen Standes des Auswärtigen Wechselkurses*, St Gallen.

Kann. E. (1935) 'Copper notes in China', Central Bank of China *Bulletin*, 2 (3) (September): 1–23.
——(1936) 'Modern banknotes in China', Central Bank of China *Bulletin*, 2(4) (December): 13–26.
Kemmerer, D. (1987) 'Kemmerer, El money Doctor', *Difusion Cultural*, Banco Central del Ecuador, 6, (December): 59.
Kemmerer, E. W. (1927) 'Economic advisory work for governments', *The American Economic Review*, IVII (1) (March).
Kerr, A. W. (1884) *History of Banking in Scotland*, Glasgow: David Bryce.
Kindleberger, C. P. (1984) *A Financial History of Western Europe*, London: Allen & Unwin.
King, F. H. H. (1957) *Money in British East Asia*, London: HMSO.
——(1965) *Money and Monetary Policy in China 1845–1895*, Cambridge, Mass.: Harvard University Press.
——(1987, 1988, 1989) *The History of the Hongkong and Shanghai Banking Corporation*, 3 vols, Cambridge: Cambridge University Press.
King, R. G. (1983) 'On the economics of private money', *Journal of Monetary Economics*, 12: 127–58.
Klebaner, B. J. (1974) *Commercial Banking in the United States: A History*, Hinsdale, Ill.: Dryden Press.
Klein, B. (1974) 'The competitive supply of money', *Journal of Money, Credit, and Banking*, 6: 423–54.
——(1978) 'Money, wealth, and seigniorage', in K. E. Boulding and T. F. Wilson (eds) *Redistribution through the Financial System*, New York: Praeger.
Klein, E. (1982) *Deutsche Bankengeschichte*, 2 vols, Frankfurt am Main: Knapp.
Knight, J. T. P. (1908) *Canadian Banking Practice*, 2nd edn, Montreal: F. Wilson–Smith.
Knox, J. J. (1903) *A History of Banking in the United States*, reprinted New York: Augustus M. Kelley, 1969.
Kock, M. H. de (1974) *Central Banking*, 4th edn, New York: St Martin's Press.
Kyrkilitsis, A. (1968) 'The Greek banking system: a historical review', *Revue Internationale de l'Histoire de la Banque*,vol. 1.
Lair, L. (1967) *La Banque de France*, 7th edn, Paris: Banque Editions Techniques et Professionelles.
Landmann, J. (1910) *The Swiss Banking System*, US National Monetary Commission (61st congress, 2nd session, Senate doc. no. 401), Washington: Government Printing Office.
Lee, Sheng–Yi (1986) *The Monetary and Banking Development of Singapore* rev. edn, Singapore: Singapore University Press.
Leggett, W. (1984) *Democratic Editorials: Essays in Jacksonian Political Economy*, L. H. White (ed.), Indianapolis: Liberty Press.
Lévy, R. G. (1911) *Banques d'émission et trésors publics*, Paris: Librairie Hachette.
Lezana, A. O. (1956) *Monografia sobre el regimen monetaria de la republica oriental del Uruguay 1829–1955*, Montevideo.
Logan, W. H. (1839) *The Scottish [sic] Banker*, Edinburgh: Fraser & Crawford.

Ma, Tak–Wo (1987) *Currency of Macau*, Hong Kong: Urban Council and Meseu Luis de Camoës.

McCallum, B. T. (1986) 'Bank deregulation, accounting systems of exchange, and the unit of account: a critical review', *Carnegie Rochester Conference Series on Public Policy*, 23: 13–46.

——(1989) *Monetary Economics: Theory and Policy*, New York: Macmillan.

McCammon, A. L. T. (1984) *Currencies of the Anglo-Norman Isles*, London: Spink.

McCulloch, J. R. (1826) 'Fluctuations in the supply and value of money', *Edinburgh Review*, 43 (February): 263–98.

——(1837) *A Statistical Account of the British Empire*, 2nd edn, London: Charles Knight.

McCullough, A. B. (1984) *Money and Exchange in Canada*, Toronto: Dundurn Press.

McEldery, A. L. (1976) *Shanghai Old-Style Banks, 1800–1935*, Ann Arbor, Michigan: Center for Chinese Studies.

MacFarlam, J. F. (1845) *Remarks on the Scotch Banking System*, Edinburgh: Adam and Charles Black.

McGreevey, W.P. (1982) *Historia Economica de Colombia, 1845–1930*, Bogotá: Terca Mundo.

McIvor, R. C. (1958) *Canadian Monetary, Banking, and Fiscal Development*, Toronto: Macmillan.

Macleod, H. D. (1866) *The Theory and Practice of Banking*, 2nd edn, London: Longman.

MacPherson, D. (1805) *Annals of Commerce*, vol. 4, London: [n. p.].

Makinen, G. E. and Woodward, G. T. (1986) 'Some anecdotal evidence relating to the legal restrictions theory of the demand for money', *Journal of Political Economy*, 94(2) (April): 260–5.

Malcolm. A. [n.d.] *The Bank of Scotland, 1695–1945*, Edinburgh: R. R. Clark.

——(1950) *The History of the British Linen Bank*, Edinburgh: T. & A. Constable.

Mangold, F. (1909) *Die Bank in Basel, 1844–1907*, Basel.

Marichal, C. (1988) *Historia de la Duda Externa de America Latina,*: Alianza Editorial.

Marion, M. (1914–28) *Histoire financière de la France depuis 1715*, tome IV, Paris: A. Rousseau.

——(1934) 'La Fondation de la Banque de France' in *History of the Principal Public Banks*, The Hague: Martinus Nijhoff.

Meisel, A. (1988) 'La historia monetaria de Mauricio Avella: Hamlet con tres principes', *Ensayos sobre Politica Economica*, Banco de la República, 13 (June): 100.

——(1990a) 'Los Bancos Comerciales en la era de la banca libre, 1871–1923', in *El Banco de la República, Antecedentes, Evolucion y Estructura*, Bogatá: Banco de la República.

——(1990b) 'La creacion del Banco de la República y las teorias sobre Banc Centra: Porque 1923', in *El Banco de la República, Antecedentes, Evolucion y Estructura,* Bogatá: Banco de la República.

——(forthcoming) 'Los Banco de Cartagena, 1874–1925', *Lecturas de Economia*, Medellín.

Meisel, A. and Lopez, A. (1990) 'Papel Moneda, Tasas de Interes y Revaluacion durante la Regcneracion', in Meisel, A. (ed.) *El Banco de la República, Antecedentes, Evolucion y Estructura*, Bogatá: Banco de la República.

Meisel Roca, A. (1989) 'Las bancos commerciales en la era de la banca libre, 1871–1923', unpublished manuscript, Bogatá: Banco de la República.

Menger, C. (1981 [1871]) *Principles of Economics*, trans. J. Dingwall and B. F. Hoselitz, New York: New York University Press.

Merrett, D. T. (1989) 'Australian banking practice and the crisis of 1893', *Australian Economic History Review*, 29(1): 60–85.

Mints, L. (1950) *Monetary Policy for a Competitive Society*, New York: McGraw–Hill.

Mirabeau, Comte de (1785) *De la Caisse d'Escompte*.

Mullineaux, D. J. (1987) 'Competitive monies and the Suffolk system: a contractual perspective', *Southern Economic Journal*, 54: 884–98.

Munn, C. W. (1975) 'The Origins of the Scottish Note Exchange', *Three Banks Review*, 107: 45–60.

——(1981) 'Scottish provincial banking companies: an assessment', *Business History*, 23 (March).

Munn, C. (1981) *The Scottish Provincial Banking Companies, 1747–1864*, Edinburgh: John Donald.

——(1982) 'The development of joint-stock banking in Scotland 1810–1845', in A. Slaven and D. H. Aldcroft (eds) *Business, Banking and Urban History*, Edinburgh: John Donald.

Munro, N. (1928) *The Royal Bank of Scotland*, Edinburgh: R. & R. Clark.

Nardi, G. di (1953) *Le banche de emissione in Italia nel secolo XIX*, Turin: Unione Tipografico–Editore Torinese.

Nataf, P. (1982) 'Free banking: a workable system', in *Competitive Money and Banking*, with introduction by L. H. White, Greenwich, Conn.: Committee for Monetary Research and Education, monograph 37 (November): 3–4.

——(1984a) 'Competitive banking and the cycle', in *History of Economics Society Annual Meeting*, vol. 2, Pittsburgh, Penn. (23 May): 3, 17–18.

——(1984b) 'The business cycle theories in mid-19th century France', *History of Economics Annual Meeting*, vol. 1, Pittsburgh, Penn. (22 May): 2, 12–13.

——(1987) *An Inquiry into the Free Banking Movement in Nineteenth Century France, with Particular Emphasis on Charles Coquelin's Writings*, San Diego: William Lyon University.

——(1990) 'Le système bancaire français au XIXe siècle', *Marchés et Techniques Financières*, nos. 20–1 (July–August): 51–4.

Naylor, R. T. (1975) *The History of Canadian Business, 1867–1914*, 2 vols, Toronto: James Lorimer & Co.

Nelson, W. E. (1984) 'The Imperial administration of currency and British banking in the Straits Settlements, 1867–1908'; Ph.D. dissertation, Duke University, Durham, NC.

Neufeld, E. P. (1964) *Money and Banking in Canada: Historical Documents and Commentary*, Toronto: McClelland & Stewart.

——(1972) *The Financial System of Canada: its Growth and Development*, Toronto: Macmillan.

Ng, K. (1988) 'Free banking laws and barriers to entry in banking,

1838–1860', *Journal of Economic History*, 48: 877–89.

Nicholson, J. Shield (1893) 'Scotch banking', *Journal of Political Economy*, 1 (September): 487–502.

Nolan, P. (1923) *The History and Mystery of Banking in Ireland and Elsewhere*,? Desclee, DeBrouwer & Co.

O'Brien, G. (1921) *The Economic History of Ireland*, New York: Augustus M. Kelly. Reprinted 1972.

Ollerenshaw, P. (1987) *Banking in Nineteenth-Century Ireland: The Belfast Banks, 1825–1914*, Manchester: Manchester University Press.

Onoh, J. K. (1982) *Money and Banking in Africa*, New York: Longman.

Ou Chi–luan (1932) *Kang–chou chih yin yeh* [Native Banks in Canton], Canton: [n.p].

Pardo, M. C. de (1973) *Monedas Venezolanas*, 2nd edn., 2 vols, Caracas: Banco Central de Venezuela.

Parkes, H. (1852) 'An account of the paper currency and banking system of Fuhchowfoo', *Journal of the Royal Asiatic Society* 13: 179–89.

Parnell, H. (1827) *Observations on Paper Money, Banking and Overtrading*, London: James Ridgway.

——(1833) *A Plain Statement of the Power of the Bank of England and of the Use It Has Made of It; with a Refutation of the Objections Made to the Scotch System of Banking; and a Reply to the 'Historical Sketch of the Bank of England'*, 2nd edn, London: James Ridgway.

Pecquet, G. M. (1990) 'The tug of war over southern banks during the Civil War: a property rights approach', paper presented to the Durell Foundation Conference 'Money and Banking: The American Experience', Washington, May.

Pelaez, C. M. (1981) *Historia monetaria do Brasil*, Rio de Janeiro: IPEA/INES.

Pender, H., Otto, G. and Harper, I. R. (1989) 'Free banking in Australia', mimeo, Australian National University and University of Melbourne.

Pick, A. (1986) *Standard Catalog of World Paper Money*, Iola, Wisconsin: Krause Publications.

Plumptre, A. F. W. (1940) *Central Banking in the British Dominions*, Toronto: University of Toronto Press.

Pope, D. (1987) 'Bankers and banking business, 1860–1914', working paper in economic history no. 85, Australian National University, September.

——(1988) 'Did Australian trading banks benefit from scale economies and branch networks during the nineteenth century?', working paper no. 111, Australian National University, May.

——(1989) 'Free banking in Australia before World War I', unpublished manuscript, Australian National University, Canberra.

——(1990) 'Australia's payments adjustment and capital flows under the international Gold Standard 1870–1914', working paper no. 141, Australian National University, August.

Postlewaite, A. and Vives, X. (1987) 'Bank runs as an equilibrium phenomenon', *Journal of Political Economy* 95(3) (June): 485–91.

Pressnell, L. S. (1956) *Country Banking in the Industrial Revolution*, Oxford: Clarendon Press.

Prober, K. (1957) *Historical numismatica de Guatemala*, Guatemala City: Editorial del Ministerio de Educacion Publica.

Quarmby, E. (1971) *Banknotes and Banking in the Isle of Man, 1788–1970: A Guide for Historians and Collectors*, London: Spink.

Quintana, R. R. (1971) *Apuntes sobre el desarollo monetario de Guatemala*, Guatemala City: Banco de Guatemala.

Quintero–Ramos, A. M. (1965) *A History of Money and Banking in Argentina*, Rio Piedras, Puerto Rico: University of Puerto Rico.

Rait, R. S. (1939) *The History of the Union Bank of Scotland*, Glasgow: John Smith.

Ramon, G. (1929) *Histoire de la Banque de France*, Paris: Grasset.

Redish, A. (1983) 'The economic crisis of 1837–1839 in Upper Canada: case study of a temporary suspension of specie payments', *Explorations in Economic History*, 20 (4 October): 402–17.

——(1984) 'Why was specie scarce in colonial economies? An analysis of the Canadian currency, 1796–1830', *Journal of Economic History*, 44 (3 September): 713–28.

Renard, F. (1990) 'Le suicide des banques françaises', *Le Monde* (14–15 October): 1 and 15.

Reserve Bank of Zambia (1983) *The Currency Media of Southern Rhodesia (from the Time of the Charter to 1953) of the Federation of Rhodesia and Nyasaland (from 1954 to 1963), of Rhodesia (from 1963 to 1979) and of Zimbabwe (from 1980)*, Harare: Reserve Bank of Zambia.

Rich, G. (1988) *The Cross of Gold: Money and the Canadian Business Cycle 1867–1913*, Ottawa: Carleton University Press.

——(1989) 'Canadian banks, gold, and the crisis of 1907', *Explorations in Economic History*, 26 (2 April): 135–60.

Riesser, J. (1911) *The German Great Banks*, trans. M. Jacobson, US National Monetary Commission (61st congress, 2nd session, Senate doc. no. 593), reprinted New York: Arno Press, 1977.

Ritzmann, F. (1973) *Die Schweizer Banken. Geschichte – Theorie – Statistik*, Bern: Paul Haupt.

Rivarola P. J. B. (1982) *Historia monetaria del Paraguay*, Asuncion: Imprenta El Grafico.

Rochac, A. (1984) *La moneda. Los bancos y el credito en El Salvador: material para analizar su evolucion*, 2 vols, San Salvador: Banco Central de Reserva de El Salvador.

Rockoff, H. (1974), 'The free banking era: a re-examination', *Journal of Money, Credit and Banking*, 6: 141–67.

——(1975a) *The Free Banking Era: A Re-Examination*, New York: Arno Press.

——(1975b) 'Varieties of banking and regional economic development in the United States, 1840–1860', *Journal of Economic History*, 35, 160–77.

——(1986) 'Institutional requirements for stable free banking', *Cato Journal* 6(2) (Fall): 617–34.

Rogers, K. A. and Cantrell, C. (1989) *Paper Money of Fiji*, Dallas: International Bank Note Society Press.

Rolnick, A. J. and Weber, W. E. (1982) 'Free banking, wildcat banking, and shinplasters', Federal Reserve Bank of Minneapolis, *Quarterly Review* (Fall): 10–19.

——(1983) 'New evidence on the free banking era', *American Economic Review* 73: 1080–91.

——(1984) 'The causes of free bank failures: a detailed examination', *Journal of Monetary Economics*, 14: 267–91.

——(1985) 'Banking instability and regulation in the US free banking era', Federal Reserve Bank of Minneapolis *Quarterly Review* (Summer): 2–9.

——(1986) 'Inherent instability in banking: the free banking experience', *Cato Journal*, 5 (Winter): 877–90.

——(1988) 'Explaining the demand for free bank notes', *Journal of Monetary Economics*, 21: 47–71.

Romero, C.A. (1987) 'Historia monetaria en Colombia, 1880–1909', Tesis de Economia, Universidad Nacional, Bogatá.

Root, L. C. (1895) 'New York Currency', *Sound Currency*, 1–24.

Roover, R. de (1974 [1954]) *Business, Banking, and Economic Thought in Late Medieval and Early Modern Europe*, Chicago: University of Chicago Press.

Ross, A. (1910) *Chile 1851–1910: Sixty Years of Monetary and Financial Questions and of Banking Problems*, Valparaiso: Imprenta Westcott & Co.

Ross, V. (1920) *A History of the Canadian Bank of Commerce; With an Account of the Other Banks which now Form Part of its Organization*, 3 vols, Toronto: Oxford University Press.

Rothband, M. N. (1988) 'The myth of free banking in Scotland', *Review of Austrian Economics*, 2:229–45.

Rowe, C. F. (1967) 'The coins and currency of Newfoundland,' in J. R. Smallwood (ed.) *The Book of Newfoundland*, St John's, Nfld: Newfoundland Book Publications, Ltd.

Rudin, R. (1985) *Banking en Français: The French Banks of Quebec, 1835–1925*, Toronto: University of Toronto Press.

Saint–Aubin, C. (1795) *Des Banques particulières*, Paris: Pougin.

Salin, P. (1990) *La Verité sur la monnaie*, Paris: Editions Odile Jacob.

Salomons, D. (1837) *A Defense of Joint-Stock Banks*, London: Pelham Richardson.

Salsman, R. (1990) *Breaking the Banks: Central Banking Problems and Free Banking Solutions*, Great Barrington, Mass.: American institute for Economic Research.

Sayers, R. S. (ed.) (1952) *Banking in the British Commonwealth*, Oxford: Clarendon Press.

Schedvin, C. B. (1970) *Australia and the Great Depression*, Sydney: Sydney University Press.

Schedvin, C. V. (1989) 'The growth of bank regulation in Australia', paper presented to the Joint Universities Conference 'Regulating Commercial Banks: Australian Experience in Perspective', August 1989.

Scheiber, H. N. (1963) 'The pet banks in Jacksonian politics and finance, 1833–1841', *Journal of Economic History*, 23: 196–214.

Schenck, Fr Von (1953) *Viajes por Antioquia en el ano 1880*, Bogatá, Banco de la República.

Schuler, K. (1985) *Hands Off! The History of Canadian Free Banking*, mimeo, Fairfax, Virginia: George Mason University.

——(1988) 'The evolution of Canadian banking, 1867–1914', unpublished manuscript, George Mason University, Fairfax, Virginia.

Schull, J. and Gibson, J. D. (1982) *The Scotiabank Story: A History of the Bank of Nova Scotia, 1832–1982*. Toronto: Macmillan.

Schumpeter, J. A. (1942) *Capitalism, Socialism, and Democracy*, New York: Harper.

Schweikart, L. (1987) *Banking in the American South from the Age of Jackson to Reconstruction*, Baton Rouge and London: Louisiana State University Press.

Schweizerische Nationalbank (1957) 'Schweizerische Bibliographie über Geld Währung und Notenbankwesen', *Mitteilungen der Volkswirtschaftlichen und Statistischen Abteilung der Schweizerischen Nationalbank*, 40, Heft.

Scott, W. (1826) 'A third letter to the editor of the Edinburgh Weekly Journal, from Malachi Malagrowther, Esq. on the proposed change of currency', in *Thoughts on the Proposed Change of Currency*, New York: Barnes & Noble, 1972.

Sechrest, L. J. (1988) 'White's free banking thesis: a case of mistaken identity', *Review of Austrian Economics* 2: 247–57.

——(1990) *Free Banking: Theoretical and Historical Issues*, Ph.D. thesis, Arlington: University of Texas.

Sedillot, R. (1979) *L'Histoire du franc*, Paris: Sirey.

Selgin, G. A. (1987a) 'Free banking in China, 1800–1935', mimeo, George Mason University.

——(1987b) 'The stability and efficiency of money supply under free banking', *Journal of Institutional and Theoretical Economics* (September): 435–56.

——(1988) *The Theory of Free Banking: Money Supply under Competitive Note Issue*, Totowa, NJ: Rowman & Littlefield.

——(1990a) 'Banking "manias" in theory and history', mimeo, Department of Economics, Athens, GA: University of Georgia.

Selgin, G. A. and White, L. H. (1987) 'The evolution of a free banking system', *Economic Inquiry* (July): 439–57.

——(1988) 'Competitive monies and the Suffolk System: comment', *Southern Economic Journal*, 55: 215–19.

——(1990) 'National bank notes as quasi-high-powered money', unpublished manuscript, Athens, GA: University of Georgia.

Servais, E. (1942) *La Banque de France*, Paris: L.G.D.J.

Shearer, R. A. and Clark, C. (1984) 'Canada and the interwar Gold Standard, 1920–1935: monetary policy without a central bank', in M. D. Bordo and A. J. Schwartz (eds) *A Retrospective on the Classical Gold Standard, 1821–1931*, Chicago: University of Chicago Press.

Shen, L. Y. (1939) 'Chinese currencies: old and new', Central Bank of China *Bulletin* IV(3) (September): 217–25.

Shinjo, H. (1962) *History of the Yen*, Kobe Research Institute for Economic and Business Administration, series no. 1, Tokyo: Kinokuniya Bookstore Co. Ltd.

Shiu, G. M. C. (1990) 'Free banking in China: a preliminary study', unpublished manuscript, George Mason University.

Shortt, A. [1990] *History of the Bank of Nova Scotia, 1832–1900*, Halifax: Bank of Nova Scotia.

——(1986) *Adam Shortt's History of Canadian Currency and Banking 1600–1880*, Toronto: Canadian Bankers' Association. (Reprints articles from the *Journal of the Canadian Bankers' Association*, 1896 to 1925.)

Simpson, N. (1975) *The Belfast Bank, 1827–1970*, Belfast: Blackstaff Press.

Smith, A. (1937 [1776]) *An Inquiry into the Nature and Causes of the Wealth of Nations*, New York: Modern Library.

Smith, V. C. (1936) *The Rationale of Central Banking*, London: P. S. King.

——(1990) *The Rationale of Central Banking and the Free Banking Alternative*, London: P.S. King. Reprinted 1990, Indianapolis: Liberty Press.

Soley Guell, T. (1926) *Historia monetaria de Costa Rica*, San José, Costa Rica: Imprenta Nacional.

Somers, R. (1873) *The Scotch Banks and System of Issue*, Edinburgh: Adam & Charles Black.

Soyeda, J. (1896) 'Banking and money in Japan', in *A History of Banking in All the Leading Nations*, 4: 409–544. New York: Journal of Commerce & Commercial Bulletin.

Sprague, O. M. W. (1977 [1910]) *History of Crises under the National Banking System*, Fairfield, NJ: Augustus M. Kelley. Original edn, US National Monetary Commission, (61st congress, 2nd session, Senate doc. no. 538), Washington: Government Printing Office.

Stanley, P. W. (1974) *A Nation in the Making: The Philippines and the United States, 1899–1921*, Cambridge, Mass.: Harvard University Press.

Stokes, M. L. (1939) *The Bank of Canada: The Development and Present Position of Central Banking in Canada*, Toronto: Macmillan.

Subercaseaux, G. (1922) *Monetary and Banking Policy of Chile*, Oxford: Clarendon Press.

Sumner, W. G. (1896) *A History of Banking in the United States*, in W. G. Sumner (ed.) *A History of Banking in All the Leading Nations*, reprinted 1971, Fairfield, NJ: Augustus M. Kelley.

Sylla, R. (1972) 'The United States 1863–1913', in R. Cameron (ed.) *Banking and Development: some lessons of History*, New York: Oxford University Press.

——(1976) 'Forgotten men of money: private bankers in early US history', *Journal of Economic History*, 36: 173–88.

——(1985) 'Early American banking: the significance of the corporate form', *Business and Economic History*.

Tamagna, F. M. (1942) *Banking and Finance in China*, New York: Institute of Pacific Relations.

——(1965) *Central Banking in Latin America*, Mexico City: Centro de Estudios Monetarias Latinoamericanos.

Tavedikoul, T. (1939) *Le systeme d'émission des billets au Siam*, Paris: A. Rousseau.

Thomas, C. Y. (1965) *Monetary and Financial Arrangements in a Dependent Economy; A Study of British Guiana, 1945–1962*, Mona, Jamaica: Institute of Social and Economic Research, University of the West Indies.

Thornton, H. (1802) *An Enquiry into the Nature and Effects of the Paper Credit of Great Britain*, edited and with an introduction by F. A. Hayek, Fairfield, NJ: Augustus M. Kelley, 1978.

Timberlake, R. H., Jr (1978) *The Origins of Central Banking in the United States*, Cambridge, Mass.: Harvard University Press.

——(1984) 'The central banking role of clearing-house associations', *Journal of Money, Credit, and Banking*, 16 (1 February): 1–15.

——(1987) 'Private production of scrip-money in the isolated community', *Journal of Money, Credit, and Banking*, 19 (4 October): 437–47.

——(1990) 'The government's license to create money', *Cato Journal*, 9: 301–21.

Torres G. G. (1980) *Historia de la moneda en Colombia*, 2nd edn, Medellín: Bogatá: Fondo Rotario de Publicaciones FAES.

Tortella Casares, G. (1977) *Banking, Railroads, and Industry in Spain 1829–1874*, New York: Arno Press.

Trivoli, G. (1979) *The Suffolk Bank: A Study of a Free-Enterprise Clearing System*, London and Leesburg, VA: Adam Smith Institute.

Tullock, G. (1957) 'Paper money – a cycle in Cathay', *Economic History Review*, IX(3): 393–407.

United States, National Monetary Commission (1910) *Interviews on the Banking and Currency System of Canada* (61st congress, 2nd session, Senate doc. 584), Washington: Government Printing Office.

Urquhart, H. C., and Buckley, K. H. (eds) (1965) *Historical Statistics of Canada*, Toronto: Macmillan.

Vanderblue, H. (1939) *The Vanderblue Memorial Collection of Smithiana*, Boston: Harvard Business School.

Vaubel, R. (1978) *Strategies for Currency Unification: The Economics of Currency Competition and the case for European Parallel Currency*, Tübingen: J. C. B. Mohr (Paul Siebeck).

——(1984a) 'The history of currency competition', in P. Salin (ed.,) *Currency Competition and Monetary Union*, Boston: Martinus Nijhoff.

——(1984b) 'The government's money monopoly: externalities or natural monopoly?' *Kyklos* 37: (1): 27–58.

Villalobos V. B. (1981) *Bancos emisores y bancos hipotecarios en Costa Rica 1850–1910*, San José, Costa Rica: Editorial Costa Rica.

Villamarin, H. (1972) *Evolucion del Derecho Bancario, Estuido General y Legislacion Colombiana, Contraloria General de Boyaca*.

Völlmy, H.-U. (1967) Zür Geschichtee des Schweizerischen geldes, Basel: Dissertation Universität Basel.

Wagel, S. R. (1915) *Chinese Currency and Banking*, Shanghai: North China Daily News & Herald, Ltd.

Waldo, D. G. (1985) 'Bank runs, the deposit-currency ratio and the interest rate', *Journal of Monetary Economics* 15(2) (March): 269–77.

Wallace, N. (1983) 'A legal restrictions theory of the demand for "money" and the role of monetary policy', Federal Reserve Bank of Minneapolis *Quarterly Review* (Winter): 1–7.

Wang Yeh-Chien (1977) 'Evolution of the Chinese monetary system, 1644–1850', Institute of Economics Conference on Modern Chinese Economic History, Taipei, August.

Weber, W. E. 'Currency competition in Switzerland, 1826–1850', *Kyklos*, 41 (3): 459–78.

Weiller, R. (1981) *Cent vint-cinq ans de papier-monnaie Luxembourgeois* Luxembourg: Banque Internationale.

Weisskopf, E. (1948) *Das schweizerische Münzwesen von seinen Anfängen bis zur Gegenwart*, Bern: Dissertation Universität Bern.

260   *The experience of free banking*

Wells, D. R. (1989) 'The free banking model applied to pre-1914 Canadian banking', *Studies in Economic Analysis*, 12(2) (Fall): 3–21.

Wells, D. R. and Scruggs, L. S. (1986) 'Historical insight into the deregulation of money and banking', *Cato Journal*, 5 (3 Spring): 899–910.

Wenley, J. A. (1882) 'On the history and development of banking in Scotland', *Journal of the Institute of Bankers*, 3: 119–45.

White, E. N. (1989) 'The regulation of banking in France, 1776–1815, or why Free Banking failed to succeed', unpublished paper, Rutgers University.

——(1990a) 'Free banking during the French Revolution', *Explorations in Economic History*, 27 (3 July): 251–76.

——(1990b) 'Free banking, denominational restrictions, and liability insurance', paper presented to the Durell Foundation conference, *Money and Banking: The American Experience*, Washington, DC, May 1990.

White, L. H. (1984a) 'Competitive payments systems and the unit of account', *American Economic Review*, 74(4) (September): 699–712.

——(1984b) *Free Banking in Britain: Theory, Experience and Debate, 1800–1845*, New York and Cambridge: Cambridge University Press.

——(1986) 'Regulatory sources of instability in banking', *Cato Journal*, 5: 891–7.

——(1987) 'Accounting for non-interest bearing currency: a critique of the "legal restrictions" theory of money', *Journal of Money, Credit and Banking*, 19 (November): 448–56.

——(1990a) 'Banking without a central bank: Scotland before 1844 as a "Free Banking System"', in F. Capie and G. E. Wood (eds) *Unregulated Banking: Chaos or Order?*, London: Macmillan.

——(1990b) 'Scottish banking and the legal restrictions theory: a closer look', *Journal of Money, Credit, and Banking*, 22 (November): 526–36.

White, L. H. and Selgin, G. A. (1990) '*Laissez-faire* monetary thought in Jacksonian America', in D. E. Moggridge (ed.) *Perspectives on the History of Economic Thought*, vol. 4, Aldershot, England: Edward Elgar.

Wilkinson, E. P. (1980) *Studies in Chinese Price History*, New York: Garland.

Williams, J. H. (1920) *Argentine Trade under Inconvertible Paper Money 1880–1900*, Cambridge, Mass: Harvard University Press.

——(1863) *The Chinese Commercial Guide*, Hong Kong: A. Shortzede & Co.

Williams, S. W. (1851) 'Paper Money among the Chinese', *The Chinese Repository*, 20(6) (June): 289–96.

Willis, H. P. and Backhart, B. H. (1929) *Foreign Banking Systems*, New York: Columbia University Press.

Wilson. J. (1847) *Capital, Currency, and Banking*, London: The Economist.

Wolowski, L. (1864) *La Question des Banques*, Paris: Guillaumin.

Wong H.-C. (1936) *Fukien Chai Ching She Kuan* [A Financial History of Fukien] [n.p.].

Wyeth, J. (1979) *A History of the Belize Board of Commissioners of Currency (1894–1976): Belizean Economic History*, Belize City: Belize Institute for Social Research and Action, St John's College (*Journal of Belizean Affairs*, no. 8).

Yang, L.-S. (1952), *Money and Credit in China*, Cambridge, Mass.: Harvard

University Press.

Young, J. P. (1952) *Central American Currency and Finance*, Princeton: Princeton University Press.

Young, S. Y. P. (1935) 'China's Banking Progress in the Past Decade', *China Quarterly* I(1) (September): 65–80.

——(1939) 'The development of Chinese monetary laws under the national government', Central Bank of China *Bulletin*, vol. (3) (September): 223–32.

Index

free banking in Canada 4, 79–92
free banking in Colombia 93–102
free banking in Foochow 103–22
free banking in France 34, 123–36
free banking in Ireland 137–56
free banking in New York 207–9
free banking in Scotland 4, 9–10, 14, 157–86
free banking in Switzerland 175–205
'free banking' in the US 206–40
'free banking' in US states: Illinois 211; Indiana 213–14; Michigan (1837) 211–12; Minnesota 214–15; Ohio 213; Wisconsin 212–13
'free banking' laws US 209–10, 215–6, 228
'free banking', New York-style 229
Free Banking School 32, 34, 36
free banking systems 5, 9, 15–17, 19–20, 22–6; Canada 23; England 23; France 23; Scotland 18, 23, 26; US 23;
free banking, the experience of 1–6
free banking, the origins of 8–9
free banking, the world history of 7–48
free banking's demise, causes of: crises 37–9; seigniorage 30–3; theoretical rationales 32–7
free banks: Mexico 18
free competition 3
French Free Banking School 124
French playing-card money 13, 78
Friedman, M. 1 7, 36

Garcia, R. J. L. 1
Garcia, T. 97
GDP: Australia 65–6
Georgia 209, 214
Germany 14–16, 34; brnach banking 34; note-issue system 14
Gibson, J. D. 27, 83
Gilbart, J. W. 180, 183–4
Glasgow Arms Bank 161–2, 177, 180
Glasgow Ship Bank 161–2
Glasgow Union Banking Company 171–2
GNP statistics: Canada 90; US 90

gold convertibility 28, 30; Argentina 29
gold-denominated assets 21
gold dollar 20, 86
gold pound sterling 20
gold reserves 27, 33
gold standard 21, 24–6; Canada 88; Chile 29–30; Colombia 96; Japan 37
Gollan, R. 28
Goodhart, C. A. E. 23–4
Gore Bank (Canada) 85
Gorton, G. 30, 111, 113
de Gournay, V. 123
government bonds: France 134
government note issue 16, 26; Americas 13; Australia 64; Canada 83–6; Colombia 95–6; monopoly *see* seigniorage
Graham, W. 162, 165, 177, 184
Great Britain 12–13, 15, 32–3, 39; British government 12; Central banking 32
Great Depression 26, 37; Canada 90–1
Greece 14, 197
Green, G. D. 216
Greenfield, R. L. 21
Gresham's Law (Australia) 51, 73
Guatemala 13
Gunasekera, H. A. 28
Guyana 11

Haiti 13
Halifax (Canada) 80
Halifax Banking Company (Canada) 80
Hall, F. G. 10, 67, 138–9, 144–5, 148
Hall, R. O. 103
Hamilton, H. 164
Hammond, B. 21, 25, 35, 208, 212–3, 218
Hanke, S. H. 34
Hardcastle, D. 144, 148
Hargreaves, R. P. 9, 12
Hayek, F. A. 1, 7
HBC (Canada) 90
Hepburn, A. B. 36
Hibernian Bank (Ireland) 150
Holdsworth, J. T. 207, 213, 230